KEEP YOUR
HEAD DOWN

ALSO BY DOUG ANDERSON

POETRY

Blues for Unemployed Secret Police

The Moon Reflected Fire

KEEP YOUR
HEAD DOWN

A Memoir

DOUG ANDERSON

W. W. NORTON & COMPANY

NEW YORK LONDON

I have sought to protect living persons by changing certain names and, when necessary, altering character descriptions and events. The dialogues in this book are constructed from clear memories of their content, and with an ear for the nuances and idioms of speech.

For information about permission to reproduce selections from this book, write to Permissions, W. W. Norton & Company, Inc., 500 Fifth Avenue, New York, NY 10110

For information about special discounts for bulk purchases, please contact W. W. Norton Special Sales at specialsales@wwnorton.com or 800-233-4830

Manufacturing by Courier Westford
Book design by Chris Welch
Production manager: Anna Oler

Library of Congress Cataloging-in-Publication Data

Anderson, Doug, 1943–
Keep your head down : a memoir / Doug Anderson. — 1st ed.
p. cm.
ISBN 978-0-393-06855-9 (hardcover)
1. Anderson, Doug, 1943– 2. Anderson, Doug, 1943– —Childhood and youth. 3. Poets, American—Biography. 4. Veterans—United States—Biography. 5. Vietnam War, 1961–1975—Veterans. 6. United States—History—1961–1969.
I. Title.
PS3551.N3456Z46 2009
811'.54—dc22
[B]
2009009093

W. W. Norton & Company, Inc.
500 Fifth Avenue, New York, N.Y. 10110
www.wwnorton.com

W. W. Norton & Company Ltd.
Castle House, 75/76 Wells Street, London W1T 3QT

1 2 3 4 5 6 7 8 9 0

FOR JULIE

Thence we came forth to see the stars again.
—Dante, *Inferno*

PROLOGUE

EVERY OTHER MONDAY I drive down to the Veterans Affairs Hospital at West Haven, Connecticut, for my appointment. In the waiting area, two World War II vets are shouting at one another over failed hearing aids. I find myself a seat and nod at another Vietnam vet in a leather biker vest, his long black hair woven with gray.

Some days there are Korean War vets, Gulf War vets, and even somebody from forgotten little "police actions" like the invasions of Panama and Grenada. Today there are three men I'm sure are Iraq War vets. There is something besides their youth that identifies them. They have that stunned look. One of them paces as if he were trying to climb out of himself and run. One confides in me that his wife kicked him out of the house and changed the locks. They take me back to my own war, and what happened after.

Since Vietnam, I've acquired a second self that lies dormant until he's needed. I call him *Snakebrain*. Since the beginning of the Iraq War, he's come alive. He's an early warning system for some seriously bad behavior. *Snakebrain* is good at sniffing out sham but not so good at affirming things. Sometimes he takes over the whole mind and I need someone to point this out.

After a few minutes in the waiting area, I am called in for my session with my therapist. I haven't much to say today. I'm feeling good. I haven't had any incidents of incapacitating rage, even while watching politicians on television. She is aware that I have "constricted affect," an ability to be glib about things I should really stammer and weep about. It is my way of getting along in the world—much preferable to the kind of crisis-craving life I had been leading more than twenty years ago. After my appointment, I drive back to Hartford, a little lighter.

AS A KID, I hung out with men who worked hard, fought hard, and spat tobacco. They believed that putting your life on the line for your country made you a man. My imagination was colonized by war stories, the *Victory at Sea* installments that ran for years on the TV long after World War II, and the patriotic newsreels that preceded the black-and-white movies in the theater. I wanted to be a cowboy, then I wanted to be a soldier. By way of further preparation I went duck hunting with uncles and fishing with my father. In my teens, I bought a .308 Winchester and hunted javelina in Arizona.

I ALWAYS SEEM to arrive in the middle of things. As I child, I grew up in the apartheid South that was giving birth to the civil rights movement. I remember separate black and white restrooms, drinking fountains, store entrances. I remember black men stepping off the sidewalk to let whites pass. I grew up thinking this was normal.

I was in high school after the Korean War, and people went into the service right after high school to "get it out of the way," never thinking there would be another war. No one really knew that the CIA was already in Graham Greene's Vietnam attempting to destabilize the country to such an extent that the United States would have a pretext to fight a war there. We just thought that the service was something that you naturally did if you were a man because your father had done it and his father before him. Even Elvis went into the army. I watched others go into the service and come out telling stories about the girls in Malaysia or the Mediterranean. But I was already playing drums in a rock band by then, and would enroll the next year at the University of Arizona's music department.

My first year at the university was miserable. ROTC was compulsory in those days, which meant maintaining a clean uniform with shined shoes and buckles and showing up for drill at seven AM. I hated it. Most of us hated it. Punks from the overachiever class who were headed to West Point after graduation would harass and threaten us during morning drill. We couldn't kick the shit out of them because we'd be expelled. I flunked two semesters of ROTC because I couldn't bring myself to go to class. I didn't know that within a few years I would be on my way to Vietnam.

About that time I met some people who would try to change me. I hung out with these guys who were reading Marx and complaining constantly about racism and capitalism in the United States. They lectured me on the unfair distribution of wealth and the lynchings in the South. There was a coffee shop downtown—there were still downtowns then—where folksingers sang in the tradition of Peter, Paul and Mary, Pete Seeger, Woody Guthrie, or the more homogenized Kingston Trio. This was where the young reds hung out. I'd go there and listen to music and try to get interested in communism. Their outsider style appealed to my sense of social alienation. The McCarthy witch hunts had ended not so long ago and there was a certain heroic stance taken by younger reds that was borrowed from that time. I liked the people I met there. I began to practice their way of speaking and thinking. Fighting for the underdog seemed right to me, as it had been for my grandfather Wiseman in his union days. I was also on my way to becoming a jazz musician, and I liked wearing black turtlenecks and lurking in the shadows of respectable society. The ideas inculcated by my new friends would slip into my unconscious and lie there until I went into combat against the tough and committed Communist Vietcong and NVA in Vietnam.

In the middle of my youth and my ignorance I served in Vietnam as a corpsman with a marine infantry battalion. In 1968, just home from the war, I found my friends stoned and newly political, running around naked with their hair grown down to their butts. The things they were saying made sense to me.

Vietnam was the beginning of my *real* education, but in a way that my family had never imagined. When I turned against the war I'd served in, they thought I'd I turned against them. My mother said one day, "How can you say what you're saying? You've *been* there." I told her I could say what I said *because* I'd been there. Because of this transformation of my beliefs and values I would later affiliate myself with the William Joiner Center for the Study of War and Social Consequences in Boston.

When we lost the Vietnam War and the country swung to the left, traditional patriots suffered a serious blow to their self-image. The black flags with the grim silhouetted face that to this day fly over police stations and post offices throughout the country are more about this than any fictional abandoned POWs. There are no such men, still held captive by the Communist Vietnamese, but I think the left in this country underestimated the rage these black flags represented, a rage that would fuel the Reagan revolution, as the right began to reclaim their role as patriots.

In the sixties, many of us thought we were poised at the gate of Utopia. We laughed at people who had lived longer, had seen the wheel of history turn and turn again, and who had grown a well-developed sense of irony about idealism. We ignored (or did not read) William James, who wrote that the notion that human beings improved through the course of history is "the Meliorative Myth." But being cynical is not enough. I can't help thinking the present has us up against something we've never seen before, inside or outside the country.

The amount of change I experienced during and after the sixties, the amount of traditional hard-wiring I ripped out by the handfuls, was not a trip through strawberry fields. It nearly cost me my life and sanity.

Until recent years, I never planned anything—merely caromed between one impulsive choice and the next. I lowered my head and drove blindly into what I perceived to be a storm always breaking. I was an edge junkie. The only way the world seemed real to me was if disaster was at hand. The only way love made sense was if it was hot or chaotic. Like many people of my generation, I managed to continue this addiction to intensity late into life.

But just as often I have taken risks that bore creative fruit. I've rejected jobs that might have brought material comfort and remained loyal to my creativity even while doing soul-deadening things for a living. I have worked in grocery stores, been a trim carpenter, a word processor, computer operator, a worker in a marble mill. I have driven a cab and sold products I didn't believe in over the phone. I have bartended, worked in a bookstore, and taught classes in universities and prisons.

I have started three careers and abandoned two: I wanted to be a musician then I wanted to be an actor then I wanted to be a writer. I could very well have added a fourth: visual artist. An old friend, a talented actor, once told me, that I'd never "make it" because "if you can do more than one thing, you're dead." Now *he's* dead, murdered in a dope deal—and I'm still breathing. Perhaps I have arrived at an understanding of William Blake's infernal proverb: "If a fool would persist in his folly he would become wise."

I AM FORTUNATE to have become a storyteller, to have found a life in books. I don't think I would have made it otherwise. I believe that imagination is a survival tool and that writing and reading are the best way to grow it. This belief came to drive my writing and teaching.

Because my father was absent and my mother was at work, I spent a lot of my childhood alone. I read every book in the house. I read the King James Bible and struggled through the *thees* and *thous* to the great fleshly stories. How hot the dust of the road must have been to Jesus' feet, and how sweet when someone bathed and anointed them with oil. I thought of this in the summer when hot pavement or beach sand burned my feet. I couldn't understand why they treated Him so badly; neither could I understand why He grew the soldier's ear back after Peter whacked it off (I was hoping Peter would take out the whole cohort). Why did people stone Mary Magdalene? I'd figure it out later. I didn't get Job, but I would. Having been to the zoo, I could smell the inside of the ark, and wondered why Noah had invited the mosquitoes.

I survived much of high school by drifting off during class. My ability to fantasize did not help my grades, but it alleviated the boredom and alienation. When we read Poe out loud my mind would skitter crabwise off to some dark wonder as the class moved on without me. I would be brought back suddenly by being called on to speak, and I'd be lost. I developed a cyclopean mind's eye. I loved *Hamlet*. In those days, they actually *taught* Shakespeare in high school, the real thing, not the gutted texts they're using now—they've updated the language and killed some of the poetry—and I could tell you all about how cold the stones were at Elsinore. Milton's Satan, trailing fire in his descent, lit up the inside of my head and let me see the demons there.

I claimed, for appearances, not to be interested in such things. When I hung with the guys and lowered my recently deepened voice and bragged about the hot moves I was going to put on my date after the game on Friday, there was no point in discussing how much I liked a certain line in *Macbeth*, like ". . . ere the shard born beetle with his drowsy hums hath rung night's yawning peal."

Even the girls would have stepped back and stared. So there I was after school slamming my helmeted head against the helmeted heads of others in scrimmage. I was tall and strong, but a mediocre athlete who tried out for sports because I hoped it would get me a girlfriend. It didn't.

I never internalized television the way I did books. Television seemed to me a filmed circus; it still does: a Roman circus. It is the kind of thing you can enjoy while doing something else, like paying bills. Books you can wander into and get totally lost and then

come out changed. The worst times in my life have been when I
was too distraught to read.

I BEGAN WRITING late in life. I wrote plays and stories, and
then found poetry to be a vehicle for my lack of patience and need
for *immediate* expression. I did not begin to publish until my for-
ties. My first full-length book of poems came out when I was in
my fifties. When I received the Kate Tufts Discovery Award in 1995
for *The Moon Reflected Fire* I was introduced to Kate Tufts, who
had endowed it. I was sitting in a room at Claremont Graduate
University with Tom Lux—who had won the larger Kingsley Tufts
Award—when she strode into the room and said, "I'm so pleased
that this year's awards went to some really *disreputable poets.*" I felt
validated.

In January 2000, I returned to Vietnam with a delegation from
the Joiner Center to visit poets and writers who had at one time
been shooting at me. Vietnam, which had changed me, changed
me again in a more gentle way. It seemed in many ways to be the
last piece of a picture I had spent more than thirty years trying to
complete.

There is a pile of books next to my bed. Martin Buber is there
with John Banville, Hegel is there with crime fiction by David
Peace. There are new books of poems by C.D. Wright and Marie
Howe, and two of my favorite books by Dorianne Laux. I'm reading them simultaneously. I've always been this way. The house is full
of books. My office is so full I can't work in it anymore, nor can
I find anything. There are books in the bedroom, the living room,
on shelves, and stacked against the wall or strewn on the floor by
the couch. There are books full of notes and Post-its and there are
books lying open as if something has escaped from them and is
running around the house. There are boxes of books I intend to
sell, knowing that I will buy some of them back again.

Mornings I sit propped up on pillows with my laptop and work.

The dogs sleep, wake, scratch, whine to be walked. Fall is in the air. Around me are attempts at organization: syllabi for the fall semester, book orders, Xeroxed handouts for students.

Every semester a student will complain that I always assign readings that are full of suffering and despair. Why does Tess of the D'Urbervilles have such terrible luck? What did she do? I tell them to go to the library and make a list of happy books. I tell them it will be a very short list. Stories are about how we snatch what happiness we can from calamity, how we love in spite of whatever life hands us, how good people are destroyed and the evil prosper, how we lose our dreams and find new ones.

These students are in thrall to Eros. Their bodies are still growing. They are in love with the tricky shifts of self and love as the soul finds itself. Even though their peers come back from Iraq in body bags, they cannot help but be drawn toward the force of being young. Perhaps this is as it should be.

My own youth began in the 1940s in Memphis, Tennessee.

ONE

1

I DON'T MIND being on the German side because I know I'll be American next round. Our rifles and machine guns are sticks. There is an occasional plastic cowboy or aluminum cap pistol, but they don't make toy rifles in 1948, at least the kind that would stand the punishment we give them with our leaps and falls and shoulder rolls, and we are forced to imagine our guns from the shapes of our sticks. We are either German or American, because nobody wants to be the Japs, with their thick glasses and buck teeth. The war ended three years ago, but the thrill of victory still hangs over the working-class culture of Maple Drive in Memphis.

My constant companions are Raymond Wallace, Jockey Smithwick, and Cole Michaels. Jockey has a fort built into his garage. The front wall is a thick, double layer of plywood and two-by-fours. There is a slit in the front through which projectiles may be shot. Jockey's ammunition is arrayed in different potencies. In big jars there are walnuts, mud balls, and bolts. His chemical and biological ordnance is piss-soaked oranges, to be used only in extreme circumstances. Nailed to the inside of the front slot is an inner tube that serves as a giant slingshot to propel the ordnance. Jockey is towheaded with a swagger and a one-cornered John Wayne grin. Raymond is short and plump and smart. He knows how to operate a jigsaw so we can make our weapons and our wooden boats that we float in the chemical-stained water under the trestle at the end of the street.

I am a privileged member of the fort, and may withdraw within its confines in case of attack. We don't talk about who might attack us. Niggers? Well, we'll deal with them when they come. Kids from the other side of town? We don't know who will attack, but we are ever vigilant. Meanwhile there are the war games for practice, Germans and Americans. We snipe, we ambush, we assault. We are very, very crafty. Then we hear our mothers calling us for dinner and, lingeringly, we say our goodbyes. *Doooooouglas, you get home right now. Rayyyyyymond.*

WHEN I TURNED SIX, my mother had not yet explained to me where my father was. He had been in the Aleutian Islands with a PT boat unit for four years during the war, so I scarcely knew him. I have few pictures of the two of us. One is of me riding on his shoulders. He's wearing his navy blues and my grin is mediated with fear, as if to say *I don't quite trust this guy who has, without my permission, quickly mounted me on his shoulders.* He'd come home on leave a couple of times, but I don't remember that. On one of these occasions the picture was taken.

There is something about the photos that spoke of who he was. They seemed posed—*devoted father returning after service to his country*—and, later, pictures of him, in a white shirt, slacks, shined shoes, and tie, hair impeccably combed, bowl of pipe resting in the cup of his hand, seated in a leather chair. This pose said *patriarch, breadwinner, disciplinarian.* Of course he was none of these, although he had worked hard to create the images, repeating them through three different marriages and sets of children. He had a portable collection of symbols: a set of Reader's Digest condensed books, which said *culture,* a piece of driftwood on whatever mantelpiece, and an old pistol grip, sawed-off shotgun that was given to him by a sheriff friend who had confiscated it in a raid. The driftwood said *taste,* the shotgun said *crime does not pay.* The four children sired in his first two marriages said *virility.*

My father always told two stories, and over the years, each time I would visit him, I would hear them, pretending not to have heard them before. One was about a shaving kit he lost during a blizzard in the Aleutians, which he tried to retrieve, only to find his steps buried in deep snow. This had a parable quality: *time waits for no man*. The other was about a Japanese mini-sub pilot who, having abandoned his sinking sub in the cold water near the PT boat base, found an American navy uniform several sizes too large for him and snuck into the chow line, looking like a bundle of laundry. I liked that one. These stories were so polished the corners were worn off. They edited themselves into sleek cameos. The stories went with the driftwood and the Reader's Digest condensed books.

It may be that I only knew my father from the outside, and therefore his carefully crafted symbols were my only means of understanding him. The only time I saw him as fully human was just before his death in 1987, when I visited him in Memphis. He was carrying an oxygen tank and wearing a nasal cannula. He could scarcely walk from the car to his office without stopping to breathe. That day he managed to squeeze out a tear, perhaps his one expression of being sorry for leaving me without a father. He had always seemed embarrassed around me, as if he had some responsibility for my existence, but didn't quite know who I was. As if I were an illegitimate son who had wandered into his life from some past mistake and demanded to be recognized.

WHEN I WAS seven and my mother and I were on the bus headed to my grandparents' house, I finally asked her where my father was. He'd been gone a year. Since silences in my family were respected; I'd never asked. But that day I said, "When's Dad coming back?" My mother said, stiffly, "Your father won't be living with us anymore."

I remember once, in the Maple Drive house, I was sleeping in my parents' bed when I heard a scuffling and muffled crying. I woke up to see my mother struggling with my father. He was trying to get a piece of crumpled paper out of her fist. He tore the paper in two, then began to pry her fingers open. He retrieved the rest of the paper, and my mother fell in a sobbing heap on the floor. He saw me peeking out from under a sheet and reached over perfunctorily to pat me on the head.

After the divorce, my mother sold the Maple Drive house and moved over to a place at the corner of Arlington and Airways Boulevard, just a few miles from Elvis Presley's Graceland. My grandparents' house was an easy walk from there and became my day-care center. We ate dinner there almost every night.

My maternal grandmother, Birdie Bradberry Wiseman, cooked three meals a day, every day, until two weeks before she died. I remember her in the kitchen on a steamy summer day, a sheen of sweat on her forehead and her dress soaked down to her waist. She let the ash of her Chesterfield grow long and somehow managed never to drop it in the food.

On chicken days, she went into the backyard, snatched a chicken up by its head, and wrung its neck precisely three times, the fat jiggling on her big arms. She brought the chicken in and plucked it, the pin feathers sticking to her sweaty cheeks. She gutted and washed it, stuffed the giblets back in, and put it in the oven. When this was done, she pulled a chair into the corner of the kitchen across from the stove in front of the oscillating fan, sat, and, nod by nod, fell asleep. She had a huge mole on her right temple that looked like a blackberry, which she refused to have removed, and which grew over the years. I got up close and stared at it. When the timer rang she straightened in her chair, lit a new cigarette, and opened the oven to baste, after which she returned to the chair.

I never asked her for her recipe for barbecued lamb and I wish I had. Apparently she had given it to whoever asked her for it, but always managed to leave out one essential ingredient so that all efforts to reproduce it failed. It was her pièce de resistance, the mention of which could bring the whole family together. It came out of the oven black, tart, and salty, and I couldn't get enough of it. In the summer we had big pitchers of sweet ice tea floating mint leaves from the garden. Also from the garden we had big tomatoes and okra. I loved the tomatoes and loathed the okra, which I would hide under the little lump of mashed potatoes I got away with not eating.

Once a week an old black man in a mule-driven cart would round the corner onto Larose Avenue, singing softly and resonantly, *watermeh-lon, sweet peas and fresh liiiiiima beeeans*. He would sing each vegetable as if it were an unrepeatable creation of God. My grandmother would dig around in her coin purse and hustle out to meet him.

On chicken days there was the giblet gravy on the potatoes. There were turnips also, which, like the okra, I learned to cover with potatoes. There were collard greens and black-eyed peas, which I loved.

When the family lived in Kentucky during the Depression there was a saying: "Taters and beans on Wednesday, beans and taters on Friday, and lard in between." But in Memphis, we had roast beef with gravy—not just any roast, but a big one. The full table, three generations of my mother's family present at it, would be quiet except for the slurps and grunts of eating, a language of suffering no longer endured. My grandmother's laborious cooking was a language of both love and gratitude. Since I'd never had to eat lard or go without a meal, and since words were not the principal form of expression in the family, it would take me a long time to understand this.

In Kentucky they had a big garden that they shared with a black family down the bluff. The father, Totten, would work the garden alongside my grandmother in return for which he would take home half its yield. The children from the two families played together.

But in Memphis, I was the only child at the table. The vigorous eating was in harmony with the general social uplift after the war. The Depression was long over, and we had beaten Tojo and Hitler. Uncle Fred had risen from laborer to carpenter to a contractor who could read blueprints and work with architects. My grandfather, whom we called Pop, had not worked since he hurt his neck on the job. The injury coincided with the introduction of a television into the house. He spent most of his remaining life at the right end of the couch, getting up once a week to mow the lawn. Although well by then, he refused further employment and had a steady pension.

In the years after World War II there were lots of family get-togethers, minus my father, whose name was not mentioned. Aunt Frances and Uncle George and my two cousins, George and Freddy, would come from North Carolina, and Uncle Fred and Aunt Rosie would come in from Raleigh, where they'd built a house.

The attitudes of poverty carried over unconsciously into this new age. When Uncle Fred bought his first new car he left the plastic covers—that were meant to be removed—on the seats for a good year after. He made us wipe our feet when we got in. When he parked, he would take down the license numbers of the cars in front and in back of him.

The men stood around the kitchen sink and drank Wild Turkey, and I stood knee-high and invisible and listened to the stories. The only man in the family who ever saw any actual fighting was my uncle George, who had been wounded in the head and the neck while in the airborne artillery. He was what they called a "mustang." He worked his way up through the ranks from buck private to warrant officer, and then to lieutenant colonel. Later, he'd been a general's aide and had a certain amount of authority when he spoke about the war. He was still in the army and would be until his drinking got him passed over for promotion too many times. Uncle Fred had stayed stateside in the Seabees. Regardless of the amount of combat they'd actually seen, they spoke as if the war had been the biggest adventure in their lives. And it had been.

Despite the horrors Uncle George had experienced, he only talked about things that were at least partially funny. I remember him complaining that his silk-lined sleeping bag had been shredded by an incoming artillery round. He did not talk about how grateful he was not to have been in it at the time, merely what it cost to have the thing reassembled from shreds.

Being a war baby meant an immersion in the drunkenness of victory when the war ended. When we went to the movies, I'd see the newsreels from World War II. *Victory at Sea* was on the television every week. I imagined the faces of the kamikaze pilots moments before they crashed into the American aircraft carriers in a boil of flame and black smoke. I rooted for the deck gunners as they directed their tracers toward the incoming planes, and cheered when one was hit and went spiraling down into the sea. It seemed as if there would always be war, and we would always be winning it. But the Korean War got lost in the shadow of World War II, and most of the imagery that appeared in my drawings from that time is either about Japs and Americans or cowboys and Indians. Sometimes I got the historical periods mixed up. In one drawing, an unfortunate cowboy tied to a tree is about to be roasted in a big fire set by some petroglyphic Indians. The grinning hero, depicted in a cowboy hat, swings in on a rope from the bow of a huge, World War II–era ship. He was coming to the rescue—one of my constant themes. There is an illustrated story about American planes coming to the rescue of a town with skyscrapers that had been attacked by Japanese planes. The caption for panel two reads: "The yak featers were saprsed by three U.S. featers" (*yak* being my phonetic rendering of "Jap"). Strangely, below, in the city of tall buildings, there are cowboys. In another drawing, the Yaks are bombing a city, and its people are trundling out of town bent under huge bundles of possessions. I don't know if this image of civilians came from a newsreel or from listening to Uncle George's stories, but it is an image I would encounter later in life, in another war with frightened people trying to get out of a hot combat zone.

In another story, I am sent on a mission to get the cavalry and bring them back to rescue the fort that is being attacked by Indians: "I ran as fast as I could airrus zinged by." In the end, the fort is victorious. My stories always celebrated victory. Isn't that what happens when Americans come? The title of this story is *Wor;* the opening line reads, "I was 8 years old whin the Indein wor came. My mother would all ways haf to work."

I have two *Life* magazines from the month I was born. The magazines are entirely filled with the imagery of war. The woman on the cover of one is wearing a Montgomery beret, and all the women's fashions have a military cut with padded shoulders. All the stories are about "our boys" or the support workers at home. All the ads are related to the war. In one, a young soldier and his wife look up at a little house on a hill with a white picket fence. The sun is rising behind it. Tire companies picked up the call to ration rubber and nylons.

One of my drawings reflects that kind of wartime mind. In two panels, one above and one below, is a medic. In the first panel he is dressed for combat and is holding a poster that says "GIVE BLOOD." The lower half of the poster is cut off. In the next panel, the lower half appears. The same medic has hooked up a plasma bottle to a rifle stuck in the ground by its bayonet, the plasma drip running down into a wounded soldier. The caption reads "–SOME DAY YOU'LL NEED IT." It does not say "Someday you *might* need it," but you WILL. The wounded soldier is grinning, looking out at the viewer, saying in a dialogue bubble, "I'm Lucky." I did not know, of course, how prophetic this drawing would be.

Back in the kitchen, I'd get bored when the men began to get drunk, to repeat their stories, and I'd move to the living room. There the women were in high form, gossiping at the speed of light. They'd all had their hair done to look like Loretta Young. When they saw me listening, they began to spell things. My aunt Frances was saying "that b-a-s-t-a-r-d." My mother told them I could spell better than they thought. My mother had an imperious manner when changing the subject, speaking in a queenly and implacable tone through which she indicated that she did not wish to pursue a subject. This was accompanied by lifting her chin to gaze over everyone's head at the horizon. This time, they were talking about Charles Renagle, a carpenter friend of the family's who was always drunk and had "a woman in every bar." But I was not to hear the rest of that one.

My aunt Frances had a cigarette going in every ashtray in the house and was beginning to annoy people. She rattled her ice cubes when she wanted her drink refreshed. Uncle George heard it from the kitchen, like a shepherd hearing the bell of a lost goat, grabbed a bottle, and went into the living room to replenish her. Then he returned to the kitchen, where the men were laughing heartily. At a certain point, my aunt Frances would have a "spell," or start an argument, or get disoriented, and a scarcely more sober Uncle George had to wobblingly escort her to one of the bedrooms. It was a dance they did until death.

These were mostly good days for me. The mood was up in the house, and the poisonous depressions had not yet set in. I had the run of the place. I would go into the attic, dig around in my father's abandoned photography equipment, or the magic kit he used for his act at the Chicago World's Fair. I would wave the wand, pull brightly colored scarves out of long silver cans, and open little concentric eggs to find nothing.

I would open Uncle George's footlocker, where he kept a captured German rifle, packed in grease, and a series of etchings of dachshunds behaving in very French ways, sniffing the bottoms of coifed and pink-bowed poodles. There was a box that belonged to my grandmother I never opened. It was devoted to the first-born, Mary Wiseman, dead of leukemia at four. In it were her little dresses and dolls. I had seen these things one day when I came up and found my grandmother weeping over them.

Their house became the container of my imaginative world. I had no siblings and my imagination became my companion. In the bathroom that surrealist artifact, the douche bag, hung from the shower head, with its long tentacle and nozzle, and it became in my imagination a deep-sea beast. During bath time I would take it down and play with it along with my toy boats, its long red tube becoming the terrifying tentacle of a giant squid, its spouting nozzle a storm against which my imagined crews floundered and fought.

At night, before I slept, I made up stories in which I was a wounded hero, heavily decorated and cared for. I imagined a sister who would sleep with me for comfort, or a sweet-faced nurse who'd stroke my brow and ease my pain. And sometimes I whispered into the oscillating fan, my words returned as a chord.

IN DECEMBER 1966 I have completed my training at Field Medical Service School at Camp Lejeune, North Carolina, where I have been learning how to give combat medical support to a marine infantry unit. We have been stomping around breaking the ice of the frozen swamps, preparing for the jungle. I am given a Fleet Marine Force uniform with a caduceus on the left sleeve. I get five days' leave before I fly to the staging battalion at Camp Pendleton, California. My grandmother is dying and I go to Memphis.

My mother is there, and a doctor. My grandmother is to be moved to the hospital the next day. I know enough to know that this means *palliation*. This means *easing her into a coma*. The doctor lets me practice my intramuscular shot technique and give her some Demerol. I do it expertly and leave no hematoma. My grandmother smiles and says she felt nothing. Compared to the pain of the cancer, I don't imagine she would.

My grandmother is graceful in her dying. I have never seen her this way. She was not graceful in her life, but angry and unfulfilled. Aside from muttering prayers or curses under her breath, she never articulated her rage. She would slam kitchen cabinet doors, bang pots and pans, and give a cold silence to all, so that we never knew exactly who or what she was mad at.

I came to understand her grace in dying as a release, almost as if she'd looked forward to leaving life for a very long time. Years later, I heard this wish for release from my mother, who said things like, "We live too long these days." There was a great fatigue in this statement, as if the life she had carried grew heavier each year and her pride would not let her put it down. To put it down would leave her faced with the possibility of happiness, which was too alien a world. In this family there is pride in the way one carries one's lot, and when that burden is lifted by death, it is the rightful release of one who has endured. Heaven is never mentioned.

NEXT DAY WE leave my grandmother at the hospital and go back to the Larose house to spend the night. Pop is sitting in his place at the door end of the couch watching television. When the TV first came, he began watching in the morning with cartoons. When the news came on he'd mutter "Crap." Westerns came on in the afternoon, and then more news and more muttering. Pop, being a union man, liked Fidel Castro and resented the frequent diatribes against him. Later, he refused to believe that Sputnik had ever been sent into space. "Crap," he said.

When I was little I would sit and watch the nightly boxing with him. This was a time when whites were still taken seriously in the profession, and Floyd Patterson had not yet knocked out Ingemar Johansson. When there was a match between a black man and a white man, I would root for the black boxer, just to get my grandfather's goat. "You're only sayin' that because he's a nigger," he'd say. "Hesh, Fred," my grandmother would say. "Hesh . . ." Now he is very old and has ceased cursing the news and has left the world to change without him.

That night I am awakened by the sound of a chair falling over. I get out of bed and go into the dining room where Pop has fallen against the table. I help him straighten up and hand him his cane. His arms are like sticks beneath his flannel pajamas. When he is solid on his feet, he raises his palm and nods, and continues the shuffle *tap tap* to the kitchen where he will pour a shot of whiskey to put himself back to sleep. I return to my room and stare at the oscillating fan, now still in winter.

The next morning I hear the old push lawn mower in the backyard. Pop is doing his weekly trim. He leans into the lawn mower as if it is a walker, and pushes, his cane hung over the handgrip. He gets up some momentum and then begins to run-stumble. I wonder how he is going to get along without Birdie Bradberry Wiseman to cook him three meals a day.

2

AFTER MY FATHER LEFT, the extended family made some half-hearted attempts to find suitable male mentors for me, but they had children of their own. My mother made it known to me, and to others, that she did not much like boys.

"Boys are dirty," she'd say. And then she would talk about various girl children she admired for their maturity and poise. She would take me to the houses of people who had girl children and let me play with them. I never did get excited about dollhouses, but I thought it would be fun to set one on fire.

My mother subscribed to *McCall's* in those days, which included a section for little girls in the back, featuring Betsy McCall. She was the perfect little girl in the form of a paper doll that could be cut out, along with her new clothes, and dressed according to the incoming fashions. My mother would open to the Betsy McCall page and hand me the scissors. I complied, thinking nothing of it. One day, after several such indulgences, my uncle Fred observed me placing the little dresses and shoes on Betsy. I'll never forget his face. He was appalled. Shortly, my grandmother Birdie and grandfather Fred joined in, shouting at my mother.

Uncle Fred said, "He is not a girl. What is wrong with you?"

After that there were no more *McCall's*, but my mother continued to maintain her contempt for boys. They tracked dirt in the house, were difficult to control, and they turned into men. Men, she said, had *terrible passions*.

I had an honorary uncle, Jim Nunnally, who teased me, took me duck hunting, and let me shoot a .410-gauge shotgun. He was as round and pink and bald as Elmer Fudd, and we never really hit it off. One day, when my father was away, he came over to the house with my uncle Fred and some other folks. My mother was in high spirits, and everybody had a drink. Jim went into the kitchen and returned with my kitten between two slices of bread and his mouth gaping as if to eat it. I threw a fit. I might have actually hit him. I was not amused.

When I was eight, Uncle Fred took me out on the job, which in this case was the building of his own house on Mallard Point Drive in Raleigh. I remember sitting in the front seat of the pickup, crammed between my uncle and one of his bricklayers. We stopped at a drugstore off Airways Boulevard and went in for chewing tobacco and snuff. I was given a "chaw" and nearly made myself sick trying to chew it. Uncle Fred and his friend got an enormous kick out of my reaction, but let me know that I had passed the test.

My job was to crawl around under the house and pick up all the wood chips the framing carpenters had left. When I would get lazy, or grow distracted, Fred would call to me, "Get hot on it, boy, or I'll get a little nigger boy to do it for a quarter." I was getting fifty cents.

Charles Renagle was an excellent carpenter, and was also the bricklayer. Charles was dark-skinned for a white man, had a perpetual grin, and was always performing. I would listen to him and his crew for hours as they coated the bricks with their trowels and made a perfectly straight wall. Their speech was full of words like *cunt-hair* and *pussy* and *nigger pussy*. He had the personality of a stand-up comic, but was too stupid to pull it off. One day he asked me if I knew where chocolate milk came from. I shook my head. Then he said, "Nigger cows!" and his bricklaying crew collapsed with laughter. One day he said, "You know what I'm givin' up for Lent?"

I said, "Naw."

"Cigars and nigger women." And he howled at his own joke.

Growing up without my father had certain advantages. My

father's presence would have been worse than his absence, because he would have tried to kill in me what he'd killed in himself.

My father had turned away from his own talent. He was a gifted artist and photographer. When he met my mother, he was selling mattresses door-to-door. This makes me chuckle when I remember family descriptions of him as a lothario. I imagine him offering to test the mattresses with the blushing housewives.

But after the war, with my mother's help, he went to night school to get his CPA certificate, which could be had without a college degree in those days. He became appallingly responsible after that. When I stayed with him that year in Mississippi, I would ask him for money and he would say things like, "You've got champagne taste and a beer pocketbook, son." He became the practical man, and his considerable talent fell into shadow. By then I think he considered any kind of creativity a form of degeneracy.

After age seven, I would visit my father every other weekend, in accordance with the custody agreement. He would go through the motions of being Dad, but his heart wasn't in it. Once he kissed me on the lips, a forced, awkward kiss. He was never affectionate with me after that.

He liked to go fishing by himself, and when, out of necessity, he would take me with him, I sensed that I was an obstacle to his pleasure. We would take the canoe out into a lake and sit quietly, him casting in a slow rhythm, letting the fly drift gently down on the water, scarcely breaking the surface tension. He gave me a cane pole with a bobber and a worm attached to a hook. I would get bored very early and fidget, and he would tell me to sit still, that my wiggling was scaring the fish. I would then stare at the shallows and imagine what was down there, where it became darker green beneath the sunlit patches, where it clotted in the cypress knees along the shore. I would stare down into the water by the canoe at the fish hanging on the stringer, and wonder if they knew they would be executed, gutted, and fried in batter.

My father would go out on the water to brood, letting his mind drift until the tug of a fish brought him back. He would do every-thing himself. He had a lightweight canoe that he would load on rails on the roof of his Chrysler, then unload at the fishing spot and carry to the water by himself. Most people keep a part of them-selves hidden, a place they can go when things get hard. My father kept three quarters of himself hidden. I don't know if anyone ever knew what was there, but toward the end of his life, all that he had stored away in the dark became a painful mass of guilt and fear.

My mother told me that once, when they were still married, he'd been out in the canoe fly-fishing, and the fly had been caught in a snag. In his attempt to pull it out, the fly broke loose and flew back, one of the hooks catching in his eyelid. He paddled ashore, loaded the canoe, the fly hanging from his eyelid, and he drove a long way to the nearest hospital to have the hook cut loose. Somehow I picked up his capacity for solitude and hard-headed singular survival. I also picked up his tendency to sexual profligacy, but that is a story for later. What he failed to do, however—and this is the blessing of growing up without him—was to inhibit my imagination.

After the long divorce, I continued to live with my mother in the Maple Drive house. In those days, divorces were played out in the courtroom with both parties present. It was a horrible, shaming procedure that changed my mother forever. She'd bring the shame home every day and hand it to me with her nasty remarks and her short fuse. I had to give her a wider berth than usual.

There are reasons I cannot completely hate my mother. One time she took me to Hickman, Kentucky, where she had been born in a two-room house on a bluff overlooking the Mississippi. The foundation remained, with the rust stain of the woodstove that my grandmother Birdie cooked on, and which served to heat the whole house. There was a small kitchen and a slightly larger bedroom, where my grandmother and grandfather and three chil-dren slept in two feather beds. My grandfather worked as a coal miner, then a letter carrier. He quite often drank up his paycheck and came home scary.

My mother would never have admitted to being poor, but she was. There were days they went without food. The family staples were beans and potatoes and lard. The summer garden improved the fare, but a chicken was a rare thing and beef was almost unheard of. There were, of course, catfish from the river, and bream and bass from the lakes, on the weekends when there was time to fish.

My mother's past was always off-limits, except for a few stories that got repeated. In one, she is walking home from school in one of her two dresses. (She had one for everyday, and one for church.) She crossed somebody's yard and a mean chow dog came after her. She managed to climb up a tree, but the dog tore her dress. She was stranded in the tree until the dog's owner returned and took the dog inside. When my mother came home that night in her torn dress, her mother beat her nearly senseless.

In another, she was playing on some monkey bars in a school-yard when she fell and broke her arm. Pop was called away from work to come get her. When he arrived he began to shout at her, in front of others, for being stupid. There was no fatherly comfort, no worry for her well-being or her pain. He was enraged that he would have to shell out for the doctor and would have his pay docked for leaving work early.

Her broken arm was set in an old-fashioned plaster cast by the local sawbones. When, after much too long, the cast was removed, my mother's arm had become frozen at a ninety-degree angle. The doctor's prescription for straightening it was to have her stand on a kitchen stool and grab the top of the door. Then the stool was pulled out from under her and she hung by her injured arm to stretch the atrophied tendons.

These were not really even complete stories, but little flashes in a long darkness. Other family members offered similar anecdotes, with no narrative development. The listener was expected to fill in the gaps. You were supposed to *get it* without having it explained. Uncle Fred did offer once that my mother was referred to in the extended family as "the cold one."

My mother got a job at a Memphis cottonseed oil company as a secretary. When I came home from school, I was in the house alone. When my mother had to go anywhere, I was told to stay in the house *or else*. I did not understand the phrase "latchkey kid" until much later in life, and assumed other children were locked up too.

My imagination developed remarkably in those lonely years. I wrote and illustrated stories. I invented things. I fashioned a kind of camera/movie theater made of a cardboard box with a hole cut in it. I would strip colored cellophane from empty food boxes I'd found in the trash and place them over the hole. I would close off the hallway by shutting all the doors and create total darkness. Then I would shine a flashlight through the cellophane. This was, in fact, a pinhole camera without the film, inside of which images would appear opposite the pinhole. If I'd known to lay a piece of sheet film against the back of the box and time the exposure by covering the hole, opening it, and covering it again, I could have taken pictures. But I imagined movies against the far side of the box, ghostly figures moving in a red fog.

Occasionally, my mother would hire a maid to clean the house. She never had the same maid twice, and I think it was because of me. I was acting out a lot in those days, and I would do things like follow the maid around and make messes where she'd cleaned. I overheard one maid saying to my mother at the end of the day, "I can't work for you no more, Mrs. Anderson. Everywhere I clean up, that child go and mess up."

And I would do more alarming things. I had an electric train in my bedroom, and when I'd grown tired of watching the thing run in circles, tooting its horn, I began to use the platform on which it ran as a drawing table. One day, I drew a picture of a man who had been beheaded and castrated. Drops of blood fell from the severed head and genitals. When I was done, I went in the kitchen and presented it to my mother. She seemed genuinely alarmed, saying things like, "That poor man, you've cut off his head."

In my family, psychology was held in the same contempt as communism. Much later, as a last resort, I was taken to a Memphis clinic for observation. I was put in a room with a very nice woman psychologist, shown ink blots, allowed to build a model airplane, and given other less fun activities to perform while she observed. Other than providing me with things to do, she was not intrusive, but sat a short distance away and smiled.

I loved the inkblots. I could make them anything I wanted. I could spin stories from them that made the silent woman smile. I don't know what was determined by the psychologists, but my mother, after I had been to the clinic two or three times, summarized the psychologist's findings by looking at me from a great height, her expression rigid, and telling me that they'd said *I was disturbed*. I've always wondered what else they said.

I had begun to grow rather rapidly around age seven, and my mother had begun to beat me commensurate with that growth. She had always been quick with a slap. I had an early memory of her slapping me when I was in the high chair. I had dropped some food on the floor. This was the way she'd been raised, and this is what she knew to do. But at age seven, my mother ceased completely any kind of affection, physical or otherwise, and increased verbal and physical punishment. Unlike my father's perfunctory swats—as if he were training a dog with a newspaper—my mother's beatings were impassioned. Her red face and furious eyes were a part of the terror I experienced. I was made to take off my pants, stand on a heat register—not to be tortured by the heat, but to give her a confined target—and was beaten with belts and sticks. She would swing hard and raise bloody welts on my legs that would afterward begin to bruise. In those days, there was no social services agency to check on children who came to school with bloody welts on their legs. Besides, I wasn't the only one showing up in that condition. The response would be more likely *I wonder what he did to get those welts?* I can't remember what the beatings were for—not a one of them—but I remember the beatings themselves in excruciating detail.

Her verbal punishment consisted principally of remembering every bad thing I had ever done and reciting the list back to me when she was angry. These tirades were something like a prosecutor building a case against the most egregious of criminals. There was a leer in her voice when she recited these crimes, as if describing some kind of grisly murder to a jury. I would have dreams for years after of being locked in a cell below the schoolhouse, understanding that I was to be executed in the morning, but no one would tell me my crime. Apparently being male was enough. And, at that time, I had begun to look like my father.

A therapist told me once, during a discussion of nature and nurture, that she had early on been a fan of nurture only. "But now," she said, "I am more and more impressed by nature." I have watched episodes on *Animal Planet* where young animals, injured or motherless, are taken in by veterinary types and nurtured until they can return to the wild. At a certain point, a lion cub becomes an animal that can kill you. All the care in the world cannot make it otherwise. Apparently, I was going to be a boy.

The beatings and condemnations continued until I was eleven years old. My mother swung to hit me one day and I reached out, grabbed her wrist, and held it. We both understood at that moment that I was stronger than she was, and that there would be no more beatings. The verbal condemnation continued until much later in life, when I finally refused to speak to her for two years.

Many years later, after the war, I asked my mother why she had stopped loving me when I was a child. She was visibly shaken by the question, and her words stumbled. She said things like, "I liked you when you were little. But then you began to grow. It wasn't normal. When you were seven, your head was too big for your body. There was something wrong with you."

There were girls on the block down toward the Jackson Avenue end of the street that I had brief, poignant encounters with. There was a family that lived mid-block where the street dipped and the storm drains were. They lived in a house raised up over the street on a knoll. I knew the family to say hello. One day I wandered into the yard and the father was sitting on the front porch with his chair tipped back against the gray-shingle front wall. I had a few words with him during which he said, "You ever tell a lie?"

"Naw."

"That's the biggest one you ever told."

He laughed a kind of *huh huh huh* laugh that made me nervous, so I went around the back of the house where three little girls were sitting around an upturned washtub having a meeting of some kind. I approached and said "Hi." They did not respond and did not look at me. Finally, one of the little girls turned slightly, still not looking at me, and said, "Silence means you are not wanted. This is a secret meeting."

I continued down the street to two houses before the end, where the Weinsteins lived. The father was the local druggist, and he had a daughter named Sarah, who was two years older than I. Unlike the shorter haircuts brushed up at the edges that most girls had, she had long black hair that hung straight down her back and big, black eyes.

The Weinsteins were Jews. My mother had confided to me one day that Jews had different morals from Christians and that they swapped wives. I had no idea what it meant to swap wives, but the whispery leer with which she uttered the remark made me understand it was forbidden, and of course, made me want to know the Weinsteins.

Sarah had always been nice to me, and she invited me into the house to play. There was a black maid at work in the house who eyeballed me over her shoulder from the kitchen as I came in.

Sarah and I were silly for a while, and then she took me into the bathroom and locked the door. She pulled down her drawers but not her underpants. She told me to do the same, and I did. Then she reached over and pulled down my underpants and stared. In a while, she pulled her own down and I was left staring at the hairless cleft, the mysterious split-leaf rhododendron. It was so strange, so other to me that I never had the thought that my mother had one, or that I had come out of it.

I was less eager to touch her between the legs, but she took my hand and placed it there. This was all done with such gentle sweetness. There was no notion of shame, no leering sexiness, merely the most focused and tender curiosity. The maid began calling Sarah's name. The voice came closer, and then she banged on the door. "Open that door, child. What you doin' in there?"

She continued pounding and finally, somehow, forced the door open and found us standing there with our pants around our ankles. She began to roll her eyes and shout at us. "Your mama goin' skin you alive. Get out of there. Get out and go home, boy."

I went home and knew enough to keep it to myself. I kept a lot of things to myself and learned to edit out what might displease my mother. That didn't leave much to talk about.

This said, I am grateful to my mother for many things. She was an avid reader and made sure that there were books in the house. She believed that speaking and writing well was the way to get ahead in the world, and would not allow any double negatives in my speech, nor would she allow me to listen to country music, although I was attracted to its very real sadness. She read Shakespeare and would quote him, often, the most frequent quote being from *King Lear*. "He hath ever but slenderly known himself." And to me, "How sharper than a serpent's tooth it is to have a thankless child." She was one of the few people, besides myself, who ever read Faulkner and laughed.

Even when she was dying in a nursing home in Tucson, she read Faulkner. It is not surprising that she would hear those voices and nod in agreement with the hard-bitten ironies, the cruelty of poverty, and the chaos of sex and thwarted love. When I read *As I Lay Dying,* I hear her in the voice of Addie as she sits by the window, dying, and even in her last moments, supervising the building of her coffin.

3

WHEN I WAS TEN, my mother decided to move to the South-west. She had chronic bronchitis and believed that the dry air would be good for her. But I knew that she wanted to leave behind the pain of a failed marriage and all its geographical reminders.

She bought a green 1952 Plymouth and we set out toward Roswell, New Mexico, where she had a secretarial job waiting for her. We went south to Louisiana, stopped in New Orleans, and ate jambalaya, hushpuppies, and crayfish all across the state as we drove toward Texas on Route 10.

Most motels were not chains in those days, and each one we stayed in had its own eccentricities. However, there were certain universals. Most of them had Magic Fingers: put a quarter in a little machine and the bed would vibrate. Virtually all of them had Gideon Bibles in the drawers and bad paintings on the walls.

I was big for my age, and I shared the driving with my mother. When I drove, she would climb in the backseat and nap, her head resting where the seat met the rear window. She was in such a good mood she didn't even nag me about keeping both hands on the wheel. I suppose that she imagined she would find happiness now. I have never seen her so relaxed, so even-tempered. She was riding hope across the country, just as one dreams between the purchase of the lottery ticket and the inevitable disappointment.

Texas bored me, but as soon as we got close to the New Mexico border, the landscape became a deep ferrous red.

We visited Juarez, a sleepy little border town, and I bought a wallet with an Aztec sun on it. El Paso could have been Mars, with its rusty cinder cones and endless piles of rusty rock.

My mother was a stunning woman, much younger looking than her years. The sun had made her skin glow and brightened the blonde highlights in her hair. Slender, with dark blue eyes, she turned heads wherever she went. Men standing in line to pay at a store would surreptitiously run their fingers through their hair, or straighten their ties, before they moved into the frame to say hello, but my mother carried the hurt of her lost marriage like a deep and fatal sickness, and none of these men seemed to measure up. They were not as handsome as my father had been. They were not as witty. They appeared foolish to her, or ridiculous, but she always had admirers, men who would court her furiously, spend a great deal of money on her, and take her on outings. And she would reject them one after another.

There were caves in New Mexico, and bottomless saltwater lakes fed by underground rivers. Later, one of my mother's boyfriends told me I could swim between the lakes in the underground rivers, but that the current would be fierce. I imagined myself in scuba gear, traveling all the way to the ocean past fantastic spires of gypsum. There were obsidian and turquoise, and mica you could peel off in transparent strips. There were scorpions, centipedes, and vinegarones hidden in garages and under rocks. There was every kind of landscape in New Mexico, from the flat and desolate red-dust plains full of burrs and tumbleweeds to pine-covered mountains.

My mother rented a house just down the street from the New Mexico Military Institute. She soon made friends playing bingo, and in a square-dancing club, and she took me. I loved the dancing, and had aspirations to become a square-dance caller.

Someone—I don't know what male authority my mother had consulted—suggested that I join the Boy Scouts, and so I did. I was eleven going on twelve and they let me in early. I have a picture of myself in my neatly pressed Scout uniform, kerchief and hat, standing at attention with a solemn, priestly expression on my face as if I were about to pronounce some great truth.

I remember one Scout outing where we went camping not too far from town in a flat area with a stream and a few trees. It was raining, and the Scout leaders showed us how to dig trenches around the tents we had just erected and staked with much trouble. It was cold and miserable and wet and there were mosquitoes. After a rainy night the weather cleared and the Scout leaders decided to leave us to our own devices. This was very irresponsible, but in retrospect I imagine they had gone into town to drink beer or see girls. It was late in the evening when we got out the marshmallows and hot dogs and began to make dinner. We built a fire as we had been instructed, making a little teepee of sticks over some crumpled newspaper, and soon we had a roaring blaze.

About that time a puppy wandered into the camp and approached us playfully. Someone threw it a hot dog.

I said, "That dog's too friendly" in an ominous voice. "That's a symptom of rabies."

I had their attention then. We'd been lectured on rabid skunks, squirrels, and the like and told not to approach them. This puppy, who seemed harmless, now acquired an aura of sorts.

"You don't want to get rabies," I said. Winston Carter was climbing onto a picnic table, staring at the dog.

"Friend of mine died of it," I lied.

"His eyes turned red and his teeth and fingernails grew. They have a special hospital for rabies." More Scouts were on the picnic table now.

"They had him chained up like a dog. He snapped at everybody who came in to look at him, and the nurses and doctors wore iron gloves. I tried a pair on myself. They were heavy."

The puppy had the whole package of hot dogs now and was growling, playing with it. This added to the atmosphere.

"And you're afraid of water, so they have to pump water up your butt, which is dumb because you're going to die anyway."

The puppy pranced around the hot dogs and then tugged one out of the pack. "My mother says *hydro* means water and *phobia* means scared of. You want to kill anybody carrying a glass of water."

Winston said, "My dad said it's the fluoride. You'll turn communist if you drink that water."

"It's terrible," I continue. "You start biting yourself because nobody else will let you bite them. You bite off all your fingers and your toes. You bite off your own pecker." Winston looked down at his crotch, then at the puppy, who was on its third hot dog and getting kind of sluggish.

"Everybody's scared of rabies, so you don't have any friends. You don't have any fun, can't go out." I had begun to scare myself, and the puppy was growing slowly into the Hound of the Baskervilles. "Then you bite your own heart out and die."

By that time we had all climbed up onto the picnic tables to protect ourselves from the hot-dog-besotted puppy, which had begun to nod out. When the Scout leaders returned that evening they found us standing on tables.

I had become a skilled liar and dramatist. I once told a history teacher that I had spent three months in Paris with my mother. When mother went to a PTA meeting later that year, the grinning teacher bounded up to her and said, "I understand you know Paris," hoping for a little Francophile flirtation. That night I remember the angry cadence of my mother's high heels coming up the walk.

I had suddenly grown pubic hair. To my mother, it seemed to have happened overnight. She walked into the bathroom one day while I was taking a bath and made a remark about me "becoming a man." There was a thickness in her voice when she said it. In another, more conscious life, she might have known to knock first, but she just stood there, fixing her hair in the mirror, giving me an occasional look over her shoulder.

I had also begun to masturbate. One night I was masturbating enthusiastically and the headboard of the bed was knocking against the wall. My mother slammed the door open against the wall and shouted

"WHAT ARE YOU DOING?" She was red-faced and wild-eyed. She stalked around my room, swinging right and left and knocking things over. "I AM GOING TO GO SEE SOMEBODY ABOUT YOU. THERE IS SOMETHING WRONG WITH YOU."

The next day she went to see someone, as promised, as if it were an emergency, as if I were deathly ill or possessed. When she came home later that day her anger had shifted to the psychologist. She made a number of statements about how psychology was a bunch of "bunk." I don't know what the therapist said to her, but she never mentioned masturbation again, and I was quieter about it from then on.

I hung out with some boys who'd also just begun to masturbate, and we had several group sessions. In one of them, a boy had produced his mother's personal vibrator. In those days vibrators were not out of the closet as to their true purpose. They were described as massage or relaxation aids. We passed it around the room. We were a closed circuit, a culture unto ourselves.

On Saturdays, freed from school, we would roam, as if driven by our own little cock-headed god. On this particular day we had ridden our bicycles a distance out of town and wandered in one of New Mexico's flat, red landscapes. We stopped for a masturbation session and then moved on. We came to a dump where there was a mangy little dog someone had abandoned. It was blind. Charlie Wainscot, whose mother's vibrator we had passed around, decided that it should be killed, because it could not possibly make its way in the world. The mercy killing idea was a mask for something deeper, and I watched, horrified, as Charlie beat the dog to death with a piece of rebar. The dog yelped piteously and Charlie, swinging the rebar, wept himself, his face crimson. After that we moved on in silence, as if carrying something heavy between us.

I had left my suede jacket at the dump, but when I realized it later, I could not go back to get it. I didn't want to see the dog. It was getting late, and the red earth became a darker, blood color.

Our faces were bright gold in the slant sun and the sky was clear and fierce. I felt so far from home, and not just in distance. We walked and picked the burrs out of our socks and somebody pulled out a pack of cigarettes. We smoked and coughed and tried to forget the dog.

On our way back to the wash where we'd left our bicycles, we came upon a group of archaeologists who had discovered a burial place of some prehistoric Indians. They wore Levis, leather vests, and work shirts, boots and broad-brimmed hats. One was a pretty young woman with black hair and green eyes.

The wash had bisected a grave and there, before us, the skeleton of an ancient person was revealed in the bank.

The archaeologists explained to us what they were doing. They were painting the bones with shellac to protect them, and photographing them in place, before they removed them. They had assembled a pile of potsherds and ax heads they'd already removed and were putting them in little sacks and marking them. They were so civilized in their explanations, and we had just emerged from *Lord of the Flies* land. I felt guilty in the presence of such gentleness and patience. I was magnetized by the skeleton, and it burned into my brain where it still lives, incandescent, as I write this.

AFTER A YEAR in Roswell, my mother had not found happiness, and we moved on to Tucson.

We drove endlessly over the flat land between western New Mexico and Arizona. There were advertisements for COLOSSAL CAVE, and one that kept repeating: HITLER'S CAR, 10 MILES. HITLER'S CAR, 5 MILES. HITLER'S CAR, 1 MILE. DON'T MISS HITLER'S CAR. YOU MISSED HITLER'S CAR. I never saw Hitler's car, but someone told me it was an old Mercedes the man had once ridden in, and which somehow found its way to a little roadside restaurant in the Arizona desert.

Arizona was like New Mexico, but the landscape was less red, and there was more cactus and ocotillo. There was more water in Tucson in those days, in the rivers and arroyos, and there were even places near the river where grass grew. People had not yet taken to laying green gravel in their front yards to simulate a lawn.

The skies were crystal and there wasn't the faintest hint of the pollution that would come in the seventies. The population was about one hundred thousand, and there was little traffic in the streets, which to the south, scarcely extended past 22nd Street, and to the north, River Road. Tucson was surrounded by four mountain ranges, with the biggest, the Catalinas, to the north. The western part of the city was scarcely developed. Tucson was good for my solitude and I spent a lot of time in the desert.

My mother found a place on North Winstel Boulevard, near Speedway, and I enrolled at Catalina Junior High School, now called Doolen Middle School. Before school started I explored the desert around the house and found that there were horned toads and great numbers of other lizards. I chased and caught them, and got stuck with prickly pear cactus. I looked for Gila monsters but never found one. Once I came upon a rattlesnake and heard the rattle for the first time. It was a sound designed to make your spine fuse, to find the snake in you and freeze you in place.

When school started I had the usual social terrors. Puberty had forced me into myself, perhaps because interacting with others had become so complicated. My imagination, as usual, compensated for the disconnect by enlarging my inner worlds.

I would usually find someone like myself, an outsider or loner, and hang out with him exclusively. There was a plump black kid named Raymond Nix I immediately bonded with. We were a survival unit against mean kids who sensed our aloofness as reason to harass. Raymond, the only African American in the school, would say to them, when they pushed him to fight, "I ain't got time for you. I got other things to do." I memorized the phrase and used it liberally. I scarcely remember my classes. I would, after I came home from the war, find Raymond's picture in a *Life* magazine spread that showed the names and pictures of Americans who had died that week in Vietnam.

There was one English teacher who attempted to penetrate my solipsistic zone, repeatedly asking me why an intelligent boy like me was not doing well in school. I would hear this over and over again from teachers.

The girls in the school were growing faster than the boys, almost grotesquely, shooting up several inches higher, breasts—buds and boobs and pointies—appeared suddenly. There was complete alienation of the sexes at this stage, as if the biological surge we were all experiencing was something to be worked out in separate worlds.

I was such a dismal, unhappy student in junior high that my mother determined that I would spend my freshman year in a private Episcopal school called Crocker. It was a small school of adobe buildings and a chapel. It had a beautiful courtyard full of oleanders, and an old-fashioned, slightly mossy swimming pool.

During this time, I had fantasies about becoming a priest. I constructed a little altar on top of the bureau in my room, complete with candles and crucifix. I made vestments and other items out of kitchen towels, scarves, and whatever else was lying around and would perform communion services, intoning the texts I'd memorized at church. My religious longings, however, were soon replaced with visions of girls, real or imagined, and the little cock-headed god displaced my dreams of priesthood. Here we have the old Freudian substitution by libido of spiritual aspiration that many religions describe as the reversal of energy up and down the spinal column. Buddhists say that entering the path is like "entering the stream," except that for the spiritually minded, it is upstream against the current of desire. But I was lost in the flood that swept me before it on out to sea.

At Crocker School sex overflowed the spiritual vessel. I was flung in the direction of carnal love. When the nuns were not around, four of us played strip poker. Mary, the only girl in the group, was prematurely voluptuous. Unfortunately, she was a better poker player than the rest of us. We longed for her bra to come off and release her big breasts, but she always had us down to our jockey shorts, our erections tenting them up before she even unbuttoned her blouse. I remember her clearly, her glasses resting on the bridge of her nose, grinning at us in our red-faced thralldom.

AFTER MY YEAR at Crocker, I went to visit my father in Mississippi for the summer of 1957. It had been so ordained by the custody agreement, although my father seemed to be just going through the motions. Both my mother and father had the ability to *do their duty,* as was socially required of them, with absolutely no animating spirit. I arrived and was greeted by his forced smile, and his new wife's scarcely concealed contempt.

I ARRIVED IN Marks, Mississippi, with a mouth full of rotten teeth. I had originally planned to stay a month, as per the custody arrangement. How I came to stay a year is still disputed, but I remember it had something to do with Mandy Prue, with whom I had become infatuated. Mandy was slender, with pale blue eyes, and long mahogany hair falling around her shoulders in big curls. She ordered me around the way Southern women ordered their men around. I was her summer amusement, and when I told her I had decided to stay the year, she dumped me.

As if for further punishment, I went to the dentist three times a week to fix the damage in my mouth. My father and stepmother were silently enraged that my mother had sent me to them in such an expensive condition, especially after all the alimony. For the rest of the summer, I endured the dentist's big burr bits. The water-cooled drill had not yet been invented, and the old-fashioned ones shook my whole body and dug out huge chunks of tooth rot. I would lean over the little swirling basin and spit out the ugly mess. You can't be in love and have a toothache, said Dr. Freud, whom I would read much later in life, but, as I found, I could compound the general misery of Mandy's rejection with dental torture.

My mother had not objected, in fact, not cared much at all, when I said I wanted to stay in Marks. She wrote me regularly, letters full of advice and platitudes. I knew that to write to her about my broken heart would be pointless, would be met with derision or indifference, so I didn't bother. I was therefore hard put to write letters with more than the usual phrases. *I'm fine. I'm playing guard on the football team.* And then went on to exaggerate my feats on the field.

Marks, population eight thousand, was a bean and cotton town. Downtown was a block long. On the north side of the street was a feed store and a big grain elevator that poured grain into freight cars waiting on the tracks. On the other side of the street there was a drug store, a clothing store, a pool hall, and a couple of offices. Around the corner on Cherry Street was the movie theater. Besides the community center and the movies, there was virtually nothing to do in Marks.

My father had moved there to take a job as an accountant with a soybean oil company. My first day there I was standing in my father's yard and a jeep with three boys in it pulled to a stop in front of the house. They were my age, I would find out, but looked older, their skin cracked from the sun. They stared at me. I said, "Hi." They stared at me some more. Then one of them said, "I hear you said you could whup my ass." His hands seemed twice too big for the rest of him.

"I never saw you before." It must have been one hundred degrees, but I felt cold.

"You callin' me a liar?" He slid down from the jeep as from a horse and walked toward me. His hair was sun-bleached, and he had a piece of chain hanging from his back pocket.

"I said I never saw you before."

"You hear that shit, Jethro? He ain't seen me before. You best watch your mouth, boy."

Jethro, who was short and pudgy with glasses, said, "Haw. He's a pussy, Lester."

"You got me mixed up with somebody."

"When I get done with you, you gonna be mixed up. You gonna be wearin' your ass on your face."

He tossed this one over his shoulder to the others.

They laughed.

"Where you from, boy?"

I didn't want to tell them I lived in Tucson, so I said, "Memphis."

"Shit. You goddamn near a Yankee."

Jethro said, "They Yankees up there. And they got all the good whiskey for themselves." Mississippi was a dry state then, and people would drive the ninety miles to Memphis to get their Jack Daniels.

"I'm from Memphis, but I live in Tucson now."

Jethro said, "Whoooeee. You a cowboy?"

I couldn't see a way out of this, so I turned and slunk back toward the house.

"See you around, Tucy." I kept walking. I would be, from then on, known as "Tucy."

I told my father.

He said, "Gosh, son. Not much you can do about that, hunh? If you fight, you're just another hoodlum. If you don't, they call you names." He walked away. My father was the only person I ever knew who was not in the movies or a comic strip who actually said "Gosh."

The next morning I woke up with a jolt. My two-year-old half brother, Mark, had whacked me in the head with his mother's cold cream jar. When I sat up and looked at him, he was grinning ear to ear. He had probably heard his mother complaining about my unwelcome presence in the house and figured I deserved whacking.

Football practice started in August, and I thought if I tried out Mandy Prue would think better of me. I needed friends.

The summer heat in Mississippi was awful, and we practiced across from the cotton and bean fields. Crop dusters would come in low over the fields and, when the wind blew our way, the choking yellow cloud would drift over us. We high-stepped through rows of tires, hit tackling dummies over and over, hit each other, ran wind sprints until we dropped, did not drink water till after practice, and then in small gulps to swallow our salt pills. My team-mates hit me especially hard and tried to step on my fingers in the scrimmage pile. I was new and untested and had already backed down from one fight. I guess they wanted to see how far down they could push me before I fought back.

We wore high-topped leather shoes with inch-long, conical plas-tic cleats. Our practice uniforms were washed only once a week and were so caked with salt they could stand up by themselves. We stank so bad I ceased to smell it.

These were the days before field goals, and we didn't pass as much as they do now. It was mostly a running game. We played with injuries and were ridiculed if we mentioned them. One day I was limping down the field during wind sprints and the coach shouted, "Anderson, you look like you got Jake leg." I had to ask what that was. It had something to do with having had too much Jamaican rum.

My tormenters were my world, but I was still on the outer edge of the circle looking in. I had not proved myself.

There was a girl named Emmie in my class who reluctantly put on shoes to enter the schoolhouse. She was growing out of being a tomboy and not yet aware that she was beautiful. Or, rather, she was just aware enough to know that boys became disoriented when she was around. She had thick blue-black hair, black eyes, and a sudden bloom of lusciousness that had entirely eradicated the tomboy. I am sure that if someone had timed me from the time I sensed her presence till I was completely hard, it would break some kind of record.

I went up to her one day and said, "Hi."

"You're from Tucson. I heard about you," she said.

My face was hot.

She said, "I like your belt." I had bought that belt because the other boys were wearing them. It was wide and thick with a big buckle.

She said, "Can I have it?"

I said "What?"

She said, "Your belt."

I really wanted to give it to her. But that would have finished me in more ways than one.

"I can't."

"Why not?"

I stammered. "My pants will fall off."

From that day on, every time I saw her, we would stop and talk. She took over my mind. In class I would think about her. At night I would reach under the covers and hold myself and think about her. The Kleenex supply next to my bed was depleted because of her.

One day I was walking down Main Street in front of the pool hall when Jimmy Ray Houston sauntered up to me. He was wearing a belt that was a good half inch wider than mine. He said, "I wanna talk to you."

"Okay."

He stood with his feet apart like he was waiting for something to happen. Jimmy Ray had to work the farm and couldn't play sports in the afternoon, but his forearms were as big as Virginia hams.

He said, "Stay away from Emmie."

I said, "But . . ."

He said, not louder, but a little meaner, "Stay away from Emmie."

This was the second time I'd backed down. I still could not get Emmie out of my head, but I avoided her in the halls from then on. She avoided me also, having been, no doubt, given the same warning.

There was something about Jimmy Ray that let me know I would get more than the usual ass-whipping. Truth is, beyond my

hero fantasies I never liked fighting, but I was beginning to understand that I was going to have to appear to like it.

The number three had a certain deadliness to it, and the third
time I backed down just about finished me. I was in choir practice
and Will Willis—Wild Willy—was staring at me from the other
side of the room. We were in a circle, and I could not help but look
at him every time I looked up over the sheet music. He shouted at
me, "Stop lookin' at me, boy."

"Now, boys," said Miss Holland, our choir director.

I stopped looking at him, but every time my head came up over
the music to watch Miss Holland, my eyes would come directly in
line with his. The third time he came across the room at me and
threw a flurry of punches. I grabbed onto him to stop the blows
and we rolled on the floor. When I looked up, Miss Holland and
the girls had left the room, and the other boys in the class were
grinning, settling in for the fight. "Hit him with your elbow, Tucy.
You got a shot at his face." I threw an elbow but Wild Willy ducked
it and knocked the wind out of me on the next punch.

The vice principal, Mr. Lewis, who had been described to me
as "mean enough to go bear huntin' with a switch," came into the
room, grabbed each of us by the collar, and shoved us into the hall.
He marched us past classrooms full of grinning and gaping kids.
"You in for it now, Tucy," someone shouted.

He sat Willis down in a wooden chair next to the secretary and
said, "Don't you move, son." Mr. Lewis pushed me on ahead of him
into his office and closed the door. He took a paddle down off the
wall and said, "Put your hands on that desk." I waited for him to
hit me. He said, "Son, I thought more of you than this. I thought
maybe you'd teach these idiots some manners. You can go all day
without sayin' *ain't*. Why can't you set an example for these boys?"
He whopped me on the butt. Real hard. I let out a yelp. He hit me
two more times and the tears leapt from my face. Then he pushed
me out to the secretary's alcove.

"Get in here, Willis." On the way into Lewis's office, Willis looked at me and laughed. "You won't see a tear on my face, Tucy." I listened from outside the door. Willis got five swats to my three. When he came out his face was red, but there were no tears. He stared at me and grinned.

I had to do something. It was lunchtime, and I walked out the side door of the school toward the cafeteria looking for somebody to hit, I didn't care who. I saw Henry Downs, our three-hundred-pound center, exiting the cafeteria, wiping coconut meringue pie from his mouth. The closer I got to him, the bigger he got. He had a head like a full moon. His eyes were squinty, and his nose was flat and covered with blackheads. He looked at me stalking toward him and stopped in his tracks. He stopped chewing whatever he was chewing. I strode up to him and hit him as hard as I could right on the nose. It made a soft *thwat* sound and his head did not appreciably move. His mouth was open and I saw the remnants of pie under his tongue. I hit him again, and a little bit of blood trickled from his nostril. Then he hit me. The next thing I knew Kyle Elliot was helping me to my feet and the coach was grinning at me. "You two get on in the gym." A gleeful crowd had gathered.

I wobbled up the gym steps after Henry and the coach produced two sets of boxing gloves. Somebody, I think Jethro Turner, was tying on my gloves. When the gloves were on tight, the crowd pushed us toward one another. I was beginning to get my balance back. I swung at Henry and he batted my fist away. I kept swinging, and he kept batting my punches aside until my arms were so tired I couldn't punch anymore. Then he simply pushed me hard and I fell on my ass. He waddled out of the gym and into the bright sunlight, and finally I was alone on the gym floor.

Things got better after that. It was known that I would respond to mistreatment with enough energy to get somebody's clothes dirty, and people let me be. Just to make sure, I went after Kyle Elliot once because he said something smart, I forget what. But the way he said it was nasty, so I hit him. People stopped calling me Tucy with a sneer. They changed it to "Tucson," pronounced with long, accented first syllable, "Tooson." I don't think anybody but girls called me Doug.

That afternoon, after a few congratulatory slaps on the back and some advice about boxing, I was walking home and saw Henry Downs over by the Coke machines eating peanuts as fast as he could. He seemed to be crying. I walked over to him. He washed down some peanuts with a swig of Coke. His face was wet. He said, "Why'd you do that? I ain't done nothin' to you." I felt awful. But he said hello to me every day after that, and after a while, we became friends, although I never saw him except at school. He was a private boy and went home every day after practice.

4

THERE WAS A little community center downtown in Marks where we went every Friday night. There, we danced to Little Richard, Bobby Blue Bland, Elvis, The Everly Brothers, and Chuck Berry, to songs like "Blue Velvet" and "Unchained Melody," slow dances that left us red in the face and hard in the crotch. To an observer we were no doubt comic, the boys' hips thrust forward for contact and the girls' butts stuck out to avoid the same. We looked crippled, or as if we were about to have a seizure and the girls looked strained, as if they were trying to disarm a bomb.

Around the corner at the movies, white people sat in the first-floor seats and entered from the front. Black people sat in the balcony and entered from the side door. I used to look up at the balcony, where the cigarette smoke rose and was broken into shafts by the projector lights, and wonder what they thought about all the white people on the screen, their loves and their wars.

We all went to the movies. It didn't matter what was playing. There would always be movie stars to feed our fantasies, and if you were lucky enough to have a date, there was the promise of a breast brushing your arm, a moist held hand.

My time in Marks was up, and indeed, in my mind, I had gone long before.

Back in Tucson in 1958, I entered Catalina High School and was instantly out of my depth. A large number of the students were from upper-middle-class homes and some of them lived in the Country Club Estates near the mountains. The children of doctors and lawyers, they were sophisticated, were headed to good colleges after graduation, made good grades, spoke French, won chess matches, and excelled at athletics. We called them *highrollers* without really knowing what the word meant. The most datable girls were of this group, not because they were more beautiful than the others, but because the way the dressed, sat, carried themselves, spoke, and dismissed with a look made them objects of desire. Some of them were actually having sex, unlike the rest of us, who talked about it constantly but knew nothing beyond the texture of our hands.

The guys I hung with wore shirts with the collars turned up, or black T-shirts, Levis that hung on our hips and were stopped just short of falling by thin, blue suede belts. We wore thick-soled black shoes with taps on the bottom, which were good for fighting. We gathered in the halls and tried to appear menacing.

One of the most desirable girls in the school was Linda Ron-stadt. She was a sylph in those days, a German and Spanish mix, with black eyes and a confident stride. It was said in the halls that she was talented and lived in her own world. I once saw her in a pink spaghetti-strap dress, and it impaired my concentration for the rest of the day. Even then she had a voice like pure water. In some ways, she was an odd girl out, having parents of mixed ancestry, a father who owned a hardware store downtown and a small ranch north of town where she kept horses. But she was tough, even then, and the school cliques seemed not to interest her. I think of her now and wish I'd had some of that whatever it was, but I was too busy trying to be liked.

One day, after high school, I would drive to California with her and bass player Bob Kimmel. I was going to Los Angeles to find work as a drummer, and she and Bob would form the core of The Stone Poneys, a terrific band whose music was colored by Bob's jazz background and seemed to point toward the innovation of the later sixties. But she became too famous too fast and was shortly on her own.

I had an argument with her on that trip. Trying to impress her by saying I was above country-and-western music, she surprised me by talking about all the country music she liked. She talked about it like a musician and a poet. I held my position and she hers and we didn't speak for half the trip. But I knew that she knew more about music than I did, and I knew I also liked country music and still do.

My first dating experiences were painful, and they did not get better during my time at Catalina. This was the late fifties and very early sixties. Birth control pills had not been put on the market, and abortion was illegal. I remember one date when the girl clung to the opposite door handle of my mother's car and gave off a smell like hot truck brakes. When we got to her house, she didn't even wait for me to come around to open her door. She was gone and the porch light went out. There were stories of pregnant girls who'd gone to Mexico for abortions and had bled to death, or had died from horrible infections.

All the guys I ran with had condoms in their wallets. We called them rubbers. We got them in service station bathrooms, where the mechanics had blackened the sink with their greasy hands. There were Trojans, and one other brand, and there was another little machine that had a substance you could smear on your penis to retard ejaculation. It was called something like *For Her Pleasure*. The rubber machines all had a disclaimer that read "FOR PREVENTION OF DISEASE ONLY." It seemed to imply that the only people who used rubbers were those who went to whorehouses.

There were stories about special condoms, French ticklers, that could drive women crazy. There was something desirably smutty about going into a dirty bathroom to get condoms. We smirked when we emerged into the bright sunlight. Then we'd put the condoms in our wallets so that the rubber ring was visible through the leather. When we took our wallets out to pay for our Cokes, especially when there were girls present, we made sure that the rubbers were visible. *Always ready,* it said.

My emotional life was another matter. This was something you didn't discuss with the boys. If you had a girl who was giving you

trouble, you were "pussy-whipped." I foolishly attempted to penetrate the cliques where the most popular girls were. I was mirror-
ing, I suppose, my mother's contempt for her own class. This was
usually a disaster. Girls would tell you they would go out with you
and then cancel at the last minute because one of the popular guys
had asked them. One tall beauty, a Mormon, Andrea, led me on for
a while, then dumped me. I was unable to hide how I was feeling,
and my mother kept picking at me until I told her why.

Her response was, "That girl is too beautiful for you."

All the philosophy, all the religion in the world was not up to
dealing with sex. The body was the realm of the devil. It would
be years before I could imagine a compassionate God, one who
had mercy, as Milosz wrote, "for those entangled in the flesh." But
a young boy's sex marches in his shadow like some half-human
thing, something snake-spined that glows white hot as an affront
to appropriateness.

Playboy was just on the stands, and most of my images came
from movie magazines: Jayne Mansfield, Marilyn Monroe, their
breasts just contained, perhaps hanging by a nipple, promising to
spill out of their gowns. I almost collapsed while watching Elizabeth Taylor, in *Raintree Country*, her full breasts burgeoning from
her gown, posing for a photograph. This was at the peak of the
Great American Breast Fetish ushered in by *Playboy* magazine. The
great, gleaming, blow-brushed breast was a symbol of plenty and
comfort, balm for the warriors' wounds and wholesome nourish-
ment for our great country.

My mother had started dating in earnest. She was working as
a secretary at Hughes Aircraft, and every few months she'd bring
home somebody who worked there. There was Fat Mack, and then
there was Harold the engineer who had a Porsche and went to
rallies, then Arnold—who her friends referred to as the "gigolo."
There were others less memorable.

Fat Mack would bop me on the shoulder when he came to visit,
like we were going to be pals in a manly man sort of way, or, hor-

ror of horrors, that he was going to step in as Dad. None of them ever said anything real to me. On the other hand, I wasn't easy to know, sealed off in my own world and boggled by hormones. Some of the men showed a genuine interest in me, but most just went through the motions, were baffled, or found me an obstacle to their intentions. Each one of these men—some after only a few dates—would finally be set down at the dining-room table, where my mother told them she didn't want to see them anymore. Then they'd get up and walk quickly out the front door with heads down, their jaws set, avoiding my curious gaze.

Getting rid of them didn't seem to trouble my mother at all. Sometimes she'd even sing after—usually a church hymn—or start cooking, or otherwise go on about her business. Arnold was the only one who, by disappearing, rejected her. He had convinced her to buy a used Mercedes because he liked to be transported in style. Arnold did *not* have a car, did have a pencil-thin mustache, and was very gentlemanly. He was *cultured* and could say things about art and music that impressed my mother. He said I had "fine bones in my face." He reminded me a little of my father: internally absent and externally respectable. His loss did not greatly bother my mother either. But we were stuck with the old Mercedes, which then began to fall apart. After Arnold's exit, I went out to the garage and twisted the hood ornament until it broke off, an act that sent my mother into a rage. By and by we got a Nash Rambler station wagon, which amused my male friends at high school because the seats could be reclined, an advantage on dates.

My mother went to bars a lot with her boyfriends and began taking me along. I occasionally observed that at least some of her dates were stifling their annoyance at my presence. In retrospect, I wondered if I was there as a sexual buffer.

I was enchanted by the bars, the womblike feel of the dark and in it, the red lights, the apothecary-like display of bottles, the false depth of the bar mirrors and then the stage lights that lit the pearl of the drum sets and the gold of the horns. There was always music

at the bars. Partly because of this I was determined to become
a drummer. In those days the local musicians tried to incorpo-
rate a little improvisation into the cocktail set. Most were refugees
from New York or Las Vegas and they brought with them seriously
good jazz chops. I watched the drummers intently and copied their
moves on the practice pad when I got home, scarcely aware of
what was going on in my mother's world. I owned a snare drum
with which I began to drive my mother crazy.

Then my mother began going with her dates to strip clubs. She
took me along. There was no checking ID at the door, and I could
come and sit if I was accompanied by an adult, and if I did not
drink liquor. There were sweet alternatives for the under-aged, in
the form of the gendered Rob Roy or Shirley Temple. I didn't stop
to think—people don't generally like to think about their parents
having a sex life—that these excursions to strip clubs might be
intended to put a little charge in the middle-aged mojo. I never
knew whose idea it had been to go to a strip club, but my mother
did not appear to be disgusted, or even nervous, in the presence of
bare female flesh.

I was fascinated by the strippers. They aroused me, of course, but
in a kind of mythological way. I am now convinced that strip clubs
are home to some kind of inverse religion, a place where the con-
gregation worships undulating pulchritude in the old pagan way,
but then I was simply stunned into reverence by these larger-than-
life women. I remember one stripper in particular, at the Elbow
Room. She came onstage in a little sparkly silver halter and hot
pants, trailing feather boas, and danced for an imaginary guy on a
chaise longue stage left. At certain points, when she was imagining
the imaginary man's responses, she would do a take to the audience
and wink. She was a Harlow blonde and, when unclothed, revealed
a sleek, gleaming body. She brought a vulnerability onstage that
made me like her. I thought that if you touched her she would
bruise like a magnolia petal. Her spike heels tilted her round little
butt up, and, at intervals, she would bend over and present it to the

audience. As she danced, I became detached from the raw sex she was pedaling and saw her as a nice person, somebody who, if she had kids, would take care of them. There was something neat and tidy about her act, and she seemed genuinely sweet. She could be cooking Thanksgiving dinner, so domestic was her attitude.

At the height of her routine, she took one of the feather boas and began to caress the enormous erection grown by her imaginary man on the chaise lounge. She turned to the audience, opened her eyes wide, and formed an O with her lips. The audience laughed. All this time I was thinking what a great mom she would be. She was tender. I don't think anybody else saw it. The simian howls and the riotous female laughter she elicited were tuned to some other station.

And, of course, I was attentive to how the drummer followed her closely and gave her a roll or a rim shot boost where required.

In Tucson, among my mother's friends, drinking was as natural as breathing, although my mother's tastes became more varied. She began drinking margaritas and tequila sours and other drinks specific to the Southwest. My mother had a friend, Anita Ennis, who lived in a trailer park off Oracle Road, in a section of orange groves. She had supplied her little trailer with a front yard of green gravel and pink flamingos. Anita lived on a small inheritance and seldom left the trailer. A clock on the wall had all fives on its face, so she could never be accused of drinking before five. This alcoholic humor permeated everything in our lives and was a variant of the drinking culture I'd grown up with.

Tucson had a kind of exotic reputation in those days, and a stretch of Oracle Road called Miracle Mile had a kind of naughty feel. It was full of motels for quick sex and extramarital shenanigans. There were places like the Hula Hut, and Manny's Hoof and Horn. All these places had music, and I became addicted to them.

I had acquired a set of Ludwig drums in black diamond pearl with Zildjian cymbals, and played well enough to get into a band that was being formed by some kids who lived in the Country

Club Estates: Gary Silverman, Manny Neeman, and others. David Feder, who was a friend of both, let us practice in his living room, and soon became de facto manager. We added sidemen as needed. Kurt-somebody on bass, Jerry Simms on trumpet—at the time an odd choice for a rock band. Jerry was the champion rope climber from the gymnastics team, and Kurt was a wrestler I'd met while trying out for the wrestling team. I had been on the outside looking in, but the band brought me into another sphere, the upper-middle class of the estates. I spent a lot of time at the Silvermans' house. I was welcomed, fed, respected, and treated as a member of the family. They were Jews, and I liked the *Jewishness* of the household: the dinner conversations, the bar mitzvahs and the Passover seder I was invited to. What I was observing, of course, was a real family that acted like a family, but never really having experienced this, I assigned the quality to Jews. I began to fantasize that I was really Jewish, that since my mother's maiden name was Wiseman I belonged somehow in this household. I made up a story that my grandparents upon arrival at Ellis Island had their name changed from Weissman because the immigration guy couldn't spell. My Jewish friends found this very amusing, since many of them were leaving the tribe to become Marxists or atheists. They indulged me with good humor. I was educated by them in racial matters, as well, because during this time many Jews were aligned with the civil rights movements.

I became sharply aware of my own family's racism. I discovered that my unconscious was informed by it and endeavored to change my ways. Merely having the thought that it was wrong did not change one overnight. It would take a long spiritual struggle to disinherit the programming. I saw the damage that racism could do to children growing up within its suffocating smallness. I owe much of this awakening to the Silvermans.

I would also receive a musical education in that house. Peter Silverman, the older brother, had lived in New York City and played jazz there. I spent hours listening to jazz with him, taking in his views. I discovered that I could *see* music. Synesthesia is quite common in musicians. I had always been able to do it, but only just became aware that it was wonderful. I closed my eyes and saw peacocks' tails or gold rivers of sound, the bass line coming through in black ovals and the drums black lines, dots and silver bursts.

I became good at identifying particular musicians by their styles, and Peter would give me "blindfold tests" (emulating the feature in *Downbeat* magazine): he would play records and ask me who was playing.

He played Diz and Bird and 'Trane until I was steeped in bop and could follow its threads into later music. I could observe the evolution of a player's style (old Miles into new Miles). My own drumming changed accordingly. I began to reject the heavy bass drum and rim shots of rock and learned to float just on top of the beat, reserving the bass for accent and rhythmic variation, and to embellish phrase endings with my left hand, change ride cymbals and sticks to brushes as required. It was perhaps the first time I felt in control of anything at all. I started to read music.

After I graduated from high school I began playing professionally. I joined the musicians' union and began to get jobs with established groups. Alcohol wove its way through this time, and I began to drink along with the older musicians. I was tall for my age and nobody questioned my presence in bars. I began to play in some of the clubs my mother had taken me to on her dates.

One night I went home with a jazz singer I was backing at the Sky Room with the house band. We'd all gone to the Press Club for drinks after the gig, and, as she socked away her screwdrivers, she put her hand on my thigh, and pretty soon we were on our way to the Tidelands Motor Inn where she was staying. Her breath had that chemical scent that hard-core alcoholics get, and there seemed to be a pall over her beauty. I would recognize her later as an alcoholic, but that night I was astonished. She seemed to want to eat me alive. During the next three days she acted slightly embarrassed at the club, especially since the musicians all knew what had happened and were talking out of the corners of their mouths about it. Later I would understand that she'd gotten drunk and gone to bed with an eighteen-year-old, but then I was hurt by her sudden coldness. We never got together again.

When I didn't come home that night, my mother became hysterical and started calling the other members of the band. The band leader replied that I'd probably "shacked up" for the night, a phrase my mother berated me with for days after. There was no point in trying to be honest, telling her how emotionally confused I was by the woman's behavior. All she could do was berate me, and at times she sounded as if she were attacking my father instead of me.

But I was hooked. Older women would give me sidelong looks. I knew what they were thinking. I became worldly very quickly while maintaining an air of innocence.

One night a bisexual couple came into the Sky Room, bought me a drink, and asked me to sit with them during the break. When I sat with them, they got right to it. They wondered if I'd like to join them for the evening. I politely declined, and they politely accepted it. They seemed like nice people, but I was not queer, as the word was in those days. However, I had entered the demimonde, such as it was in Tucson, and planned to make the most of it.

I worked in Mac McCann's Dixieland Band—Mac, with his ice-tea glasses full of gin and short span of wakefulness before he passed out, alternated between periods of Jesus and binge drinking; I never got to know who won. I worked with trumpet player Pete Flanders, who looked at the world with a leering good humor. These musicians were different beings in the daytime. The night versions, glowing with alcohol and the full-blooded eroticism of the music, contrasted sharply with the daytime rehearsals, the gray faces, bloodshot eyes, and cheeks full of swollen capillaries. When you are young, there is a notion that you live as part of a separate species, one that will never experience age or debility. But some part of you knows. The part of me that picked up a drink whenever they did certainly knew, but I kept that part caged. I was resilient. I could get falling-down drunk at night and get up in the morning, do ninety pushups, and enter the day shiny and hopeful.

I worked steadily as a drummer and was always the youngest member of the band. I worked with Rob Caley at the Twin Flame Room. I worked with Woody Keys and Johnnie Pinella at Smiley's. Keys, hunched over the piano in his sports jacket, reminded me of a crumpled paper bag. The house band at Smiley's played for strippers and comedians from eight to midnight, and then opened up for jam sessions after hours. Smiley himself stood at the back of the house, just visible within the outer edge of the stage lights, and chewed his cigar. His face was always deadpan, thus the name. We interpreted his mood by how vigorously he chewed his cigar; there was virtually no other way to tell. When the club was not making money he chewed harder, and he had been known to fire people while in this mood. But Smiley's was doing well in my time there. There were the regulars for whom the club was probably their only social life, and there was royalty in the form of a mafioso referred to as Joe Bananas, who would arrive almost nightly with his entourage. In the group was a linebacker-sized man not much older than I who was a bodyguard and enforcer for Joe, and there was whomever Joe brought along as guests. The Mafia was very present in Tucson in those days, and I passed the Bonnano house every time I turned north on Campbell from Elm Street.

And there were the whores. Vicky—referred to behind her back as Vicious Vicki—and Rhonda were a pair. They were very high-priced girls who knew everybody. Rhonda was tall and blonde and Vicky was svelte with shoulder-length black hair and retro bangs. When she was not talking, she was elegant. When she opened her mouth, even jaded rounders flinched. She had a particularly nasty way of verbally castrating men she didn't like. I remember her thrusting her hand down some poor guy's pants and saying, "My, what small balls you have."

Vicky and Rhonda liked me. They would not have sex with me, however. I was eighteen and they had principles.

My evening routine was typically this: go to the club, play two shows and three dance sets, then break for a bit at midnight. When the other musicians showed up carrying their instruments, the house band would return and allow them to sit in. One night a famous movie star's brother came in. The star was making a movie in town and had brought his brother along. His brother was completely drunk, snarly, and defensive. Not easy being a famous movie star's brother. In any case, he dabbled in drums wanted to sit in. I let him. He managed to get through a tune or two.

There were other brothers of the very famous. Jerry Van Dyke, brother of Dick, came in and did a stand-up slot for a week. The musicians liked him. He was cheerful, physically fit, and clearly had a life elsewhere.

The strippers who came through were all a little damaged. I have never met one who didn't carry some deep hurt, but I couldn't guess what it was in those days. Now it seems perfectly clear: Someone who parades her nakedness in front of men for a living discovers very quickly what a body is worth and what utter fools men can be—a truth that sooner or later inspires contempt, with roots somewhere in a murky family history.

The Keys brothers, Woody and Jim, had an act in Las Vegas before coming to Tucson. They reveled in their Las Vegas days but never alluded to why they left. They were both serious drunks. They were also terrific musicians and played jazz with spirit and finesse. Woody was on the wagon when I was working with him. Then one night he went off the wagon. I saw him at the bar drinking his first beer in many months and trembling while Johnnie Pinella bent over him in concern, trying to talk him out of it. It was not long after that that a singer came through, I can't remember her name, but I remember she was good-looking, and a not bad singer, and very soon she and Woody were having a fling. She would come into the dressing room and take off her clothes and sit butt-naked in front of the mirror to put on her makeup. We all tried to get a peek, but it was Woody she wound up with.

I was not as innocent as other people thought I was, which gave me a kind of strategic cover. I would stand nearby when the older guys took their smoke break and listen to their conversations with fierce attention. I would adopt their worldly talk as my own and attempt to shock my friends with it.

In conversation, everything was coded in sexual terms. Or mortally grotesque.

"Don't let anybody see that bottle. If Liquor Control gets a hard-on for us, we're fucked."

"Danny's eyes look like two fried eggs."

Danny had been drinking a lot the night before.

Or, "I bet she'd push back real hard," when discussing a woman who had just walked by.

Then they'd tell stories, like the time Vicious Vicki and Rhonda took Joe Bananas' bodyguard in the back room of the store he managed and amused him alternately while the other stole dresses off the rack.

The guys got a kick out of my moon-eyed amazement at the world they swam in. They would occasionally, in my presence, poignantly envy my youth. There was a lot of sadness there, and comments about life wasted, and *if I had known then what I know now . . . youth is wasted on the young.*

D U R I N G   M Y   L A S T year at Catalina High my mother had been preparing to join the Foreign Service as a clerical assistant—these days called an administrative assistant. She passed all her exams and the background check, and six months after I graduated, left the country for her first posting with USAID, in West Cameroon. I remember crying at the airport and feeling desolate. I realized that my mother could barely stand me, and couldn't wait for me to graduate and be on my own.

While abroad, she sent me a lethal combination of money and relentless criticism of my character. Her exit had a powerful effect on my life. I began to grow, that is, I began to develop a musculature and went up a couple of shirt sizes. I began lifting weights. I went to Steinfeld's Department Store and bought two rifles and a pistol. I began to go hunting. I shot javelina in the hills around Tucson. I lay in the brush with a scoped .308 and blew the heads off prairie dogs and jackrabbits. I had acquired some kind of Hemingway streak, or unearthed it from my Southern collective unconscious. I wore button-down shirts and Levis or chinos. I slapped on Canoe aftershave lotion. I tried to look like a frat boy when I started at the University of Arizona in the fall of 1961.

I continued to play professional gigs for the next two years while I studied music at the university. I became quickly bored at school because there was no percussion major and I didn't like the trumpet, suggested as a substitute. I had to take piano class and practice in little snot-stained practice rooms in the basement of the music building. I flunked music theory. I hated music school. There were too many overly serious people, and I was starved for life.

At the Sky Room, the house band often backed stand-up comics, and I had the good fortune to back up Henny Youngman, Dave Madden, and others less illustrious. I was quite good at kicking their punch lines with a rim shot or cymbal burst, or a combination of moves. I got into it. I inhaled their comic timing and let it show up in my life.

BY 1963, I was leaving music. I played a gig here and there, but, probably because of my experience backing stand-up comics, I had become fascinated with acting. My first role was one of Dogberry's watchmen in *Much Ado About Nothing* at the university main theater. This was one of many impulsive changes I would make in my life, as if life were nothing more than a sequence of such changes, and as if I would always be young and could do such things any time I wanted and nothing had to be planned.

In the summer of 1963, when I visited my mother in Washington DC, prior to her posting to USAID in Santo Domingo, I acted the minuscule role of Rugby in *The Merry Wives of Windsor*, directed by Donald Driver. The cast was made up of professionals and members of the community.

During this visit, my mother asked me, for the first time, if I was sad. She said that I had a "strained expression" on my face. The strained expression was probably my then full-blown alcoholism and my daily hangovers. This was the only time in my life she asked such a question.

I returned to the University of Arizona in the fall of 1963. In November, John F. Kennedy was assassinated. No president had been assassinated in my lifetime and I sensed a dark shift in the country, and in myself. Vietnam was beginning to break the surface of American complacency and there was a rumor that the draft was coming. I realized that my bad grades made me vulnerable to the draft and I made another impulsive decision: I joined the Navy Reserve and became a hospital corpsman. My drill instructor in boot camp warned me that if I were a corpsman I might be transferred to the marines. But large-sized marine units had not yet been sent to Vietnam, and I didn't think they would be. A few months later, they were.

Two

5

Quang Nam Province, early 1967

THE STEWARDESSES ARE somber; one is crying. As we deplane, she touches my arm and says "Good luck." It's getting to them. These women have been at this a while, have ferried over thousands of troops and watched them deplane in the sure knowledge that just down the tarmac occupied coffins are being loaded onto transports headed home.

Our boots are shiny and unscuffed and our jungle utilities are crisp and new until the heat hits us and they go black with sweat. We walk across the shimmering tarmac, smelling the new country, apprehensive but still full of stateside swagger. There are mountains to the west of us, and shacks and shantytowns all around, separated from the base by sand-bagged bunkers and coils of concertina wire. The smell of jet fuel is overpowering.

On the plane we talked or slept, but now we are silent, trying to take it in. A slight chill snakes through the heat and into my gut, as if I am mounting an executioner's scaffold.

We have been trained in anatomy and physiology, materia medica, and combat first aid. It is very likely that we will use only the last. Some of us have seen mortality in hospitals and have cared for the returning wounded, but none of us have tried to treat a casualty under fire.

We muster in front of the First Marine Division administration building. A bored lance corporal comes out with a clipboard and checks off our names. All during the flight we have been bragging about the cushy duty stations we are going to get. We talk about air-conditioned hospitals and hospital ships. We become silent as all but one of us are assigned to infantry companies. Hilliard, the undertaker's son, goes to graves registration in Da Nang, where he will process the outgoing dead.

I watch men I'd been trained with get separated into groups going to different units. I look over at Webber. He was a long-distance runner in high school, but now he looks as if someone could break him over his knee. I wave to him. He waves back and climbs into his assigned truck. I will never see him again.

We head out through a section of Da Nang I would come to know as Dogpatch, dirt poor and heavily infiltrated with Cong. The streets are swarming with people on bicycles, barefoot women carrying double baskets of vegetables or rice from poles balanced across their shoulders, dirty-faced kids, some without pants, and an occasional dog, too old to eat. The place smells of fish sauce and sewage. A grinning kid runs beside the truck, lights a string of firecrackers, and we jump. I realize how tense I am. It is February 1967, and Vietnamese are celebrating Tet. We do not yet know what the next Tet will bring, or, for that matter, what Tet is. We don't know that Tet of 1968 will forever be associated with American loss and failure. We don't know much at all about anything, and we are magnificently full of shit. We are mostly working class and a year out of high school. I am twenty-three, four years older than the average infantry grunt, and I don't know anything either, apart from the masks I use to cover my fear.

We swing through Dogpatch down to Highway One past the Third Marine Air Wing and MACV (Military Assistance Command, Vietnam) headquarters, past the Australian Special Forces compound on our left. We leave the shantytowns behind and are in the American Zone now, with its neat compounds. We pass the naval hospital on our right and see the Marble Mountains in front of us. From this angle all five mountains seem to morph together into one. But we have no idea that there are five of them, or that each one is named for one of the Chinese elements: earth, water, fire, metal, and wood. We enter the village of Nui Kim Son. Kids run beside the truck and shout at us. We catch phrases in a pidgin gathered from three wars: "Hey GI you give me MPC?" "Hey GI you number one." "You give me cigarettes?" "You give me C rats?" "Hey GI you want beaucoup boom-boom number one?" One day a prostitute in this village will say to a corpsman in my company as he injects her with penicillin, "Oh, Americans, they beaucoup hairy and ug-ry."

At the southern edge of the village there is a gate flanked by two ARVN soldiers with M1s. They pull back the barbed wire and let us through. The marine gunner swings his M60 to face the tree line to the west and chambers a round. Two riflemen lean against the wooden rails facing the other side of the road and lock and load. One of them says to me, "We in Indian country now, boy."

When we leave the village, we are in open country, with sand and rice paddies to the left and tree line to the right. We slow to pass a group of engineers out sweeping the road for mines. Then we turn left into a big compound composed of a triangular berm bulldozed up from sand. Just above the berm I can see the roofs of the battalion buildings. A marine swings back a gate covered with barbed wire, and we enter between two sand-bagged bunkers. Some of the buildings are on the ground, and others are up on stilts and covered with tent canvas. One by one we dismount the truck and are assigned to our platoons. There is one corpsman per squad, three squads in a platoon, three platoons in a company, and three infantry companies plus headquarters and Supply Company, tanks and artillery—in a battalion. The chief hospital corpsman tells me I'm assigned to Lima Company, third platoon, first squad.

The squad leader says to me, "You'll go on your first patrol in about ten minutes."

He must see my fear, because he adds, "Everything's OJT here. Get used to it."

From the battalion aid station I pick up my "unit one" medical kit, with battle dressings, morphine syrettes, tourniquet, scalpel shaft and blades, sutures, copper sulfate pads, atropine, nitrofuracin, bacitracin ointment, and a jar of malaria pills. The squad leader hands me a Colt service-issue .45-caliber pistol and two clips of ammo to, as they say in Field Medical Service School, "protect my patient." A gunnery sergeant said to me, "Hell boy, it's to shoot yourself to keep from being captured. They'll cut your fucking balls off." I put on my web belt with holster and canteen. I slide a magazine into the .45, and awkwardly pull back the slide to chamber a round. I look up and a marine with an M60 machine gun resting across his shoulders is watching me, his eyes hidden in the shadow of his helmet, shaking his head. His utilities are sun-faded, his boots covered with fine dust.

I meet the other members of the platoon and we are told to saddle up. I meet people called Cherenski, Corcoran, Jeter, names I would later that year write on casualty tags. The other corpsman, Williams, a round, baby-faced kid with wire-rimmed glasses, is soon to be rotated out. I will replace him.

On the way out of the command post, Corporal Rochetti, the machine gunner, tells me to stay fifteen meters in front of him, and fifteen meters behind the man in front. He says, "Don't come snugglin' up to me, Doc. If the dinger sees two of us together, that's where he'll aim." We file out through the main gate.

It is the "cool" season, but I am losing water by the gallon. We move briskly across a paddy dike, through a village where the children and old people hang back and drop their eyes. The young women are hidden from us, always, and the young men are fighting either for the ARVN or for the Cong. Their absence is conspicuous.

We pass on through the village and into the sand. Three hundred meters out, we enter another dry, cracked mud paddy and cross through it to sand dunes on the other side, and then toward hills covered with scrub pines. When people think of Vietnam, they think of jungle, but the landscape is constantly changing, from sand and scrub near the ocean, to elephant grass in the central highlands, to huge expanses of rice paddies, which become terraced near the mountains. There the jungle actually begins, triple-canopied and so dark you can hardly see at noon. Today we are in the sandy stretch between Highway One and the ocean, an area I would come to love because of the wind off the South China Sea.

The point squad of the platoon is at the top of the first hill when the cracking and popping starts. Someone shouts, "Corpsman up!" from the front of the column and I start running, struggling for footing in the sand. I'm the only one up and moving and I am aware of the concentration of fire pulling my way, the hiss of the .30-caliber rounds and the occasional bumblebee buzz of a heavy machine gun. My fear is crushing. Everybody else is down on their bellies returning fire.

The ambush is classical. Fire is coming from three directions, but I don't know this because I'm scared to death. I am all lungs and heaving chest and rubbery legs. I stagger off toward the left and a marine grabs me by my shirt, and points me on up the hill. I do not have to be told to crouch down as I run. The rounds coming by my head are like rattlesnakes. I know what they are the first time I hear them and they require no interpretation.

Inside the tree line I feel safer. At the front of the column, the point man is down. Williams is there before me, and I begin to assist him, unwrapping battle dressings. The point man has been shot in the lower right back, and the bullet exited just below and to the right of his navel. A glistening blue loop of intestine extrudes from the wound. He is writhing and screaming and the marines are trying to keep him quiet. The Cong have begun to use his screams to walk their mortars up the hill. Scythes of shrapnel skitter through the branches. Trees splinter, and the air is full of the scent of pine resin and cordite. Pieces of trees come sifting down on us. Williams, hands remarkably steady, injects him with morphine in the brachial artery. He quiets a little and begins to whimper.

I hear the whopping rotors of the medevac and its gunship escort coming in. The Huey escort marks our left flank with a red smoke rocket and circles back to fire rockets and strafe. In less than a minute, the gunship suppresses the enemy fire and a marine runs down the hill to mark the landing zone with a yellow smoke grenade. The medevac pilot uses the smoke to land into the wind as a squad fans out around it to form a perimeter. Williams and I load the wounded point man in a poncho and run into the blowing sand to heave him on the chopper where another corpsman is waiting. Williams shouts something to the other corpsman, who can't hear a word. He shrugs and starts checking the man's pupils with a flashlight. The chopper lifts off, circles back into the wind and up. Then a sniper rakes the landing zone and we are on our bellies again. I hear two rounds hit the chopper, *whack whack,* but it banks off toward Da Nang and climbs quickly out of rifle range.

We never saw them. This would not be the only time. I had been shot at for the first time and not been hit. These were the easy days, before we began to engage the NVA regulars moving in for the Tet Offensive. Today I learned how to distinguish fire direction and gauge distance; if a muzzle is pointed toward you, it makes a flat sound that is unforgettable. I also learned that you can find cover anywhere if you're scared enough. I learned this in fifteen minutes. It would keep me alive through the harder days. Some people never got that chance.

THE VIETNAMESE FARMER loves his independence. He is overtaxed by the Vietnamese government, but he has something the Saigon bureaucrats, in their Western suits and gold teeth, don't have. Except in the cities and big villages, he lives in another century. He is an artist. His village is hidden behind a neatly trimmed hedgerow, the high palms visible above it, inside which the thatched hooches are swept clean with a handmade broom. He drinks sweet water from a well, raises pigs and chickens, plants sugarcane and *bui* (grapefruit), and has a flourishing garden. He needs nothing from the outside. He farms with a water buffalo, a young boy or girl sitting on its hump, goading it gently with a stick as it pulls a wooden plow. In the mountain jungles, these villages bloom suddenly, as if they are a natural outgrowth of everything around them. I have seen this image over and over in old Chinese and Vietnamese paintings. This farmer is a system complete in himself. He shits in his own garden. He owns no expensive farm implements that need parts or oil. He wants things to stay this way.

He gets up at dawn, eats heartily and works alongside his family in the fields. In the late afternoon he rolls a single cigarette, and squats in the shade in front of his hooch. He watches three and sometimes four generations of family live and die in a continuing tapestry. He is a Taoist, animist, Buddhist, or Catholic who is still tuned to the stars and the changing seasons. His sense of natural time is irritated by a need to produce enough so that a corrupt government can take its greedy cut. But he gets by.

He gets by until the Americans come. If he is older, he remembers the French and the Japanese. He knows to dig a shelter under his hooch big enough for his family, to listen to the gossip passed from village to village telling him that the Americans are in the area. He knows to send his pretty daughters, or sometimes his whole family, to another village before they come. He can read the flared nostrils of the water buffalo, the barking dogs, and he knows the soldiers are close. Sometimes he can smell them. He learns to be subservient before power, in the old Confucian way, eyes down, even when he wants to kill.

He fears the Vietcong also, who come into the village at night to be fed or hidden. He is caught between two armies, but he is more sympathetic to the Vietcong. He shares a language and a culture with them, and they smell as he does. They are accurate with their assassinations, unlike the Americans, who kill civilians as a matter of course, their weapons too big for precision. He agrees with what the Vietcong say about the imbalance of wealth in the country, although he has seen governments come and go, and promises made and broken.

He wants his sons and daughters to be married and to know their children. His teenage sons have already been taken from him. One

is in the ARVN, the other in the regional Vietcong. He knows they
don't have a choice, except perhaps the angry son who went to the
Vietcong—a dangerous choice, but more honorable. His universe
is thrown out of balance by the Americans. His roosters wake him
several times a night as the illumination flares pop overhead, eras-
ing the stars. He knows that his two dogs need to be eaten before
the Americans shoot them. He knows that the Americans will burn
down his hooch, shoot his pigs and water buffalo, so he saves his
piasters to buy new ones. And he prays.

BRUGER, THE SQUAD leader, is a good old boy with sloping
shoulders, a buzz cut, and a very red neck. Of course, over here, we
all have red necks, so the social designation is irrelevant. He has a
ghost gut, that is, a way of standing that lets you know that he will
grow a gut soon, probably after he marries.

Bruger doesn't like Vietnamese. He would kill every one he
saw if he could get away with it, but he has to compromise. We
are in a village near Nui Kim Son and Bruger is lighting a hooch
on fire with his Zippo. With Bruger, to enter a Vietnamese village
is to destroy it. The thatch crackles, and the villagers are pleading
with clasped hands. Bruger laughs. He kicks over a big tin of rice.
Rochetti is lighting the next hooch as we push the villagers out of
the way on our way out.

We know that Diem—the president the Americans installed
earlier in the war and the CIA later helped murder—canceled
elections in 1956, deciding that if he held elections, eighty percent
of the countryside would vote Communist. Some people, hearing this, might question the purpose of the war, as I very soon
began to do. For Bruger, however, it is proof that all Vietnamese are
the enemy. The idea of defending some Vietnamese against others
doesn't interest him.

The next week a directive comes from battalion that we are no
longer to burn hooches. There have been complaints, and a news
reporter has videotaped some marines doing it. The video is show-

ing up on CBS, so the battalion has to give the appearance of doing something about it.

But Bruger is crafty. When we enter a village, he just rolls up a little ball of C-4 plastic explosive, sticks a lit cigarette in it, and leaves it in the thatch. We are two klicks outside the village before we see the black smoke spiraling up. The others in the squad think this is funny, except for Thompson, Corcoran, and myself; we hang back and keep our mouths shut. This is when the bouquet of razor blades opens in my gut.

We are patrolling the cluster of villages around Nui Kim Son when we see an old man coming toward us on the trail. He is very old, with cataracts and a few long chin hairs. His has his pant legs rolled up and his legs are muddy to mid-calf. He has just crossed the rice paddy to the west of the villages. He sees us, stiffens. He looks around, but there is no way around us. When the squad approaches, he drops his eyes and bows as he attempts to pass us on the trail.

Bruger shouts *"Dung lai."* The old man stops. Jeter, on point, checks him for weapons. Then Bruger shouts, *"Lai dai."* The old man totters up to him and bows, his hands clasped, a forced smile on his face. His legs are shaking. Bruger begins to search him more thoroughly than Jeter. He pulls an ID card and a wad of money out of the old man's waistband. The old man begins to cry and bob his clasped hands up and down. "Where you goin' with all this money, Papa-san? You gonna buy a B40 rocket?" The old man has no idea what Bruger is saying, although some in the squad are laughing. I am having a bad time with this. I notice that Corcoran and Thompson are not amused. They are deadly silent.

Bruger stuffs the old man's wad of piasters—probably twenty cents' worth—in his thigh pocket and looks at the ID card. Bruger shouts,

"Where VC?"

"Khong biet" (I don't know) the old man says bowing, and now crying.

"Gimme your Ka-Bar," Bruger says to Rochetti. Rochetti hands him his combat knife. The old man is now terrified, has pissed himself. "No VC! No VC! No VC!" he cries, pointing to his ID card, which Bruger holds over his head, just out of reach.

Bruger pockets the ID card and the money, leaving the old man with his open palms begging for their return. Rochetti is laughing, and Jeter begins to laugh too. I never took Jeter for a sadist—I still don't—but he wants to be liked too much. Corcoran has turned his back. Thompson stares off into the scrub. Bruger is scheduled to be rotated out soon. I'm counting the days.

We leave the old man pleading and move on to the next village, Bruger and Rochetti clinking the tops of their Zippos back and forth.

THE BATTALION STAFF officers, major and up, with a few exceptions, see the *idea* of a war. They make decisions based on experience in World War II and Korea. Some, as younger officers, saw jungle fighting on Pacific islands, but many have no idea what goes on at the squad level in Vietnam. The basic fighting unit in Vietnam is the squad. The typical squad leader is not more than twenty years old. He can call in mortars. He carries an M79 grenade launcher and has under his command men armed with M16s, M60 machine guns, pistols, rockets, fragmentation and phosphorous grenades, and the means to alter the history of an event in the "morning" reports.

ONE MORNING WE are introduced to two young Vietnamese in jungle utilities. Sergeant Mau, assigned to the battalion to do local PR for the Americans, is thin, with fragile hands and long nails on his little fingers in the Mandarin tradition. He appears to have not done much physical work. He carries an old M1 carbine and wears an ARVN uniform.

The other Vietnamese is a Hoi Chanh. He is former Vietcong who has come in under the "open arms" amnesty program. In return he will help us hunt his former comrades. He is powerfully built and handsome, in a recruiting poster sort of way. I notice he never looks at you until you're not looking. He has been outfitted with an M16 and a full set of jungle utilities, new jungle boots, and a map in an acetate pocket. He only travels with company-sized operations. I figure this is because they suspect that without a senior officer present, we'll kill him. And yet, somehow, he is the star. People ignore Sergeant Mau, who is looking paler and skinnier all the time. But the deep respect for the enemy that lies beneath the fear and hatred makes Hoi Chanh our daily fascination.

WE ARE ON a night patrol east of the battalion CP. I am suddenly flattening myself in the sand, bright muzzle flashes up front. No one is hit. We've surprised a solitary Vietcong who's fired a burst and run. When it is over, Bruger looks around like he's sniffing the air. We have just passed a fisherman's hooch, and Bruger wants to go back and take a look.

"Thompson, go check out that hooch."

Thompson ducks into the hooch. I can see the candles flickering when the door hanging is brushed aside. Bruger follows him in, with myself and Jeter. An old man and woman are sitting up in their bed staring at us, their eyes glassy.

"They actually have a bed," Thompson says.

Bruger walks around to the other side of the bed. It is about six inches off the ground. You wouldn't think anybody could fit under it. Bruger reaches under the bed and drags out a little Vietnamese by the shirt and stands him up. He is old enough to have long chin hairs and is dressed like a fisherman, in white, instead of the usual black pajamas.

We are crowded into the hooch, ducking our heads to keep from hitting the roof. The Vietnamese are so small we look like Visigoths in a doll shop. Bruger pats the man's back. "Sweat. This little fucker's been running."

We dig around in the hooch and find no weapon.

On the way out, Bruger turns and points at the old Vietnamese couple. "We'll be back to see you, you cocksuckers."

Corcoran says to Bruger, "They can't help it, Bruger."

Bruger says, "Who the fuck pulled your chain?"

Bruger ties the prisoner's hands behind him with a length of nylon rope and pushes him ahead of us, back toward the CP. Bruger explains on the radio we are bringing back a captured VC and not to shoot us at the main gate. We fire a green star cluster at the gate and they let us in. We push the Vietnamese into the CP toward the officers' bunkers. Bruger shoves him into a bunker, and I can see, in the light of the Coleman lantern, the faces of the Hoi Chanh, Sergeant Mau, and some Americans I have never seen.

Bruger says, "I'd hate to be that poor son of a bitch." Is he expressing compassion? I doubt it. I go back to the corpsman's hooch. I can't sleep. I expect to hear screaming, but all is silent except for the roosters, crowing at a flare.

SERGEANT MAU GOES with us on a patrol into the villages south of Nui Kim Son. We set a perimeter to provide him security while he talks to the village chief. We take out our C rations and eat. I smell chicken cooking. I walk over to the chief's hut and look in. Sergeant Mau is having chicken and rice with the chief. They also have some Tiger beer and American cigarettes. Sergeant Mau offers me some of the chief's chicken, but I tell him I just ate. I sit with them for a while. The village chief ignores me. He is talking in a low voice to Sergeant Mau. I am not hungry for food. I'm hungry to know something. I ask Mau what they're talking about.

Mau says, "Worried about his crop."

I think, hard to grow rice with tanks crisscrossing your paddies.

I walk back through the village as the marines are cleaning up to go. In a few minutes, Sergeant Mau emerges from the chief's hooch, smoking, and looking around as if for a hammock.

Bruger shouts, "Saddle up."

Sergeant Mau takes his time, stretches, and exhales a long, easy cloud of smoke, as if to ask why they are in such a hurry.

Bruger watches him with a hatred so pure it could start a fire.

We move out of the village and on to the next.

ROCHETTI HAS WORN out the barrel on his M60 and gets a new gun. We set up just outside of Nui Kim Son and wait for him to adjust the sights. Two eight-year-olds are walking along a paddy dike west of the village carrying schoolbooks. One has a red shirt, the other a blue. Rochetti aims the M60 at them and fires. The rounds pull to the left. The children are running now. Rochetti moves the rear sight and fires another burst. Rounds pull to the right, splash into the paddy. The two children pull off their shirts and blend into the landscape. "Fuck," Rochetti says. He looks at me. He says, "Doc, why don't you run along that paddy dike so I can sight in." I don't think this is funny but I force out a laugh. It is a harsh *haw!* It is a laugh I'll have from now on.

I WALK INTO the enlisted men's club that night and Jeter is being loud and voluble. "He's gone! Took his new M16 with him and dee-deed on out of here."

"Who's that?" I ask.

"Hoi Chanh, Doc. First platoon took him out to look at a weapons cache, and the next minute, he's gone. Right out from under the skipper's nose."

Bruger says, "Cocksucker knows the layout of the CP now. Those fucking mortar rounds will be on target next time. Get one right through the roof of the chow hall."

The table is full of empty beer cans. It is Bruger's going-away party. I can't wait till he goes. I hope he gets ambushed on the way to Da Nang. I drink the whole can of San Miguel in two gulps and open another.

"And they sent Sergeant Mau back to Da Nang."

Bruger says, "Ain't he the sorriest slope you've ever seen?"

"Fucker won't eat our food."

"Gives him the shits."

I walk over to the bar and order another beer.

The bartender says, "You in a hurry, Doc?"

"Naw, just dehydrated."

But I am in a hurry. I am going to do some serious drinking: humorless, relentless, and complete.

That night I wake up and smell myself. In my drunken sleep, I've pissed my cot. I go outside and wipe off my air mattress. The night is quiet except for a few tracers floating up into the sky off toward the mountains, and then the distant popping of the rifles.

Everything is wrong with this place, this war. I can't talk about it. I can't share what I think and feel. When I've complained about the treatment of civilians to Corcoran, he just says, "I know, Doc. Not much I can do about it."

I still have most of my tour yet to serve. I don't know how I'm going to make it. These guys don't read books and I don't play cards.

I'm not alone. I see the red tip of a cigarette rise and temporarily illuminate a face. It's Sterling, the new corpsman from Kilo Company. I walk over to him and light a cigarette.

"Who pissed?" he asks.

"Me."

"Just as long as you don't shit." Pause. "This is fucked," he says.

"Yup."

"I mean, it's really fucked."

"You don't have to convince me."

"We're fish out of water."

"Feels that way."

"Think about it. Most of the corpsman are generally people who don't fit. Bookworms. Artists. Neurotics. If we didn't know how to treat a sucking chest wound, they'd kill us on sight. Fucking jarhead motherfucking rednecks."

"There's a few good ones."

"Name ten."

"I don't know ten. Not any of them I can be real with. Maybe Shepard."

"Who's that?"

"Platoon commander."

"Hey, he went to college. He can tell the difference between a pussy and a goat's ass."

We sit quietly and take in the night. There is a heavy firefight going on down south. There is always something going on down south.

My mouth is dry. My head hurts. I see something in the shadow on the other side of Sterling.

"Is that a six-pack?"

"What's left of one." He hands me a piss-warm beer.

"This sailor," says Sterling, "was walking along a road somewhere and a man says to his wife, 'better lock up our daughters.' So the wife shoos the two teenage girls back in the house. A few minutes later, a marine comes by. The husband says, 'I guess we better lock up the cows too.'"

We laugh and are then silent. Two helicopters pass over to the west and head south. Another flare. A rooster crows. I am afraid to go back and close my eyes, because I can't control what I'll see. I'll stay up and listen to the pulse in my neck.

6

IN THE EARLY days of April 1967, things are not so bad. When I joined the platoon, just after three big ugly operations down in the Que Son valley that left hundreds dead and wounded, I found myself among angry men. I had not been through what they'd been through, and I began to understand that some of the things they did, some of the reactions they had, came straight out of Hell. It did not excuse the mistreatment of civilians, but it made it more understandable. Add a dose of racism (gook, slope, slant), and you had hate and retribution overflowing the container. But now, the survivors of those operations—men like Jeter and Rochetti—have recovered some and are beginning to laugh again, swagger.

The fighting I see is mostly squad-sized actions in response to snipers and hit-and-run ambushes. We have learned to spot the booby traps. Jeter claims he can smell them; some are composed of an explosive made from bat guano. We are assigned mostly to patrol the sandy, scrub-pine-covered area between Highway One and the ocean. The night patrols near the South China Sea are the best, the fierce heat and mosquitoes blown away by the sea wind, and fewer enemy—they do not want to find themselves between us and the water. We sit in the soft sand, wait for the ambush that never happens, and listen to the boom of the surf.

When we get Luster, straight from Pendleton in shiny boots and clean greens, we think it would be a good time to break him in on point. About 2200 hours we leave the CP and head east, straight for the ocean on a routine security patrol. We are relaxed, moving quietly at a good pace. The trail drops down quickly as we near the beach, marking the last typhoon-driven surf line, and then a young Vietnamese with a rifle steps out on the trail in front of Luster. Luster raises his rifle, but does not shoot. He shouts, "Halt. Who goes there?" The Vietnamese vanishes into the scrub and the rest of the squad lights up the scene with tracers, following the rabbit run they imagine the Cong to be taking. Rochetti mutters, "Jesus fucking Christ. Halt who goes there?" Luster hangs his head. We begin to kid-giggle and Bruger says, "Shut the fuck up." We sweep the scrub. No body, no blood trail, gone.

All the way back to the CP we can barely contain ourselves. Rochetti slaps Luster on the helmet and mutters, "Halt who fucking goes there? Why, it's Luke the Gook, Motherfucker, who do you think? It's Sammy the Slope." Bruger tells him to shut up but he laugh-snorts through it.

We are not mad at Luster. We are delighted by his innocence. He humanizes us, and the razzing we give him is gentle, even from Rochetti. The next morning, Jeter swaggers out to the piss tube—a length of pipe thrust into the sand principally so everyone will pee in one place—stretches his arms way above his head, and pisses. When he sees Luster sheepishly exiting the shitter, he shouts, "Hey Halt, you sleep good?" Luster flinches. Within the squad, Luster is referred to henceforth as "Old Halt."

Later, when I walked into the battalion aid station to restock my battle dressings, there was a colonel sitting inside with his head down, covered with mud. After a few shots of Scotch, he'd tried to drive from the CP to the Tu Cau bridge and had to drive off into the ditch to avoid the VC who stepped out in front of him on the road to ambush him. He spent the night crawling through the bush to escape while the Cong hunted him. He was not in a good mood. I suspect the chief corpsman had given him something for anxiety. Maybe the relative calm of the battalion area was driving him bugfuck and he had to go out and get into trouble to feel like a soldier.

I stock up on malaria pills as well and head back out with the
squad. That day we are assigned to patrol the area south of the CP.
The heat makes the landscape shimmer, envelopes everything in a
haze. We stop in the shade of an old pagoda to rest.

Jeter seems to grow more enthusiastic daily. He says, "You hear
about the black syph?"

Rochetti says, "Here we go."

"They got this syph over here you can't cure. Fuckin' Cong
inject it into the whores in Saigon so we get it. Your dick drops off
and your head caves in. And then you die."

Corcoran says, "Jeter, you ought to sell encyclopedias door to
door."

Rochetti rolls out his little drop cloth to clean the M60, and the
cleaning rod and oil can seem to clink into place on the mat as if
choreographed. "Where'd you hear that, Jeter?"

"Hospital in Da Nang. When we went up to see Muller. Doctors
were talking about it."

I had been with him on that trip and heard no such story.

Rochetti eases the recoil spring out of the M60.

Jeter continued. "And some of them whores got razor blades
sewed up in their pussies. Take your dick right off." Corcoran lets
out a disgusted sigh, gets up, walks away.

Watching Rochetti's samurai diligence, I think about cleaning
my pistol. I am a lousy shot with a .45. I was practicing one day
and Rochetti said, "Doc, you might as well throw it at them. Get
yourself a shotgun."

Jeter says, "The reason why you can't hit anything, Doc, is you
don't practice. That .45 is a fine pistol. My pappy could shoot the
nuts off a gnat with one."

We could be on a camping trip. We haven't seen any real action
for a month. Rochetti puts the 60 back together so fast he could
be lighting a cigarette. He rolls the cleaning rod, oil can and patches
up in one motion and puts the kit in the top external pocket of

his pack. Then he brushes his teeth. I haven't cleaned my pistol. I haven't brushed my teeth.

Jeter says, "They got some round-eyed pussy up at China Beach. Nurses and Red Cross girls."

Rochetti says, "They only put out for officers."

"They ain't met me yet." Jeter grabs his crotch.

Rochetti says, "Jesus."

THE NEXT DAY we are on a routine patrol south of the battalion CP. Jeter is on point. We step down into a dry rice paddy from a tangle of brush. Jeter is about ten meters out into the paddy when we see some branches move in the far tree line. Jeter fires at the still-moving bush and begins running toward it firing short bursts, tracking the movement with his tracers. He stops suddenly, turns around. The rest of us haven't moved. Jeter is all by himself out in the middle of the paddy.

Corcoran shouts, "Jeter, I didn't tell anybody to assault that tree line. Get your ass back here."

Jeter looks stunned. "This ain't the fuckin' Corps *I* joined."

Corcoran says, "Shut the fuck up, Jeter. Now."

When we finally do reach the far tree line, we find the remnants of a fire, still warm, and a rice sifter tipped up on its side to hide it. We smell human shit.

That night, we return to the same area, sit in the bushes, and wait. No fire. No smoke. No moving bushes. On Corcoran's command, we get up and move toward the tree line. When we are about five meters away, we hear the clicking of safeties and drop to the ground. We are out in the open and my heart feels as big as my head. Jeter says, "Aw, come on. Them's grunts. Ain't no Cong gonna make that much noise."

Corcoran hisses, "Shut the fuck up."

A flare pops overhead and we are lit bright as day. We're fucked, I think.

Then a squad of marines rises from the brush directly in front of us.

"Fuck," shouts Corcoran. "Where are you guys from?"

"Mike Company," somebody shouts back.

"That you, Singleton?"

"Yeah. We almost lit your ass up."

Jeter says, "Ha fuckin' ha. I told you so. Whaddya thinka that, Halt? Ain't no Cong gonna go clickity fuckin' click. Ha fuckin' ha." He grins at Corcoran.

There is a kind of hysteria growing in the platoon. It has been rising in the relative peacefulness of this short time, an unfed snake uncoiling in the spine. When you have seen mass violence and then there is none, Snake wants to play even if he has to create the game.

The squad from Mike Company moves out toward the ocean. We complete our patrol and head back to the CP.

WE GET OUR news from *Stars and Stripes*. It gives us casualty reports, more or less, and some very benign "news" from home. It's the GI poetry section that begins to say something. It's terrible poetry ("you sit home sipping ice tea / while we bleed to keep you free"), but the inferences of class hostility are apparent. There is a searing resentment in the poetry. It talks about who gets to fight wars and who gets to stay home. There is no sophistication in this poetry, but there is heart. It could have made a difference if Americans had known how to read it. But they didn't read *Stars and Stripes*.

The news seeps through on Armed Forces Radio in the form of song lyrics. Country Joe and the Fish tell us "Ain't no use to wonder why, Whoopee! we're all gonna die."

WE ARE TAKING a break just inside a tree line near the Vinh Dien. Jeter is patting the ground and whispering, "Go to sleep. There, go to sleep." I walk over to him and watch. There is a cloverlike plant that recoils from the touch and flattens itself against the ground. Jeter has found a patch. "Ain't that some shit?" Jeter whispers. It is so hot I think I can hear the landscape crackle.

NEXT WEEK WE are sitting in ambush just inside the tree line looking out over a paddy across from a village. Dawn is brightening the spun-glass ground fog and the grass is wet. We wait. It rained all night, and the mosquitos haven't yet found us. It's a morning to feel almost good. We mostly wait in ambushes, and as long as I've been here, we haven't caught anybody, although they've caught us plenty of times. A scrawny cat moves paw by paw into the tree line. When he gets to us he stops, raises his mangy head, and sniffs the air, then walks right through us, unimpressed. We wait. Luster eases into a firing position and the others follow. There's a bright orange patch coming from the village across the paddy, about fifty meters out. It gets larger and in a minute we see it's a Buddhist monk walking across the paddy dike. He steps into the tree line and freezes when he sees us, nine rifles pointed his way.

Corcoran says, "*Lai dai,*" which, in his Georgia accent, sounds like "lie die." The monk looks confused. Then Rochetti says, "*Lai dai* motherfucker!" The monk guesses his intent from his tone and kneels down. When in doubt, kneel. There is a thick worry vein in his forehead.

Corcoran asks him for his ID, and calls his name into the CP. The radio crackles back and Corcoran hands him back his ID. He's seventeen years old. Corcoran says, "*Di di,*" and the monk gets to his feet and bows, and then starts to walk toward the trailhead. Just as he picks up his pace Rochetti trips him, sending him sprawling forward, a green orange rolling out of his robe.

Corcoran says, "That's enough, Rochetti."

The monk gets up slowly, looks around, bows again, and starts to walk away. Rochetti lunges at him and he jumps.

Corcoran says, "Let him go, Rochetti."

Rochetti looks toward the monk, now jogging down the trail, and grins. "He was about to piss his pants."

Jeter says, "Robe. He don't wear no pants."

Rochetti says, "Lost his faith all of a sudden."

Luster says, "He was shakin' like a dog shittin' a peach pit."

Jeter says, "He weren't scared. Them Boodasses don't care if they live or die. Chaplin said so."

Rochetti says, "Bullshit."

"No lie," says Jeter. "They die one minute, then they come back as your cat. Can't get rid of 'em."

Rochetti says, "Got to watch those little fucks. Cong dress up like monks all the time."

Jeter says, "And girls, they dress up like girls."

Rochetti says, "Why, you fuck one?"

Jeter says, "Fuck you, Rochetti."

Corcoran says, "All right. Jeter, you take point."

Jeter says, "Aw, fuck."

THEY BRING OUT the mail on the resupply trucks. I'd almost forgotten it was my birthday. I'd just turned twenty-four. From my uncle George, who knew what grunts needed in the field, I got treats that contain tastes that C rations excluded: tinned paté, anchovies, little packages of fine cheeses, a salami, Swiss chocolate, and, marvel of marvels, several one-ounce bottles of whiskey, the kind you get on commercial jets. I passed some of the goodies around and stuffed myself with the rest. I saved the booze for later.

I got a letter from my father that contained various pieces of canned fatherly wisdom. This was an important birthday, he writes. He seems to be trying to be Dad awfully hard after all these years. He writes, "Keep your head down son. Those bastards are trying to kill you."

I pass the letter around for laughs. *Gee, Dad, I would have never known otherwise.*

7

JETER SAYS, "FUCKIN' cowboy," and slaps a magazine into his rifle.

Rochetti says, "We gonna kill him."

You'd think from the stateside recruiting posters these guys would look like Achilles and Hector. Except for Rochetti, handsome and powerfully built, and Thompson, blue-black and iconic, both of whom could actually pass for Homeric warriors, most of them are anything but. Jeter is slope-shouldered and chicken-chested with just the legal limit of tattoos (he says that in Kentucky if you have more than three visible tattoos you can't get a driver's license). Corcoran is one of those people who should stay out of the sun and is always red as a diaper rash, and Cherenski has more wens than a witch. They've all got snakebrain. They'll all go to the wall.

Lieutenant Shepard tells us what we've known for weeks: "There's three of them. One's got the blooper." A *blooper* is an M79, usually carried by a squad leader, a little handheld, breach-loading grenade launcher that a skilled operator can use to drop a round in somebody's lap at a hundred meters. It has a flip-up sight, but most of the guys who are good with them just eyeball the trajectory. It's good at close quarters, too. You can load a buckshot round and fire point-blank into a line of Cong. But when you use it with grenades it makes a *bloop* or *thunk* when it's fired, like a little mortar. The enemy are not supposed to have them. They aren't supposed to have bouncing betties either, but they do, and marines have been

stepping on them ever since the NVA overran an ARVN compound near Hoi Anh two months back.

A team of three Cong have been killing marines, one or two at
a time, for weeks. There's the one with the blooper—we call him
the Mad Seventy-Niner. He travels with two snipers. Grunts speak
of him with respect and in the same breath swear to kill him.

"One dead slope," says Jeter.

"Gotta find him first," says Corcoran.

Rochetti says, "Who says there's only three of 'em?"

You can hear adrenaline in the chatter.

"Skipper. Says there's a cadre."

"Skipper don't know shit. What's a cadre?"

"Hey man, the skipper's righteous. Down south I saw him up
dodgin' rounds, draggin' his radioman around during a firefight.
Skipper's okay."

Rochetti says, "Gook with the blooper's a bad motherfucker."

"Yeah, but we gonna kill him."

"Step right out on the trail and fuck with you."

"Who'd he kill to get a blooper?"

"Didn't kill nobody. Just took if off an ARVN."

Rochetti say, "Chickenshit motherfuckers. One incoming round
and they're slippin' in their own shit."

"Yeah, if they ain't they *own self* Mr. Charles." Thompson is so
black on this moonless night he looks like an empty set of jungle
utilities sitting on some sandbags. He is talking about how the
ARVN can change sides when the shit gets heavy.

"We gonna kill this fuck."

"This ain't no ordinary slope. "

"Naw, he ain't no local yokel. He's hard core."

Cherenski hands me a rocket round. I'm a noncombatant, a navy
corpsman with minimal combat training attached to the marines. I
say, "I'm not a fucking pack mule."

Cherenski says, "Fuckin' lazy motherfucker is what you are.
Here's another one."

"Hey, Doc, you can carry me piggyback," says Thompson. "I'm too sensitive for all this humpin'. I hear your legs is strong."

Lieutenant Shepard walks over and says something to Sergeant Spinner who walks over and says something to Corcoran.

Corcoran says, "Let's go. Jeter, you got point."

Everybody hates point, but Jeter always bitches. "I had point yesterday."

"Thursday. You had point Thursday. Let's move."

Jeter half whispers, "Cocksucker."

Spinner says, "Watch your mouth, boy."

We're up and moving now, toward the main gate. We are the point squad of the point platoon of a company of three platoons. The plan is to envelope anyone between Highway One and the South China Sea and pin them against the Marble Mountains. *We don't know it but there are VC inside Kim Son Mountain.* We are going to find the Mad Seventy-Niner. We are going to fuck him up once and for all. One by one we lock and load as we pass beyond the wire. A flare silvers the sand in front of us. The far trees look like inkblots. The company files out into the sand and picks up the pace. B52s are working off in the mountains to the west. I watch the arc light, and in two heartbeats hear the low rumble of the bombs.

Another flare pops overhead. We lengthen our intervals and clear our heads. *Flip the switch now.* You can stay awake three days on snakebrain. Problem is, you can't put it back to sleep after the war. A sharp sound will jerk you wide awake, and then it's all night up and looking out the window on an empty street, but we don't know that yet. The flare fades to an ember and drifts off into the tree line. *Never guess we're coming, would you Mr. Charles?* Cherenski stumbles in the sand and his gear rattles.

Spinner turns on him. "Boy, you make more noise than two skeletons fuckin' on a tin roof."

We've tightened rifle straps, made sure our canteens are full or empty so they don't slosh, taken care not to wash with sweet smelling soap like Irish Spring. Truth be told, unless we're sitting ambush or listening post, we want them to know we're here. We are in the habit of looking for trouble. We want the contact. Then we can call for artillery or air, even if that way Mr. Charles always gets off the first round. This is called "search and destroy."

The skipper radios Corcoran that we're to sit tight and wait. We do the marine version of "digging in," which means that we don't dig in, but find natural cover and make a perimeter. We set the watch and send out the first patrol. The other platoons do the same, and we have to take care not to ambush each other. We hunker down for the night. Rochetti pulls his poncho over his head and lights a cigarette.

I walk over to second squad to talk to Sterling, who's on his first patrol. "How ya doin'?"

"So far so good. These mosquitoes are unbelievable."

"You got repellent?"

"Yeah, I got some of that greasy shit."

"Be sure and put it around your ankles and on the top of your head." Sterling has still got a stateside buzz cut.

"Thanks."

He looks scared. Well, so am I.

I walk back to my squad and find a place in the sand to hunker down.

Jeter says, "Last week a recon plane took all these infrared pictures of the jungle and they found all these big patches of heat, like there's a whole shitload of people down there."

"Keep your voice down, Jeter."

"So they call in B52s and tear up a whole grid square and when they send in grunts next morning they find hundreds of dead howler monkeys."

Corcoran says, "Go to sleep, Jeter. Who told you that?"

"Guy at China Beach."

"Go to sleep, Jeter."

It's probably a lie, but in this war, the facts are harder to believe. Like what happened next.

I'm assigned radio watch till ten, then Thompson takes over. We've been told to sleep with our boots on. I ease back into the soft sand and instantly drift away. I am sitting in a restaurant in Milwaukee. While at Hospital Corps School in Great Lakes, Illinois, I find this city more fun than Chicago. The women are friendlier, less contemptuous of servicemen. I go to Milwaukee whenever I get liberty and, more often than not, find a free place to stay the night. It's bitter cold, and I'm having the best bowl of beef and barley soup I've ever had. I love the cold, the way the women come into the diner and brush the snow off their parkas, pull off their knit caps and shake out their hair. I love the smell of coffee, the steamed-up windows.

Milwaukee is the last place I have a lover before coming to Vietnam. Patty is a sweet interlude. Patty with work-shirt blue eyes and milky skin and baby silk hair. When we've fucked ourselves silly, we walk out on the jetties of Lake Michigan and let the wind make ice in our hair. But Patty does not appear in the dream. I wait for her to come into the restaurant. She doesn't show. The wind howls.

Then I am sitting straight up and marines are scuffling through the sand all around me. My ears are still ringing from the blast. Corcoran is on the radio, "Actual, this is Three Alpha, come in." I don't hear what's being said on the other end, but Thompson tells me something's going on over near first platoon. There's a rattle of small-arms fire off to the south. Puff the Magic Dragon is circling down near the ocean, tracers, like molten ingots, stream down from it, then we hear the growl of the Gatling guns. Puff is one of two C-130s armed with twenty-millimeter Gatling guns that can cover every square inch of a football field in thirty seconds. The other called Snoopy. The big parachute flares cluster together in the sky about a half klick away.

We listen to the radio and wait. Corcoran says, "Fuckers crawled up on an LP, about ten of 'em, and heaved satchel charges on 'em."

Jeter says, "Damn. Ten against three. That's real brave."

But we don't know how many there were. The revisions begin while the rifle barrels are still hot.

Lieutenant Shepard shouts, "Saddle up," and we begin pulling on our gear.

Corcoran is disgusted, humiliated. He turns away from the radio and says, "They're pickin' 'em up in pieces. They'll have to go back when it's light."

Our anger is searing and silent as we move east. Good thing there are no civilians between us and the ocean. Jeter holds back a branch so it won't slap me in the face, and I do the same for Thompson coming up behind me. The pines are thickening around us as we move.

Corcoran passes word back to stay alert, "We've got them coming our way." I hear safeties being clicked off all the way up the column. There is a burst of automatic-weapons fire at the head of the column and we hunker down. Word comes back we've got one.

Spinner can't raise second platoon on the radio so he sends Jeter up the column to see what's happening. Jeter is back in a snap.

"Got two of 'em. One's the Mad Seventy-Niner."

"Naw."

"No shit. They got the M79. The other guy had an AK."

Thompson says, "Praise the Lord."

"Fuckers stepped out on the trail right in front of them. Just like fuckin' Jesse James."

I hear Jeter go into embellishment mode.

"Fucker's deader 'n shit. Lyin' there with his dick standing straight up." His eyes get big. "Does dying give them a fucking hard-on?"

I say, "When you shoot them in the brain stem. Probably shit his pants too."

"Damn."

We hook up with second platoon on our right and begin a sweep down to the beach. Gray light of overcast dawn, thrum of surf, the smell of the fecund South China Sea. We hold ten minutes, and then start moving again, very slowly, Snakebrain luminous and burning away the gray light.

There is a leprosarium in an old French village near the beach, run by Catholic priests. We know the Cong take their wounded there at night and the doctors have no choice but to treat them. We are almost to the ocean when we see two priests leading a group of Vietnamese men down to bathe their leprous sores in the salt water. Among them we see young men with obvious gunshot and shrapnel wounds. They grin at us sheepishly. We can't touch them.

Rochetti says, "Who needs a fucking bunch of priests. Let's kill 'em and say they got caught in a cross fire."

Shepard says "Can it, Rochetti."

Rochetti butt strokes the air with the M60, "Motherfucker! Motherfucker! Motherfucker!"

I haven't eaten since yesterday, and my hunger feels like battery acid. We move down to the beach. As far I can see, marines sit in the sand. The lepers kick off their sandals, strip, and wade into the incoming tide. The priests stand by the water and watch. The Vietnamese are chatting now, laughing, the surf raising them up and dropping them down into the trough as they paddle out. The sea is as gray as the sky. We watch them lift up, disappear behind the wave, then up again on the next. They are looking back at us. The wind brings us their laughter. We watch them.

Then Jeter says, "What the fuck," pulls off his boots, his pants, and wades into the surf. I think of howler monkeys. One by one we stack our rifles and follow him. Second squad gives us security as we swim and later, we them. I breathe in the salt mist and close my eyes, Snakebrain still bright as a starlight scope. I feel the wave lift me and open my eyes. The Vietnamese are about fifteen meters away. One smiles at me.

8

SPINNER IS SHOUTING at us. We are running without yet
knowing what is happening, locking and loading on the run, hop-
ping to pull on boots, slapping on helmets, stumbling under the
weight of our gear across a dry paddy into the hedgerow of the
opposite village. The firing starts before I enter the hedgerow and
I can hear the whooping of the marines. Just inside, the bodies of
NVA regulars are already thick on the ground. Plumes of white
phosphorus shoot up from the other side of the stream that divides
the village, and then the far tree line boils over with napalm. I don't
know if I hear screams or the hiss of burning thatch.

I see Jeter firing into a corpse with his M16. The corpse is dancing. Jeter is red-faced, like a thwarted child. His eyes are all pupil.
This is the kid who most often makes me laugh, who makes me
feel most protective, the eighteen-year-old whose parents had to
sign for him when he joined up at seventeen. He empties one
magazine and slaps in another. He fires again into the corpse. The
corpse dances, arms and legs flail, the flat face peeling off the shattered skull, the pink-blue brains scattering, the ground black with
blood. Jeter stops suddenly, looks dazed.

I say, "You all right?" He stares at me. Then he kicks what's left
of the corpse, and it flops over like a doll. He runs toward the
stream where they're still fighting. I don't see the ones begging
for their lives. I don't see the ones who try to hide in the stream
and now float facedown, the stream bright red. Then the firing
stops and Spinner gives the order to line up the bodies for the
count.

Lieutenant Shepard wanders toward me, dazed. He says, "Anyone hit?"

"Don't know yet." I look at him but nobody's home. Jeter, who has been standing among the bodies staring into the burning tree line, sits down cross-legged and wipes down his rifle barrel with a rag. Rochetti is jumping up and down and shouting, "Get some, motherfucker." He's not home either. Where are they? Where am I? I think I'm making the rounds, seeing if anyone's hit. The whole engagement takes less than five minutes.

Marines come dragging dead NVA by the heels, lining them up in rows. Others start rifling the bodies, dumping out their packs.

"Thirty-nine," Spinner shouts into the radio. He's beaming. Everybody's got what they want from the bodies. Belt buckles, personal contents of packs are strewn over the ground. I pick up a cheap notebook, marked *Cahier,* its binding falling apart. What looks like songs or poems are written on the graph-paper pages, and a not bad drawing of Ho Chi Minh.

Spinner is shouting, "Saddle up." We mount the idling amtracs that grunt to a start and head north to the LZ. A Huey gunship stalks tree level on our flank. Some of us are already sleeping. Rochetti's tipping up a can of C-rats peaches, drinking the last of the juice. I light a cigarette.

Two Sea Knights are waiting for us at the LZ in the middle of a dried paddy, two others are circling, waiting to land. Yellow smoke drifts up from the landing zone. We board and lift. On board, the hum of the engines puts me to sleep.

I don't remember the ride back from the Da Nang airstrip to the battalion command post. My blackout extends so far back into sober time that Sterling has to tell me after the fact. We've been in the field seven days and we stink. I'm covered with mud, blood under my fingernails, stumbling toward the sound of beer cans opening.

Somebody shouts, "Hynuh!" and starts flinging cans of beer up in the air. I catch one. "Hynuh!" One hits Rochetti in the head.

"Motherfucker!" he screams, and looks around for the thrower. Sterling has acquired a case of beer somewhere, trying to hide it by his hip. He reaches into it and tosses another one to me as we stumble toward the corpsman's hooch.

Inside, two corpsmen from first platoon, Bayley and Higgins, have got a quart of Johnnie Walker Red circulating. Bonitas, second platoon sergeant, has his arm around Bayley. "Goddamn you should have seen those fuckers run." I drink about a pint of scotch on the first two swigs, and Sterling snatches it away from me. I chase the scotch with a San Miguel and watch the bottle travel back to Sterling's trunk, where he foolishly sets it down. When he turns his back I drink another slug. Outside, Rochetti is screaming, "You cut my head, motherfucker."

"Fuck you, Rochetti," Bonitas shouts, toward the door.

"Who said that? Come out here and say that."

Bonitas pulls aside the poncho that covers the door and shouts at Rochetti, "Fuck you, you wop faggot motherfucker," then quickly closes the door before Rochetti can turn around.

Bonitas hugs Bayley and kisses him on the cheek, then lets him fall. Bayley staggers backward and knocks over the Coleman lantern. It goes out.

Sterling rights the Coleman and lights it with his Zippo.

From outside the door, Rochetti screams, "Come out here you fucking spic fucking jumping bean motherfucker."

I look up and Bonitas is staring at me. I look away. I look back and he's still staring. "You call me a spic?"

I say, "Rochetti called you a spic."

"You called me a spic again, you fucking *pendejo* fuck."

"Rochetti . . ." but I can't get the words out. Bonitas slugs me, and I block it with my shoulder. I turn my face away from the next blow, and he slugs me in the ear. Bayley and Sterling wrestle Bonitas to the floor. I stagger toward the door and out into the sand. Rochetti's standing there. He says to me, "Go get Bonitas."

I say, "Go get him yourself." My ear is ringing and I stagger toward the flicker of a film projector that's set up in the sand next to the battalion aid station. My ear is ringing and in my condition it sounds like I'm at the bottom of a swimming pool. I've a vague notion I'm going to the aid station to see about my ear, but I get distracted by the movie. There are about thirty grunts watching John Wayne, who is being sarcastic with some Mexicans.

I stagger forward and fall facedown in the sand. I get up, reach for the Johnny Walker bottle I've managed not to spill too much of, and sit down. I watch John Wayne. He's got one hand on his hip and is talking out of one corner of his mouth. I'm brain-looping the crowd, the movie screen splits focus—two John Waynes, two horses. I have to piss so I get up, stagger toward the piss tube, and unzip. There are two piss tubes. Somebody's shaking me by the shirt. It's an officer I don't know. "You're pissing on me, son." I salute. There is a lot of laughter now, either at the movie or me. He says something like, "People who drink like you oughta . . ." and then there are two of them, one with a flashlight pointed at my ear.

One says, "He's bleeding."

"Go on to sick bay, Doc."

I stagger to the aid station. Inside Chief Sims sits me down on the examining table. "Nine stitches," he says, and hooks the curved needle in my ear.

It hurts.

"Where's the fucking Novocain?" I ask.

"You don't need any Novocain. You're shit-faced."

"The fuck are you using that size suture on me for? I'm not a goddamn turkey."

"Hold still, dammit."

"Fuck you," I say. He goes on suturing. "Sit still," he shouts. Then it all goes black.

SNAKEBRAIN TELLS YOU *where the nails are, driven through a plank, smeared with shit and hidden in a shallow pit covered with leaves, tells you before you put your foot down, sniffs the funk of its maker skittering away through the thick tangle just as you arrive. Snake tells you about the length of pipe with the cartridge in it, primer sitting on a nail, waiting for you to put your foot down, the bullet straight up into your groin. Snake tells you where the punji pits are, sharpened bamboo stakes at the bottom. Tells about the Malaysian whip, sprung back on green bamboo with sharpened spikes on the whip end, trip wire stretched across the trail and covered with leaves. Tells you where the wire's strung high up to snag the radio antenna. Tells you about the five-hundred-pound bomb hung in a tree.*

CHERENSKI'S PACKING HIS seabag. We watch, quietly. He folds his jungle utilities as if they are dress blues. He lays his Ka-Bar on his air mattress and stares at it lovingly. His orders back to CONUS, the continental United States, in a plain brown envelope, lie next to the thick packet of rubber-banded letters. He's going home. It is a tender moment where we all meet and imagine ourselves as we step off the plane, hang up our uniforms for good, let our beards grow. Cherenski cleans his rifle for the last time, very slowly. He'll turn it in tomorrow.

SNAKEBRAIN TELLS YOU *the grinning ten-year-old who empties the garbage inside the battalion CP has dropped a grenade in the shitter. This is how they do it: take an M26 grenade, tie a string around the spoon, then pull the pin. The string keeps the spoon in place. Then take an old C-rats can and fill it with mud and place the grenade in the mud. Let the mud dry. Carefully remove the string. The dried mud keeps the spoon in place.*

Then, when you're not looking, the sweet kid you'd like to adopt drops the whole works into the shitter. Five minutes later, a marine comes and sits down on the shitter. Piss and fecal matter have meanwhile begun to loosen the dried mud, releasing the spoon, lighting the fuse. Five seconds later you have a dead or mutilated marine.

———————

THE ENLISTED MEN'S club is a shack up on stilts with its tin roof just visible above the sand berm. We're giving Cherenski a going-away party, which means we buy the beer.

"Get some," Jeter says. They're talking about girls the way they talk about the notches they'd put on their M16s were the stocks not plastic. They're talking about the hippie chicks they've heard about who'll drop acid in your drink and fuck you till your eyes cross then leave you with mush mind.

Cherenski says, "Twenty-four hours and a wake up."

Rochetti says, "Yeah, but you got to get to the airstrip. Ain't over till you get there."

"All I got to do . . ." Cherenski is beginning to slur, and he's got a line of San Miguels on the bar. "All I got to do is get in the truck, drive up Highway One to Da Nang, and get me on a plane."

Rochetti says, "There's wall-to-wall gooks between here and Da Nang."

"Cut him some slack," says Jeter.

"Fuck you."

"You some kind of hard dude," says Thompson.

"Just tellin' it like it is," says Rochetti. "Myself, I don't want to go home. Country's fucked."

I know then that Rochetti is crazy. Anybody who ships over for another tour in this place is deranged.

"I'm going to join the legion," says Rochetti.

Cherenski says, "Ha, see you sittin' with a beer at the Legion hall, tryin' to pick a fight with some old fart from World War I."

"You dumb shit I meant the French Foreign Legion. Pay attention."

"Fuck you."

"Fuck a bunch of students. Country's fucked up."

Rochetti doesn't know just how much, or why, or where it goes from here. None of us do.

Corcoran says, "I get your Ka-Bar."

"On my bunk," says Cherenski.

At first we think Cherenski's clowning the way he comes off that stool. He seems as if he's trying to do a flip and lands on his side. Then we see the thin stream of blood spurting from his head.

"Go get Dr. Ayala," I'm shouting. Rochetti's got him by the shirt, and Thompson's got his ankles. We're outside now, hauling him through the sand, stumbling toward the battalion aid station. A squad of marines is running toward the north berm. A flare lights up the north tree lines.

"Aaaaahhhhh God," Cherenski's shouting.

Dr. Ayala's running toward the aid station. We've got Cherenski inside on the examining table. My clothes are soaked with blood. There's blood all over the floor. Dr. Ayala's chest is covered with blood. Cherenski's kicking and thrashing, and we hold him down. He screams, "No no no no."

"Fuckin' goddamn sniper," says Rochetti.

Two rounds had come through the tin roof of the bar, and one of them got him.

Dr. Ayala's got a fifty-cc syringe full of sterile water, washing away the blood. Bone chips are sticking out of his head. I see the red-pink-gray brain exposed. "No no no no no" sobs Cherenski, but there's something wrong with his voice and it comes out *nuh nuh nuh* as the brain winds down to track the damage. "He's got about twenty ccs of brain gone," says Ayala. "Get a medevac. We can't do anything for him here."

Luster is on the radio.

I'M BACK IN the EM club. It's midnight. I'm the only one there. It's closing time. There are two holes in the tin roof. The blood has been mopped up, leaving a pink film on the plywood floor. I'm drinking as much as I can. I'd drink more if they'd let me. I haven't thought of the morphine syrettes. I'll manage to get out of Vietnam without shooting anything into my veins, but I've got oblivion on my mind. I don't like this war anymore. Come to think of it, I never did. The guys who like it don't even like it once they're too numb to swagger. I've seen them sitting there with a table full of empties looking straight into nowhere. I'd order another beer but the bartender's cleaning up. "Better hit the rack, Doc."

I stumble down the stairs and almost fall on my face in the sand. Somebody grabs my arm to keep me upright. It's Sterling, the new corpsman from second squad.

"Doc, you look like you need to keep drinking."

"Drink what?"

He tugs a half pint out of his thigh pocket.

"Where'd you get that?"

"Da Nang. When I arrived."

"Shoulda done that."

"This is fucked up."

"What is?"

"Everything. This place. I was told we were going to be helping Vietnamese fight Communists."

I say, "Whoever told you it's about the Vietnamese? It's about staying alive until you go home, then you can sit around and drink and figure out what happened."

We stumble back to the corpsman's hooch.

SNAKEBRAIN'S A LITTLE *glow breathing in the darkest place, a quiet shimmering underneath everything that's supposed to be at peace.*

9

ONE BLESSEDLY COOL morning with a hint of monsoon on the wind we are cleaning up after breakfast, smoking. Good Morning, Vietnam is on the radio and Elwell, from second squad, is moving with Aretha's "Respect."

The fight seemed to bloom out of a burst of laughter. Rochetti suddenly throws a flurry of punches at Elwell.

Lieutenant Shepard is on his feet now, watching. He tosses a C-rations can into the fire.

"Shit." Elwell turns his back and walks away shaking his head.

"Come back here, nigger."

Elwell turns and stares at him, then turns away again, but Rochetti's all over him. Elwell gets loose and backs off. Rochetti moves in and throws a punch. Elwell tilts his head and steps away. Rochetti follows.

Shepard steps between them. "Cool it. Now."

He's got his hands out to separate them, but Rochetti sidesteps him and throws another punch. Elwell bobs away.

"All right. NOW!" Shepard says.

Elwell says, "Let him go, Lieutenant. We got some business." Elwell's gone mean and cold, red in his eye.

"I'm telling you, knock it off *now*. Or I write you both up."

But he won't write them up. He never does. That's the reason they'll stop. They won't stop for a snitch, but they'll stop for him.

Rochetti turns his back and stalks over to a bush, unzips, and takes a piss.

"Goddamn shit fuck," says Jeter, and turns the radio back on. "Monday, Monday," the Mamas and the Papas, fill the silence.

Elwell stands and watches Rochetti with a hurt look. "Damn. Some kind of hopeless motherfucker."

"Can it," says Shepard.

Elwell walks away, shaking his head.

I don't know what caused that fight. Part of me wants to say it was the radio, Aretha Franklin, Rochetti's Brooklyn-accented racism. It was probably just the continual exposure to violence, the heat, the general beshittedness of the war and its mindless pursuit. I wanted there to be a reason.

Race wound its way through the war and seemed to stitch it together. It was not the cause of the war, but it was certainly a principal propellant. For some time we had been seeing, along the trails, propaganda leaflets stapled to popsicle sticks, like little Burma Shave signs. They said things like, "Black man, why do you fight a white man's war against the yellow man?" I watched Thompson and Spinner. They did not react to the signs.

One time I heard Spinner say to Thompson, "Don't you worry, nigga. Mr. Charles catch you and snatch your balls off just like anybody else."

If you grew up white in the pre-civil-rights South you got a whopping dose of racism from the whole culture. *Nigger* was used by everyone, all the time, with impunity, and became deeply imprinted in the minds of otherwise good people. Middle-class people with pretensions of liberality would say *Nigra,* or *Colored*. If you were a committed racist, your racism became a festering rage. If you became a person of goodwill, your racism would invade your unconscious and embarrass you throughout life. It was like living with a chronic disease that caught you by surprise over and over again. Healing from it became a lifelong spiritual project. It involved, for me, a vigilant and raw opening in the heart.

That the Vietnam War was in some way involved with the struggle for civil rights was no accident. On April 4, 1967, Martin Luther King, speaking at Riverside Church in New York City, observed that black and white young men who could not sit together in the same schools were killing people of yet another race in Vietnam. He also observed that the young men who were dying in Vietnam were mostly poor: black, white, or yellow. Dr. King said, "I could not be silent in the face of such cruel manipulation."

UNDER FIRE, A marine unit is a sharply disciplined and courageous organism with no individuals. But in the rear, in the base camps and training areas, racial tension hung on like ground fog. The pressure of the war turned races against one another, and we forgot that many of us shared the same social class.

I remember the chow hall at Camp Pendleton where the long lines would snake out and around the building. A black marine would be in line and suddenly ten of his friends would join him. Their hats were slightly askew, or the bills turned up and the way they moved and talked was pure revolution. The line would suddenly swell at that point and before long, twenty or thirty black guys would have cut in line.

"Fuckin' Africa," somebody would say. The white marines either stewed over it or let it go. They knew instinctively that what was happening was powered by something just beyond their grasp, and who wants a fight before lunch?

In Vietnam there was less time to think about it, but even in the short breaks, during an hour at the EM club, or a session of touch football in the battalion sand, a fight could flare up out of nowhere. It wasn't coming from nowhere. It had been purchased with blood.

Reverend King was quick to pick up the connection between the racism he'd been fighting and the racist iconography the country had created for our Asian enemy. They were the primitives we were going to "bomb back to the stone age," or they were strange and alien semi-humans who did not have human emotions and who did not fear death because of their non-Christian belief in reincarnation. Americans had not observed that probably at least 25 percent the country was Catholic. None of us, no matter how stupid, how politically programmed, could help but see the terror in the eyes of the Vietnamese when we came into their villages.

Muhammad Ali galvanized thousands of young black men, and his choice to refuse the draft spilled over into the fighting units in Vietnam. This split between Ali and the war was felt deeply by the black marines in my unit.

About this time Thompson and I became friends. It happened as I had begun to turn, as I had begun to stand, as best I could, against a war that disgusted me. Standing up, at that point in my life, was really getting up on one knee from a crawl. It would take the rest of the 1960s for me to get to my feet.

Thompson and I talked about the black/white thing. We talked about it a lot. When he was with his black friends he would pull away from me, but when he was with me alone, resting in the shade of a hooch, squatting on the trail waiting, or hanging around under the ramada outside the EM club, we were tight.

Black people are usually bored when white people talk about race, taking on kind of a flat, sidelong look that says something like, *'bout fuckin' time you looked at what was right there under your long white nose just what does it take besides a baseball bat upside your head?* But Thompson never gave me that look, or turned away, or changed the subject, or just got the fuck up and left. He listened. Maybe living all his life on the razor's edge gave him his capacity to negotiate the irony from either angle. We talked about it and we talked about girls and we talked about going home and I humped his extra grenades for him.

I had been functionally crazy for much of my tour in Vietnam. I came from a family full of the functionally crazy, a long line of alcoholics who excelled at putting one foot in front of the other in spite of being chock full of demons. I was an automaton doing my job, burning alive inside. It reached a crisis just before I was taken out of the field and transferred to the rear. I had seen the last burned village, the last dead civilian I ever wanted to see, and my loyalties were deeply divided. I was becoming a danger to myself and others, and I wanted out. I had been thinking for some time about wounding myself. There were stories from all over the country about guys who'd stick their arm or leg up during a firefight and hope to get hit so they could go home. I never saw it in my unit, but the sentiment was there. All of us wanted to go home, and something about the internal rot of the war had gotten to everybody.

All I could think about was drinking. I couldn't wait to get back to the battalion command post and go to the EM club. I drank to become unconscious, but I couldn't stay asleep. I woke in the night with the horrors, the rest of the platoon snoring away and no one to talk to. Somewhere, out there in the battalion, somebody else couldn't sleep. I couldn't be the only one with the night terror. Fear is worse when you do not believe in what you're doing, when you don't have something transcendental to die for. I'd drink. I'd bullshit. I'd get morose. I'd pass out. I'd wake up dry-mouthed with my heart trying to get out of my chest.

One time on an operation down in the Que Son valley we were moving the company along a ridgeline, across the valley from some NVA who were sniping at us. We were so tired and parched we just kept lurching forward while the rounds whizzed over our heads or hit in the dirt halfway down the slope. It must have been a hundred and thirty degrees and the spotter pilots were dropping six packs of beer in little flare parachutes from their Piper Cubs. Some of them drifted our way. The others went too far down toward the NVA. One package fell about fifty meters down the slope toward the valley, and I scrambled down after it. I could hear Ryan shouting at me, "Doc, get the fuck back here," but that beer glowed with a holy light. I grabbed the six pack and scrambled back up the hill as the enemy rifleman adjusted fire to follow me. I didn't care. Being dead might just be alright.

I freaked Thompson out one day. We were taking a break near some abandoned hooches and I explained my plan. I told him I was going to go around to the side of the mud hooch, toss a grenade around the corner, and stick my leg out past the wall. It would just fuck up one foot, I said. I needed him to witness that I'd sprung a booby trap, or that someone had thrown the grenade.

He said, "Doc, that's your whole foot."

I said, "I can do without it." I could do without a foot, but I couldn't do without a soul.

He grabbed me by the shirt, "Don't fuckin' do it."

He was looking at me with such intensity that I thought I'd actually been listened to, actually confided something that was true.

And, like a good friend, he never mentioned it to anyone.

I still have my foot.

I HAD LOST any sense of time. That my tour was up in February did not interest me. Fear makes the present swell up and force out the future. I also lost track of sequence, and often cannot remember what happened when, although I almost always remember what happened *where,* because my visual memory is strong. There are so many things I want to turn into a story in order to make sense of them. Some have taken my life up till now to write or, rather, to be included in the larger story of years.

You will not find certain things in military documents. Two men stark naked and bathing in a well when a sniper opens up on them and they start running, laughing. A new corpsman so frozen with fear his first day in the field that he could not move from where he sat and had to be sent back on the chopper with the casualties (in later life I would simply refer to him as sane). An image of the French journalist who had come with us on an operation in the Que Son valley. Her sitting and brushing her long hair just as the sun went down. Her saying to her cameraman after the mortar attack, *"Quoi? Julien? Ça va bien?"*

Strangely, I would lie at night and think of two things. One was women—I would masturbate under my poncho; anyone can understand that—but hot soup? Over and over again I would think about beef and barley soup in a place that was so cold in the winter that it would taste good, a place that was opposite this place where it was not unusual for the temperature to reach one hundred twenty-five degrees. How good sugarcane and well water tasted on such a day.

HARKNESS ASKS ME if he can borrow my pistol to go to the chow hall. Marines are required to have their weapons with them at all times. It is more convenient to take a pistol to lunch than a rifle, so Harkness takes my pistol, which has not been cleaned in the months since I had acquired a shotgun. At the chow hall, Harkness attempts to clear the pistol before entering, but the slide is stuck with corrosion. In the struggle to pull the slide back, the pistol goes off. No one is hit, but Harkness is sent to the battalion commander for an ass-chewing. He very nearly loses a stripe. I am also reprimanded, but more gently.

On the way back to battalion aid, I run into the supply sergeant, Walker, who invites me to the supply hooch where he rolls a joint. We cool our throats with beer. All my mental controls are suddenly shut off by the pot, and my mind begins to turn on itself. Any little fragment of good I have protected in myself begins to loosen and blow away. I have to drink the rest of the day to get rid of the effects of the pot.

IT IS SO hot that even the Vietnamese are listless. We are taking a break on patrol and I fall asleep on a mound of earth. I wake up and Thompson is laughing at me, imitating open mouth while asleep. "Fly gonna go in there," he says. But I don't laugh. I feel like shit. Something is twisting in my head, and I'm seeing a red fuzz over everything. I walk over to Harkness and look at him. He looks up. I say, "You a Christian?"

He says, "Yeah, I guess."

"Then how the fuck can you justify killing Vietnamese." My body is a knot, a coil of wire. Minutes ago I was fine, joking with Thompson. I'd gotten to the point where my emotions went from zero to sixty in a millisecond.

For Harkness, this has come out of nowhere. He looks stunned. He looks like he's in trouble at school. I will see this look on my aunt Rosie's face one day when I ask her why she irons everybody's underwear.

I walk away. I know now how stupid and self-righteous this was, but I was beginning to come unglued. I would stay unglued for a long time. I was disgusted with the war and would remain so the rest of my life.

WE HAVE BEEN out all night on a company-sized patrol and are stopping for breakfast and a piss break. I'm sitting with the company commander, Captain Gillis, and Lieutenant Shepard. I start talking about all the old French buildings we've just searched in the villages near the ocean. Gillis talks about the colonials and the rubber plantations. There is a long silence. We drink C-rats coffee. The captain says, "Weird war," and we are quiet again.

I see a Vietnamese man and woman walking toward us over a dry paddy. They are carrying something slung between them on a bamboo mat. They stop ten meters away, lay the mat down, and gently unroll it. Inside is a little boy, maybe four, dead and disemboweled. Flies blacken the exposed intestines and cluster around his eyes. I recognize the jagged path of artillery shrapnel across his gray skin. His father waves the flies away from his face, but they return immediately.

We stare. No one speaks Vietnamese, so the couple are spared someone saying something stupid. Lieutenant Shepard looks at me, and I shake my head. He knows there's nothing to be done. The Vietnamese man and woman stare at us with their ravaged faces.

Jeter says, "Fuck. Out playin' after curfew. Do it every time." But his voice is shaking. Everyone turns his back but me and Shepard.

10

JUST BEFORE THE November monsoons, we are sent to a place called the Desert Position, a platoon-sized compound west of Highway One in a sandy area that was once ocean. The engineers have bulldozed a triangular berm and put bunkers at the corners. Three walls are easier to defend than four, or so goes the wisdom. It didn't help the French.

We know we are going to a bad neighborhood. The previous year the position was overrun by NVA and local guerillas. NVA units are massing in the area, and we tell fewer jokes the first week there. We patch the wire, mine the perimeter, and set trip flares. We increase the frequency of patrols and vary routes. Just after lunch Corcoran tells his squad to saddle up and we move south toward the tree line. I've learned by now not to walk near the squad leader or the radioman on a patrol.

They let half the squad through before they hit us. It's a classic L-shaped ambush, and I'm facedown in the sand listening. There's a sniper in the trees on the left and a heavy machine gun and two or three riflemen up front.

Three people shout at once, "Corpsman up." I can hear the flat crack of the sniper on my left and I flinch. He's close. I hear the familiar hiss of rifle rounds intended for me and then the rest of the squad returning fire. Just inside the treeline, Corcoran is down. He's taken two rounds in the chest and is gasping.

I hear loud cracking, and the tree in front of me splinters and falls. Everyone around me flattens out on the ground. I refocus and roll Corcoran over. The exit wounds are huge and the dirt beneath him is black with blood.

Corcoran whispers, "Am I going to be all right, Doc?" And I lie. *Yeah. You're going home, Corcoran. Just stay with me now.* But he's deep in shock and before I can start mouth-to-mouth I hear him drowning in his own blood, and then the death rattle. He's gone. I pump his chest for a while but just hear the blood soaking the lungs deeper. I don't even bother with battle dressings.

The gunship that comes with the medevac is not returning fire because they don't see anything to fire at. Our ambushers are gone. And the mortars we call in just tear up a few trees. I look at a splintered stump and wonder why I'm not hit. *Snake says, I love the smell of cordite and blood.* We heave the lifeless body on board.

I don't eat that night. The rest of the squad is quiet.

In the morning, Werner, a corpsman from second squad, gets on an amtrac going back to the battalion CP. His tour is up and he's going home. He grins at us, hungover, bleary-eyed. We watch the amtrac turn right onto Highway One. We watch Luster and Rochetti swing the wire back into place.

THE NEXT DAY the resupply chopper brings in a replacement corpsman, Meyer, and a new lance corporal named Bryan. Bryan is a light-skinned black man with a visible attitude. The minute he steps off the chopper into the sand with his seabag and looks around with his full-framed pale blue shades, I feel the platoon chemistry shift. He's got a transistor radio with an earplug and moves with whatever he's listening to. More cautiously, Corpsman Meyer steps out of the chopper, his glasses held on by an elastic strap. He looks around like he's at the zoo.

Rochetti says, "Oh boy."

Lieutenant Shepard shakes hands with Meyer and Bryan and motions them over to the CP. In a minute they come out, shielding their eyes from the sun. Bryan is going to first squad, and Meyer to the medical bunker with me.

Meyer seems delighted to be in a new place, shakes my hand too vigorously, and grins hugely, "So this is it."

"Whatever *it* is, you're here."

"I detect an ironist," he says.

"You've had some college," I say. "How the fuck you wind up here, Meyer?"

I see Bryan walking toward us.

"I was a reservist and they called me up."

I told him the same thing had happened to me. I said, "Not smart going to Hospital Corps school, hunh?"

"Hey, we thought it was going to be a few advisors."

"Yeah."

Bryan eases in between us and extends his hand. "They told me in infantry training first thing I do is get tight with the corpsman so he'll come after my black ass when I get hit. Anything you need, Doc, you let me know."

I don't know what he has that I need, but I shake his hand. I say, "They told me at Pendleton to borrow money from all the grunts in my unit so they'll keep my ass alive. You got a hundred-dollar bill?"

Bryan grins and looks off toward the berm. It's clouding up toward the west. Monsoon's coming. I see Thompson watching Bryan. Thompson gets up and walks over and stands next to Bryan, towering over him. Bryan turns and looks at him. "Hey nigga, you remember me?"

Thompson says, "Yeah, I remember your sorry ass."

There is some unfinished business here. Thompson turns and walks toward the berm.

Bryan says, "That Tom's been unhappy since Cassius Clay changed his name. Can't get over it."

Thompson hears him. Stops. Thinks better of it and moves on.

Meyer perks up. He says, "Ali refused to be drafted. Whaddya think of that?"

Bryan says, "I think if I had that man's money I'd do somethin' like that too. When we gonna eat?"

I point to the pallet of C rations they've pushed off the chopper. "Dinner came with you. Go over and get some before all the spiced beef is gone." Everybody hates ham and limas, and there's already a crowd around the pallet trying to get anything but. "Go on," I say, "better grab some." We walk over and push our way into the crowd.

I wait till Meyer is done eating before I start. He's going out on his first patrol in an hour. "In an NVA ambush they try to get the radioman, squad leader, and corpsman first. They'll let the point man and a couple of guys through, and then ambush the center of the column. So stay away from radios and anyone with an M79."

Meyer pushes his glasses up on his nose and stares at me. I'm ruining his digestion.

"You don't want to look like a corpsman. First thing you do is get rid of that Unit One." Meyer looks at his brand new Unit One medical bag, then back at me. He thinks I'm crazy. I expected this.

"Break down the bag and stuff the battle dressings in your thigh pockets. Get yourself an ass pack and put the rest in."

"Ass pack?"

"Little pack that hangs off your web belt behind. Next time we're in battalion I'll take you over to H & S company. And get rid of your pistol."

"You're shittin' me."

I began carrying a shotgun when I heard we were coming to the desert position because of the stories about the previous platoon being overrun. I reach over and grab my twelve-gauge pump from the corner of the bunker.

Meyer says, "That's a sawed-off shotgun."

"You can get one of these, or a forty-five-caliber grease gun, from the tankers in battalion. Might cost you some beer. The only time you'll be using your weapon is if we're overrun. Then you'll want something that scatters. And you don't want to be seen carrying a pistol on patrol. Sniper will go for you first."

Meyer flinches.

I toss him a shotgun shell. "It's loaded with fleshets." Meyer rolls the shell in his palm, sideways.

"If somebody's down, you'll be expected to expose yourself to fire to get to them. You'll hear the rounds coming by before you hear the pop. If you still hear the popping, you can be reasonably sure you're not dead."

Meyer has broken a thin film of sweat. I'm almost enjoying this. He shakes out an unfiltered Pall Mall from the little four pack that comes with the C rations, pats his pockets for a match. I give him a light. His hand is shaking, but so is mine. Mine have been shaking for weeks.

"If the guy's down way out in front of the column, say, more than fifteen meters, take a fire team with you. You'll need cover. They'll take real good care of you. But if you freeze up, don't expect any respect. If you run out of battle dressings, cut up his jungle utilities to make a dressing and secure it with his chinstrap or belt. If you need a splint, cut some bamboo. Everything you need to treat somebody is there whether you have supplies or not. If somebody's got exposed intestine, be sure and wet the dressing before you tie it on. Don't try to stuff the gut back inside, just secure it to his side. If you run out of water, piss on the dressings. It's pure sterile saline."

Meyer looks sick. He hadn't heard that one in corps school. "Anything you want to ask me?"

Meyer shakes his head. "Fuck," he says.

"Good. Check with me when you get back." I get up, climb out of the bunker, and light a cigarette.

I hear Meyer say "Fuck," again.

I watch the clouds piling up over the Annamese range like there was a sheet of glass there to stop them. I want to tell Meyer to act nuts. Get the fuck out now. I want to tell him this whole thing is a pile of shit, and if he's smart he'll shoot himself in the foot. I look back and see the red tip of Meyer's cigarette in the bunker door.

PROBLEM WITH SNAKEBRAIN *is that it can make you a snake. You can become all snake and never get back. Snakebrain can't see the human, only the snake inside the human. Snakebrain sniffs out the evil potential in the adrenocortex of the innocent. Snakebrain sees the piss-your-pants fear of the villagers as guilt, sees a snake in every pot posing as a chicken with big scared eyes and piss-dribbling fear. You act scared, boy, you must have something to be scared about.*

BUT MOST OF them are scared all the time. They're a little less scared of the Cong who come in at night, but not much. Mr. Charles speaks the language after all. Mr. Charles can talk the talk, has assured them they'll be better than the pale pasty compradors under Nguyen Van Thieu, who pay more for imported *haute couture* than the entire return on the gross national product. Mr. Charles talks dictatorship of the proletariat. Mr. Charles talks land reform and not the sorry-assed version the Saigon plutocrats have offered. Meanwhile, here we are, a bunch of teenagers with high-tech weapons, swaggering through their village kicking over their family altars, diddling their daughters, kicking the shit out of Papa-san for fun, burning the thatch of their hooches out of the sheer meanness of hormonal excess. We've come to think Asians are the problem. We'd just as soon kill a villager as look at him. This must be Hell, the villagers think, and the Buddhists among them must wonder what the hell they did in a former life to deserve this.

Lieutenant Shepard tells the platoon sergeant first, then the squad leaders. He's being rotated to the battalion CP. We're getting a new lieutenant. Somebody named Laughlin. Shepard shakes hands all around. I feel a wave of depression.

That afternoon when the mail comes out from battalion, Shepard climbs up on the escort tank and waves at us through the black diesel smoke as the tank backs, turns, and heads east. I watch the tank till it's out of sight. I feel something solid and decent flow out my life. I feel the dark closing in. A black snake slides under the raised floor of the chow hall. I didn't see him till he moved.

JETER IS NEXT in line for squad leader. He stops joking. He alternates between by-the-book and total anarchy when taking us out on patrols. He takes us out past where Corcoran was killed, as if to make it right, to get revenge. On one night patrol we are moving very slowly into the tree line until we come to a thicket that is almost impenetrable. There is a depression in the earth, perhaps a sinkhole. We climb down into the sinkhole and form a three-sixty. We wait and listen. We wait so long that every skittering of an animal becomes, in the imagination, the rustling of Vietcong crawling up on us. I can almost hear Jeter's heartbeat. Suddenly he gives us the order to fire and the woods are lit with tracers. The radio crackles from the compound. Jeter replies, sheepishly, that we have "reconnoitered by fire" after hearing voices. In a while, we come out of the trees and fire a green star cluster to announce our return.

Later that week we go out in the morning, push through the trees and out the other side where there is a small village with three hooches. The village is deserted except for its animals, a fact that should have warned of ambush, but a depression has settled over the squad and we are not as alert as we should be. Jeter suddenly begins to shoot pigs. The rest of the platoon follows suit. The pigs squeal; one runs, dragging its unspooling guts. Bloody feathers fly from the chickens. When we have killed everything we can see, we leave the village and move into a dry paddy. A burst of fire rakes the village. *Snake comes awake in my spine.* The sniper comes close but misses, one round breaking a clay pot. We find ourselves pinned down behind a paddy dike. Jeter tells us to crawl over the paddy dike and move into the trees just to our north. As each man rolls over the dike, rounds strike the dike.

It comes my turn. I roll over the dike onto the other side and rounds kick up dust behind me. The sniper's closer than Jeter thinks, and he's adjusting his fire down. When we have all crawled over the dike and into the tree line, Jeter calls in mortars, but the sniper is gone. If there had been more than one of them we'd still be pinned down.

SINCE WE ARE not in the battalion CP there is no beer. I miss it the way the alcoholic I don't yet know I am would miss it. And when we are moved again, I am relieved. We pile onto tanks and 'tracs and head west. We are dropped off at an old French fort on top of a hill overlooking Da Nang to the north. It is a typical French fort, concrete with turrets at the three corners. There are old concrete bunkers inside big enough for a squad. I find some old French coins in the hooch I share with Meyer. We are joined by a tank that sits, toadlike, in the center of the compound. All summer there has been heavy NVA troop movement into the area from the Ho Chi Minh Trail to the west. Rocket teams have been attacking the Da Nang airstrip with regularity.

What I like about this old fort is the ramada at the base of the hill next to an old village. There is an old man there who gives haircuts and sells Vietnamese Tiger beer out of a cooler, and a little boy with a bicycle equipped with two wooden boxes on the back from which he sells homemade banana popsicles packed in dry ice. Tiger beer does not contain as much alcohol as American beer, so I have to drink a lot of it, but it tastes good. I sweat it out immediately and am thirsty for more.

We begin patrolling the area between the hill and Da Nang. It's mostly clear of trees but has lots of scrub brush that can easily hide Cong. One night Meyer comes in from a patrol, shaken. The squad surprised a young Vietnamese who ran toward Meyer while trying to escape. Meyer drew his .45 and pulled the trigger. It jammed. The boy, terrified, had stared at Meyer for an instant and was gone. Later that night, rockets lit up the sky and blew up an oil tank at the airstrip. We sweep north the next morning and find bipods used to launch rockets.

No one talks about what everybody knows. They continue to outmaneuver us. They dance circles around us, and when we actually kill some of them, it makes no difference.

WE ARE TRANSFERRED to the Tu Cau bridge for a month. The Tu Cau bridge has a reputation for strange events. The area is heavily infiltrated with NVA and a single marine platoon is supposed to hold the bridge. Bad things happen at Tu Cau. There's a huge observation tower in the compound that looks out over the bridge and a bend in the river. Last month a guy was up in the tower and a sniper shot him right up the asshole. It came out his dick and split it open like a hot dog. Then he fell off the tower and broke his neck.

Jeter said, "He *had* to die."

Then there was the grunt who came unglued. He started walking around the compound wearing two .45-caliber pistols, swaggering and trying to pick fights. Everybody laughed at first, but then it started to get scary. One night he walked out on the bridge, his hands poised over his twin .45s, gunslinger style, and told the marine sentry he was going to kill him. The sentry put a tight group of three rounds right in his solar plexus.

We've got a dawn patrol. Before we leave the compound, Jeter says, "We going up to the DMZ! Gonna go back to Okinawa first and regroup, then we're going up north as a battalion landing team."

Luster rolls his eyes. "Where'd you hear that, Jeter?"

"Mess cooks."

Second squad was hit the previous morning by a squad of NVA so we're moving slow. *They've rigged the booby trap to catch somebody sliding down the ravine.* Jeter squats and slides and trips the Chinese grenade. But we don't know we're not being hit by rocket-propelled grenades and we're on our bellies. Then Luster says, "Doc, you better get on up here."

Part of the calf of Jeter's left leg is gone. Yellow smoke is billowing up from his web belt. A smoke grenade has been set off by the blast, and I'm afraid it's going to set off the fragmentation grenade next to it. I shout "Grenade," yank his web belt off him, and throw it down the ravine. I press a battle dressing on the mangled calf. Then I realize that more than five seconds had passed before I've even got his belt off. The grenade does not detonate. If it had, I'd be dead.

Jeter says, "Hello, Doc. I figured this would happen sooner or later."

"You're going home, Jeter. Lie back and let me work." Jeter grins.

We lug Jeter to the medevac. He waves at us through the dust as the chopper lifts and turns north. On the way back I realize that I barely know half this squad anymore. Only Rochetti, Luster, and Thompson are left.

Luster says, "Doc, what's that on your hands?"

I look down at my hands. They're red and blistered from the smoke grenade. Back in the compound, Meyer smears nitrofuracin on them and wraps them in gauze. "That's a heart. Whaddya think, Luster?"

"Looks like a heart to me."

Rochetti says, "Shit. If that's a heart I oughta get one for the VD I got in Manila."

Luster, who has just become squad leader, says, "He gets a heart."

Purple hearts are a kind of currency that has nothing to do with the glory of the ribbon itself. Two hearts and you get pulled from the field, three and you go home. I don't want to think about getting the second or third. I can't depend on their being this easy.

The next day Luster, Rochetti, and I ride the mail truck to Da

Nang and get off at the naval hospital. Jeter is in the ICU in a Quonset hut at the rear of the compound. The ward is packed with wounded. I walk down the row of beds. I see a Korean marine from the ROK Division, heavily sedated, in restraints. I can't see his wounds. There is a black marine with his lower jaw missing. There is a bloody handprint on the swinging doors that go into the OR at the far end of the ward.

Jeter does not smile when he sees us. He's gray-faced and his humor's gone. Down the row of beds someone is sobbing, pitifully, like a child. A nurse says to the sobber, "Lieutenant, Lieutenant," trying to give some notion of a self back to the mangled officer. The sobbing subsides. The lieutenant's face is bandaged. In addition to the two legs, one arm is gone, and the other hand is a bloody mass of gauze.

Jeter says, "You oughta try to sleep in this place."

I've never seen Jeter without the grin, without the gleam. He looks smaller than I know him to be. We talk about a girl. We talk about a little town called Burts Pit in west Kentucky. We say goodbye and he stares at the rounded ceiling of the Quonset as we leave.

In the snack bar Red Cross girls fry hamburgers and dish up ice cream. They are plain, cheery girls with white teeth and red dishwater hands and a kind of hardness that begins to grow on people who work around misery all day. We sit down and eat our hamburgers. A Huey comes over low, whopping its rotors, and I flinch. Luster says, "You gettin' jumpy, Doc." I look out the window at the Marble Mountains. The sky is hard blue. The sky doesn't give a shit. The mountains don't give a shit. The South China Sea doesn't give a shit. We go outside and wait for a truck going south.

After a month at the bridge, we are sent on a three-day, platoon-sized patrol down south. We move east up over a rise and down again toward a tree line. They hit us just as the point man, Luster, enters the tree line. I hear "Corpsman up," and start moving. Somebody says, "Keep flat against the ground, Doc, and I'll move the cover fire right in front of you." To this day, I don't know why he thought he'd have to tell me to crawl, but there are two sets of rounds kicking up dirt in my face, his and whoever's trying to kill me. Thompson has been sent down ahead of me and I find him next to Luster, flinching, as the rounds come close to where he's squatting. Luster is lying facedown. At first I can't find the wound. The round has caught him right between the trapezius muscle and the clavicle and has bled very little on the outside. He must have been on all fours when he was hit; the bullet drove straight down into the arteries that branch out just under the clavicle, and then on down into his lungs. He bleeds out very quickly; there is nothing I can do for him. The firing has stopped.

We have to carry Luster back out of the trees to make a landing zone for the chopper. We move into an abandoned village and form a perimeter. Harkness is glaring at me. He says, "You let him bleed to death." I walk away. I don't bother to tell him that a whole OR team couldn't have helped him, much less me. I'll talk to him later. Right now, they need somebody to blame. But I feel it. I will carry that remark for years.

But I am absolved by what happens next. A Vietcong runs out of a hooch and throws a grenade at a group of marines digging in. The grenade is a dud. A marine fires a burst at him, but the round just nips him in the top of the shoulder. He stumbles and gets up to run again. Another marine throws an entrenching tool at him and hits him in the head, knocking him down on all fours, and then they are all over him. He had circled around behind us after the ambush, expecting us to move forward. He didn't expect us to double back, and we had him trapped. It is always disturbing to find out that one Vietnamese, who is scarcely taller than an American's chest, can do so much damage, can attack thirty of us with such brazenness. What's worse, this one is about fifty years old, the same age as most of our fathers.

When we go to tie his hands behind his back, we realize that he is missing one hand. It is an old wound, chopped clean. I wonder how he got it. Since his hands cannot be tied, they pull his arms back hard and tie them at the elbow. Harkness hands me his M1 and says, "Guard him." The subtitle to this comment might read, *You let Luster die. Now this guy is your problem.*

The Vietnamese is watching me very closely. There are some rifles stacked about three meters away, and his eyes keep flicking in that direction. I feel like I've been set up. They know he's going to try to run, and I'm supposed to kill him.

Sergeant Spinner walks over and looks at us. Several marines stand a few feet away and watch. Spinner looks at him and whispers viciously, "You cocksucker." Then he draws his bayonet. The Vietnamese stiffens. "I'm gonna wale with you motherfucker," Spinner says. Spinner's anger is searing, quiet. He begins to jab the Vietnamese with his bayonet, gently at first, then digging harder. He begins to jab him in the groin. The Vietnamese draws his legs up to protect himself.

Somebody calls to Spinner, and he looks up. There are two tanks coming toward us across dry paddies. The tanks stop at the edge of the village and two men, one American, one Vietnamese, jump down. Neither has any insignia on their collars, but they walk like they have rank on everybody there. They shout something at Spinner and he grabs the prisoner by the shirt and drags him to his feet, pushes him on ahead toward the tanks.

The two men are interrogators. They begin to question the prisoner in Vietnamese, very gently. They walk him over to a small stream at the edge of the paddies. They continue to question him, almost kindly, patting him on the back, murmuring to him as if they were trying to seduce him. Suddenly the Vietnamese interrogator kicks him behind the knee and he goes down on his face. He drags the prisoner to the edge of the stream and rolls him on his back. He takes a fistful of his hair and holds his head underwater for a good minute, then jerks him up and says something to him. The prisoner does not reply, and the interrogator holds his head under again. The prisoner, on his back, cannot help that the water wants to go up his nose. He chokes and sputters. The interrogator pulls him up. Both the Vietnamese and the American talk to him, again gently. I am aware that the Vietnamese interrogator is doing the torturing. The American stands by and watches for results. This is the pattern of torture in this war. The Americans do not actually dirty their hands with the suffering body. They simply reap the information. The interrogator holds the prisoner underwater for longer and longer periods of time; each time he comes up choking. They let him recover, speak to him, and then dunk him again. After a while, the prisoner says something. They jerk him to his feet. They speak to him softly. He points to the hooch that he initially came running from. The Vietnamese ducks into the hooch and comes back. He slaps the prisoner. The prisoner walks to the hooch and pokes the thatch. The Vietnamese interrogator walks to the hooch, reaches into the thatch, and pulls out an M1 carbine. The two interrogators smoke and talk to Spinner for a while. The prisoner squats and stares out over the paddies, perhaps not seeing the land, a faraway gaze, perhaps at his own imminent death. His posture seems to say *My life is over. Take my body and do what you will.*

Then the interrogators push the prisoner toward the waiting tanks. Later that day, Spinner will tell me that the tanks stopped a few hundred meters away, safely out of sight, kicked the prisoner off the tank, chained him by his ankles and dragged him till he was dead.

SHORTLY AFTER, I am pulled out of the field and assigned to the battalion aid station. Theoretically, corpsmen are supposed to be rotated out of the field after six months. Many of them are not. Thompson said, "Hey Doc we were just starting to trust you." I didn't believe it. I wonder if my increasingly unmilitary behavior had something to do with my transfer. Nevertheless, I am relieved. I begin to gain a little weight. I am grateful to wake up in the corpsmen's hooch instead of in mud or sand. It soon becomes apparent, however, that I've brought my demons with me.

Chief Hospital Corpsman Lemle, the proud and proper lord of

the battalion aid station, is a short, round, bald man with intellectual pretentions. He sees me with a collection of Faulkner stories
one day and starts talking about what he believes should be in
every young man's library. He owns, he says, *Bartlett's Quotations*.
He says that the book is an entire education in itself, and if one
were sent to prison, the book would serve to make a well-rounded
man by the time one got out.

Since Lemle has little to do except the paperwork that keeps the
corpsmen in the field supplied and occasionally make decisions
about the course of medical treatment for fungal infections, he
micromanages me. I don't mind, because by this time I really need
somebody to tell me what to do. I need to be told when to eat,
when to piss. I do not need to be told when to drink. As soon as
my duties are over for the day, I am in the EM club drinking beer.

My life is better. I have a cot and an air mattress. I have a couple
of books to read. I have Faulkner, which brings back my mother's
side of the family. I can hear their voices. And I can hear them in
the voices of the grunts around me.

I get a letter from my mother, who is by now an administrative assistant in USAID. Her time in the Dominican Republic is
up, and she is being sent to Saigon. She wants to see me when she
arrives. She doesn't seem to understand where I am, or how hard it
is for me to get to Saigon.

I get a letter from Alan Sorokin, an old friend, who tells me that
he has just returned to Tucson from Haight-Ashbury, where he has
been living for several years. He writes that he and many others
have turned against the war, and that he hopes our friendship will
not be damaged. *He has no idea*, I think. *He has no idea how much you
can hate a war.* I write him that we will have many long conversations when I get back.

I drink. I go through the day hungover. I do not know what
depression is, but I most certainly am depressed when I am not
actually shaking with fear. The relative safety of the battalion CP
has allowed my demons to roam freely. They are everywhere I

look. There is a chapel behind the batallion aid station. I go there and pray. I haven't prayed since my confirmation in the Episcopal church. I pray out loud, as if more likely to be heard that way. There is never anybody in the chapel, and I don't know what the chaplain looks like.

I have an infection under my right thumbnail from a bad splinter extraction. It is red and has started to send red streaks up my arm, so I go to the chief, expecting him to give me an antibiotic. He wants to excise the nail and clean under it. The first thing I say is, "You're not a doctor, and you're not going to remove my nail." He looks at me, stunned.

He draws up a mix of streptomycin and procaine penicillin and injects me. My ears start ringing and the room begins to spin. I can't get my breath. When I come out of it, Lemle is standing there with another corpsman whom he has called in from outside. He says, "You are allergic to either procaine penicillin or streptomycin." He says this like he has made an important scientific discovery. I stagger out into the blinding sunlight toward the EM club.

Next day I walk past Lemle's desk and I see the Merck Manual open to the chapter on basic psychiatric disorders. I'm sure it's me he's researching. I can only imagine Chief *Bartlett's Quotations* lecturing me on my psychiatric condition.

It is raining hard, pounding the tin roofs. There is a rumor of a typhoon off the coast. The chief gets a call that there are some ARVN at Nui Kim Son who need medical aid. He tells me we have to get in a jeep and drive to Nui Kim Son. I tell him that it's stupid to drive that stretch of Highway One because it's mined and not secure. He stares at me. He tells me to get in the jeep.

I am so terrified outside the gate that I am frozen the whole way. When we get there, there is nothing but rain and mud. No ARVN anywhere.

When we get back I go directly to the EM club. I am finding it more and more difficult to go outside. There is a kind of animal run I have made, a triangle that connects the EM club, the corpsmen's hooch, and the battalion aid station. I am afraid to go outside that triangle, as I must, because I have to piss and shower.

MEMORY DOES NOT proceed in an orderly fashion. One memory pulls up another in whatever order it pleases. The connections may be a color, a place. Driving through Mississippi in 1987, the smell of the delta silt brings back the funk of the paddies.

Further, the connections that memory makes are a story wanting to be. Story elements choose one another because of unobservable unconscious connections. There is a reason one memory pulls up another *particular* memory. Two things may not have happened together, but in the story they get lumped together because they fit, because, even though separated by time or space, they illuminate one another; the slow cooking of the remembering soul works things out over the years.

After three months, one of Jeter's rumors comes true. The battalion gets orders to ship out for the Philippines, where they will be refitted and trained as a battalion landing team, then returned to Vietnam further north. Anyone who is "short," meaning, his term of enlistment is less than six months, is reassigned to another unit.

I am sent to First Hospital Company in Chu Lai. The hospital is on a bluff overlooking the South China Sea to the east and the Chu Lai air base to the west, where Americal Division is beginning to replace the older army units. I don't know yet that Tracy Kidder, who would later write *My Detachment,* is a young lieutenant in their intelligence unit. I am moving farther toward the rear, and I don't mind it at all. That is, until the beginning of the Tet Offensive, when "the rear" becomes a figure of speech, and NVA begin to penetrate the defenses of every military installation in the country.

At the hospital company, I run into Meyer, who has been pulled from the field and sent down. I get a job in the administrative office, where my principal function is to type up the company commander's letters. There is nothing much to do. I drink coffee during the day and beer at night. Certain business must be attended to in the office, while piles of casualties are pushed off choppers onto the landing pads and rushed to ORs that are working twenty-four hours a day like a meat-packing factory. The first week I am there I hear some scuttlebutt about two marine guards caught having anal sex in a dumpster and then spirited out of the country to be court-martialed.

Meyer has found a dirty movie somewhere. We watch it. Two women are so horny they pray, then some stud with little fake angel wings comes through the window and everybody has a whopping good time.

Then Meyer and I get two R & R billets for Taiwan.

11

THE HOTEL MANAGER gives us an hour to settle in before knocking on our doors. Outside in the red-carpeted corridor is a line of seven very sweet-looking Chinese girls in pastel spaghetti-strap dresses.

"You pick," the manager says, his gold tooth live in the dim light. The girls are all half our height, very young, and heavily made up to look older.

I haven't smelled a woman up close in six months. I smile at a round-faced girl in a pink dress, and she puts her arms around me. I say *girl* because that's what they were. I don't want to know how old they are. They are pretending to be eighteen.

Meyer picks a tall, sloe-eyed one. The other girls, still smiling, file down the hall giggling, and the manager, Mr. Chu, invites us down to the bar for a drink.

In the bar, two Chinese boys in red vests are hanging a string of Christmas lights across the arched entrance. A depraved plastic Santa hangs over the cash register. I look at Meyer. "Fucking Christmas," he says. We have not thought about Christmas until this moment.

The girls, Lu and Cher, sit like debutantes and smile at us a little too sweetly. The whiskey spreads through me like the healing hand of Jesus. Cher puts her hand on my crotch and instantly coaxes a hard-on.

Mr. Chu is talking about American Indians. "You look," he says. "Look at faces. Big cheekbones, dark eyes. Long ago Chinese walk across the land bridge that is now Aleutian Islands and settle America. Now, you tell me, Chinese not own America. They there first. Tell me that not true."

I look at Meyer. His face is red. Lu has unzipped him and thrust her hand deep in his pants. We depart for our rooms without answering Mr. Chu, who stands in the bar's red light, gold tooth glimmering, the chandelier's tears moving in the air conditioner's blast.

A young man's sex is like a bear tearing apart a tree trunk to get at the honey. Cher has to ask me to stop. She says, "I take a break." She limps to the bathroom. I answer the knock at the door. Meyer stands with Lu. "You got that Polaroid?" I nod. "Let's have an orgy," he says.

The girls exchange furtive looks. Cher frowns, looks at Meyer.

"No," I say. The idea of having an orgy is too much for my already overloaded mind.

Meyer shrugs.

AN HOUR LATER we are walking down club row, drunk, looking for a place to drink more. I sense the girls herding us toward huge, red doors flanked by golden lions. I am liquid now and cannot really be said to be walking. I feel Cher's strong grip on my left arm. I think *peasant girl*.

We seem to be in some kind of theater. We walk up red-carpeted steps with gold banisters into a huge, tiered dinner theater. There are Chinese women onstage in red and gold, very short skirts, singing and dancing in a kick line. The huge space dizzies me and I nearly lose my balance. I feel Cher's hand tighten on my arm.

I look at Meyer, who seems to be in better shape. The music stops, and I look up to see the whole room standing and staring at us. Everybody in the theater is Chinese. It takes me a minute to understand that they are standing for us, two drunk American servicemen, fresh from fighting Communists who are very much like the ones who drove them off the mainland. I try to assume some dignity. Meyer says, "They'd never do this for us at home."

The girls quickly seat us and open menus. My gaze falls on an elegantly dressed Chinese matron who is staring at Cher with a slight curl to her lips.

The girls are in control now. They order for us. In my condition I can scarcely speak English and the only Chinese I know is *"shir-shir."*

We are served heaping mounds of Chinese food—real Chinese food—the kind Chinese eat: whole fish with the eyes still in them, squids, and many unidentifiable ingredients which, even in my besottedness, are delicious. A Chinese comedian comes onstage to raucous laughter and applause. He reminds me of Red Skelton. His timing is so sharp even a drunk American can tell when the punch line is coming.

The girls are eating hand over fist, tipping bowls of rice up to their lipsticked mouths and shoveling the grains in with chopsticks. They are eating very well. We are paying for it. They figure out the bill. They figure out the tip.

We get up to leave and, once again, a room full of one hundred plus Chinese are standing in silence with grave faces. The juggler who followed the comedian stops, the last ball drifting down to the hands of a young man who looks for all the world like your average sixteen-year-old NVA. A little glimmer of Snakebrain burns through the booze.

We walk out onto the street, more sober than when we went in, squeeze into a tiny cab, and head back to the hotel. The girls are talking a mile a minute in Chinese. Cher dabs a food stain on my shirt with the corner of her handkerchief. Meyer is staring out the window with red eyes. The pulse of the neon on the street calms me. We will sleep now. We will sleep long.

The next day, Lu and Cher take us to an arboretum on top of a hill overlooking Taipei. It's hot. We sweat alcohol. We wander into a mass of saffron-robed Buddhist monks strolling among the bright red and white tulips. I take a picture of the group, and they pose cheerfully. I notice that there are also nuns among them, unsexed by robes and shaved heads.

An old monk pushes through the crowd and asks to see my camera. He is about five feet tall, the skin pulled tight over his skull, his eyes too bright for his age. He is a child misplaced in an old body. The others bow and give him room. He is someone of importance. He grins, points at my Polaroid, and I understand he wants to take our picture. I hand the camera to him. He takes our picture and hands it to us. While we are admiring ourselves, he begins to photograph the rest of his party. He finishes the roll of film and, irresistibly, opens his hand for another. I give it to him. And then another, and so on till the film is gone. He grins and hands the camera back to me. The other monks then begin handing around the pictures. The crowd thickens with small gestures, giggling and chattering like children. We turn to go and they wave, shouting in overenunciated English, "Goodbye! Goodbye! Goodbye!" For some reason, I begin thinking of the dead. *Goodbye Corcoran, goodbye Luster.*

As the path begins to descend toward the parking lot, I look back. The old monk, alone now, watches us. He waves, "Goodbye." He watches us all the way to the waiting cab.

"Goodbye."

THE GIRLS ARE taking us somewhere. We drive to the windward side of the island to a fishing village where there are no gringos. The fishermen unloading their boats and hanging around the piers, squat and thickly muscled, remind me of Cong we've taken prisoner. Women with rags tied around their heads, nearly as muscled as the men, heave straw baskets of fish onto the docks. The fish slither into tailings of silver. One still flops. Snakebrain flickers, but I push it away.

On the way back we stop at the house of Cher's grandparents.

They are both very old and a little stooped. When I shake the old man's hand it is cool and smooth. His skin is so white and thin I feel I could easily put my finger through it. The pair stare at us without expression.

The living room of the small house is piled floor to ceiling with boxes marked Sony, Sanyo, Nikon, RCA. The boxes are unopened. Then Cher begins to tell me, in a pidgin I have not hitherto heard her speak, and which has all the marks of being memorized, that her sister and brother are trapped on the mainland by the evil Communists and she needs money to bring them over to free China.

I look at the boxes and think black market. I look at the grandparents and I think, not grandparents. I give Cher a twenty and she looks offended by my miserliness.

I need to escape and indicate that I need a bathroom. She points out back, still feigning shock. On the way out back I look into the two other rooms. I know right away which room is hers. I think maybe they are her grandparents after all. There is a picture of her with a black GI. There is a picture of an Afro-Asian child, and an Amerasian child. On her dressing table by an incense burner is a little red, sea jade Buddha, a plastic Christ, and a plastic Mary, aligned like a little trinity. On her bed is a pink teddy bear and a large, blue-eyed Disney rabbit.

The next day, back in the hotel, I get a bad case of Snakebrain. Every Asian I see is going to kill me. Every rattle of an air conditioner is an incoming round. I don't want to have sex, and Cher thinks it's her fault. She stares at me and sulks. I don't leave my bed. Meyer laughs at the fresh laundry the Chinese boy has brought up. He laughs at the half inch of scotch left in the bottle.

The girls look at us cautiously. They must have seen this before. We are somewhere they can't touch us. We do not stop to think that they have the same thick sadness within them, and that we could join them there. I will come to know that look on women's faces, the one that comes when they realize that all a woman can do, all her compassion and her delicious tenderness, cannot help.

I WONDER WHAT that old monk was *really* doing with my camera. I imagine the Polaroids, fading in candlelight, sitting next to burning incense on a family altar. I am feeling genuinely insane.

Goodbye Anderson.

Next day we are dry-mouthed and a little sick. We take a cab to the USO to get haircuts. While we are waiting, an American woman walks up and introduces herself as the wife of the American ambassador to Taiwan. She invites us to dinner.

AT THE AMBASSADOR'S Taipei residence they have prepared a big spread—appetizers, gourmet food. They are doing their bit: *American boys fighting for an honorable cause get a little taste of home at Christmas; probably not too bright, but good boys, ready to go out and die.* I feel very uncomfortable here. Meyer seems a little awed, but I am feeling cantankerous. This is a setup in which I am supposed to behave.

The ambassador keeps talking about how well the war is going, and how we'll surely win, because, unlike the enemy, we have *infra-structure*. I am tempted to say that he has no idea. I am tempted to say, you want infrastructure, watch the VC. What he thinks is infra-structure is a mass of anarchy, a South Vietnamese army in which the officers are skimming their soldiers' pay, and paying off the Cong. It's all I can do to be polite. He's hoping to hear us parrot back to him what he wants to believe so that he can say he's heard it straight from the field. I feel like I'm holding my breath during the whole visit.

After desserts and liqueurs we go back to the hotel. I can't wait to get blind drunk and pass out.

I don't remember my last day in Taipei. I don't remember saying goodbye to the girls, only that they disappeared as quickly as they had appeared. I will think of them once a day for the rest of my life. Something about them changed me, permanently. Something about poverty of people trying to make out any way they can at the edges of a war. When we left, the hotel seemed empty.

In Da Nang, we catch a C-130 going south to Chu Lai.

WHEN WE GET to Chu Lai, we head straight for the hospital company bar. It is New Year's Eve. That night the NVA attack the airstrip with Katyusha rockets. I sit with one of the marine guards on a pile of sandbags overlooking the airstrip. We watch a fuel tank explode and send boiling fire high into black sky. The enemy is probing the west perimeter of the airstrip, and we can see the incoming green tracers and the outgoing red tracers as the grunts in the perimeter bunkers return fire.

At midnight, in the middle of the fighting, two American machine gunners at opposite ends of the airstrip start firing their tracers up in the air, then drop their trajectories down until the tracers cross, and hold them there. Truck horns blare. Happy New Year. A rocket hits the ammunition dump and lights the whole airstrip bright as day. Huge parachute flares fill the sky. I shout, "HAPPY NEW YEAR MOTHERFUCKERS."

I see a doctor from the hospital company running past, buckling on a pistol. I laugh. I know the NVA are not stupid enough to attack the compound and get themselves trapped with their backs to the ocean.

"Happy New Year, Doc!" I offer him a drink from our bottle. The doctor's red rabbit eyes reflect the fire of the burning airstrip.

12

I'M HOLDING MY orders in my hand. They are stamped CONUS—Continental Limits of the United States. I'm standing with Meyer, waiting for a jeep to pick me up and take me to the airstrip in Chu Lai. Meyer has "shipped over," meaning he's signed up for four more years. Ultimately, he wants to become a SEAL.

We shake hands, and I start down the hill. One more chopper ride to Da Nang, one more night in-country, then home. Whatever *home* has come to mean. There has never been a home. The closest perhaps was my grandmother's house in Memphis, but mostly I remember moving around. There are pockets of warmth in my memory where the people around me felt, if only briefly, like a family, but I don't have the sense of going home to a place, to a group of people.

I board an army medevac going north and I'm impressed with how clean it is. No blood on the floor or bulkheads. No shrapnel scars, no bullet holes in the fuselage. The army medic tells me that they chiefly make runs from in-country hospitals to hospital ships.

At Da Nang, I hitch a ride on a jeep going up to First Med, where I'm supposed to spend the night. I drop my seabag at the hospital ward where I'm to sleep. First Med is on a hill overlooking Da Nang from the south and seems safe from direct fire, although not from mortar or rocket rounds. A new bunch of marines and corpsman have arrived and have set up tents fifty meters down the hill. I walk down to see if I know anybody. I recognize Jimmie

Neal from my ward duty at Bethesda Naval Hospital. He is sitting
with a group of grunts drinking C-rats hot chocolate.

"Can't wait to try those C-rats, hunh?"

He looks up.

We shake hands. New boots. No mud. Clean greens. These guys
look like innocence about to be violated: death, dismemberment,
misery, and madness in embryo form.

"What took you so long?" I ask.

"They just kept me painting rocks at Pendleton."

He looks at me and, for a moment, he drops the swagger and
almost seems hurt. "You going home?"

"Yeah."

We talk for a while. They think I ought to be more excited than
I am, *going home* in one piece. In fact, they look more excited about
being here than I do about going home. They just don't recognize
numb yet. I don't see it myself, or the long unwinding from it.
They haven't had the great boy's adventure stomped out of them.

"What the fuck's wrong with you, Anderson?"

"I guess I don't believe it yet."

"All that round-eyed pussy waiting for you and you can't even
shout a little?" He shakes out a cigarette and offers me one. "Strange
things going on stateside."

"Nixon being sworn in?"

"That ain't nothin'. Country's *fucked*. People running around
naked with paisley eyeballs."

"I haven't read anything but *Stars and Stripes* since I've been
here."

He looks up the hill toward the Quonset huts. "Any beer up
there?"

"Nothing but."

We order a pitcher at the EM club and talk about all the corpsmen we know, some dead by now. "Shug got killed up at Cua
Viet."

"Shug?" His eyes open wide. "Aw, no."

"Pulled a casualty behind a tank for cover so he could work on him. Tank backed up over them both."

Soon we are into our third pitcher and have moved on to other things. I'm eavesdropping on a conversation between the bartender and one of the grunts about something called the Six-Day War.

The bartender says, "Made me reconsider Jews. We could use a few of those Christ killers over here. They kick ass and take names."

The conversation moves to short-timer superstitions, and guys who get killed on their last night in-country.

"Aw, come on," I say. "Don't talk about that shit." *Cherenski's bugged eyes loom up at me from his mask of blood. I shake it off.*

The bartender tells us to stay on our toes. We can expect mortars at night.

The idea of mortar rounds makes me want to order another pitcher, but the room has begun to spin and I realize I've passed my limit. I say my goodbyes and stumble back to the ward. I flop down, fully dressed, and then the swirl of dark.

THE SHOUTING WAKES ME. I look at my watch: 0300 hours. I sit up and see a guy in the bed across from me. His legs are being held straight up in the air by two doctors. It looks for a minute like the torture of some saint, upside down, being broken on the wheel. There are blood pressure cuffs wrapped around his thighs and the doctors are pumping them tight. They inject him in both sides of the groin, probably with epinephrine, and he sucks in a huge breath. One of the doctors says, "Pulse!" The wounded man moans and flops back on the pillow.

The other doctor says, "Stay here. I'm going over there."

I hear the squish of corpsmen and doctors walking in blood.

I hear screaming and see a man being lifted from a stretcher to a bed. He's got a compound tib-fib with a spur of bone sticking up through his blood-soaked utilities. The corpsmen started cutting away his clothes.

A doctor looks at me. "Who the fuck are you?"

I tell him.

"Get up. We've got work for you."

I'm still a little drunk and my steps feel spongy.

There's a marine sitting up on a bed, holding his hand in a bloody mass of bandages. I go over and start unwrapping the dressings. I ask him where he's from.

"Quang Tri. They really fucked us up."

I cut the bandage off his hand, already swollen with infection.

"Ow," he says. "Take it easy." I irrigate the hand with saline.

"There isn't going to be anything easy about this." I pick up a hemostat and try to decide what's bone and what doesn't belong there.

In the distance, I hear rockets slamming into the airstrip.

IT'S DAWN NOW and they're still bringing in the wounded. It's time for me to go. I pick up my seabag and head outside. A jeep is waiting with two grunts in it, homeward bound. We ride down the hill and look to see if the runways have holes, but they seem to be alright. A Flying Tiger transport sits on the tarmac waiting for us, and the stewardesses are motioning for us to hurry up. They want to get out of there before the next barrage. We have no trouble hurrying onto the plane, the doors are screwed shut, and we're down the runway and gone, into the wind toward the mountains, and then a long bank out toward Da Nang harbor. I look beyond the Marble Mountains for the old battalion CP but can't find it. The marines must have bulldozed it flat when they left. Soon we are up over the South China Sea, and then up into the clouds where we can see almost nothing except the coast of Vietnam, in short flashes, moving away.

I feel the tears come up. The sun is bright on the clouds.

There are ten people on board. Three of them are a marine prisoner and his two chasers. I think, *Hell is following me home. What did that poor fuck do?* I think, *It's me. I'm outside of myself watching myself being carted off to prison.*

When, a few hours later, we arrive at Okinawa, I get on a bus with the others and drive onto the base. When we arrive at the transfer barracks, the MPs push their prisoner on ahead of me into the check-in area. They hustle him up to the desk, one on each arm, and keep close to him as they check him in with the duty sergeant.

When it is my turn, I drop my orders on the desk and ask, "What did he do?"

"Killed his CO. Fragged him."

"Hunh?"

"Rolled a grenade under his bunk."

"What for?"

"Ask *him*." He hands my orders back to me and points down the hall. "Go out that door and your barracks will be right in front of you. You want to go into town, turn left and keep walking. Can't miss it."

"Fragging" is a word I hadn't heard, but will hear a lot in the next few years. The war had taken another strange turn. People were killing their commanding officers, refusing to go into the field, and smoking opium-laced marijuana. People were arriving in-country with peace symbols on their helmets. I don't know it yet, but morale is crumbling in the infantry units, especially the army units in the south, mostly draftees. Squad leaders were taking their patrols just outside the CP and then calling in checkpoints as if they were actually completing the patrol. But they were sitting on their butts smoking. Some kind of deep rot was happening inside the military, and this war had caused it. The sewer of politics had backed up onto America's hitherto spotless heroes.

The old wooden barracks at Okinawa have bunked men from three wars. Built in the World War II style, they are homey and quiet. I spend a lot of time lying or sitting on my bunk. When I look at my hands, I don't know whose they are. This body doesn't seem to belong to me. I feel like I snuck out of Vietnam in someone else's body. I get up and walk down to a little Japanese restaurant and eat.

Next morning I go over to the storage building and retrieve my Fleet Marine Force uniform. The corpsman's FMF uniform is just like a marine's except that the caduceus and rank insignias are black, an odd hybrid of the two services. Mine is in the style of the old Eisenhower jacket, a few of which were still in circulation. Most marines will scarcely talk to a sailor except to pick a fight, but they respect their corpsmen.

We are allowed to wear civilian clothes here. I go to the PX and buy a button-down oxford cloth shirt and a pair of tan pants. I attempt to reconstruct myself prewar, remember what I wore, what I looked like. I cross the street and get a haircut from an Okinawan barber.

He grins and says, "You have 'Nam tan."

I tell him to leave it long and trim it.

"You go home, hunh? You lucky. Some they don't go home."

He's got a big autographed picture of a young Bob Hope and another of Martha Raye stuck to the top of his mirror. His radio plays, "Monday, Monday."

I've never had a massage. That evening I ask the duty sergeant where I can get one. I walk there in the rain. A plain, middle-aged woman invites me into a room with a mat on the floor and tells me to lie prone. The massage is delicious. She gets up and does the thing they're famous for, a meticulous walk down my spine with her toes expertly plying my vertebrae, popping each one separately. I am surprised at how light she is. She motions for me to roll over, and when I do I present an erection that is not likely to go away without attention, one born of long deprivation, suddenly awakened by safety and quiet. We renegotiate the price, and she kneels with her back to me to do it. This modesty touches me. Her hair in a tight little bun, she is the image of chastity as she strokes my cock with a rather practiced and detached technique. Another woman walks through with a stack of towels and smiles at me as if she were smiling at a baby. She says something to my masseuse and they share a laugh. After I come, she wipes me off as if she were wiping food off a baby's chin, dabbing, making sure, then giving one final dab to the head of my cock that says, *There, you're done. Go home.* I put on my clothes, and I pay her. She keeps her eyes averted. Outside, it has stopped raining and the air smells sweet.

After two weeks of heavy eating and drifting in and out of sleep it's time for me to go. The destination is Los Angeles. The transpacific flight is interminable. I begin to wish I'd brought something to read. I talk to the stewardesses, the other grunts on board. There is nothing but the Pacific Ocean. We stop on Guam to refuel, and I pick up some duty-free whiskey. There is not much on Guam but an airstrip and the famous duty-free store.

After another interminable flight we land at Edwards Air Force Base and deplane. It is two o'clock in the morning. The place is deserted excepted for the five or six people on my flight. We are directed to baggage claim, and then to US Customs. I find this strange. I tell the agent I'm not a tourist and he shrugs.

"You like going through dirty laundry?" I ask him.

He shrugs again. "Everybody's got to do this. It's the rules."

He's much younger than I am, or seems so. There is an absence of snake in him that makes me realize I'm home.

What he isn't telling me, what I'll find out later, is that people have been coming home from Vietnam with enemy ears, heads, fingers, AK47 assault rifles, grenades, mortar rounds, and pure Southeast Asian heroin with a big street markup. There are guys coming back hooked who won't be able to afford their habits stateside. The prisons are filling up with vets.

He tells me I can repack my seabag and move on. I climb aboard a bus headed for Long Beach, where I'll wait out the last two weeks of my enlistment.

————

SNAKE OPENS ONE EYE. *Tongue flicks pink. I'm awake and there are city noises. Dirty freeways and dirty air. Snake says, Look, there it is. A whole shitload of humanity with their asses on fire. For what? These people could give a shit about you. See that convertible there with all that young stuff just back from the beach? Smell the suntan lotion? This is California, big guy. These people couldn't give a fiddler's fuck where you've just come from, except some of those college types that might throw something at you because you've just come from the big kill zone. I'll tell you something, though. One sugar cube of your anger could run them for weeks. You're going to have to learn how to live with these folks or you'll make a real mess, dig? Now, you're already pulling away from me. You're saying, Snake, now, you go back to the jungle. I don't need you anymore. But that isn't the way it works. Once you wake your snake you got to feed him, son. You've got to keep him interested in order to keep him under wraps. And you'll have plenty of opportunity. See, the war isn't over. It's going to pop up here, inside people's heads. People are going to throw their shit at you because they've been asleep so long they don't know they're just like you.*

WHAM! *What was that, oh, just an empty truck going over a pothole. Scared you, didn't it? Now, if I were you, I'd keep a lid on it. Alcohol will do. Opiates are better, but you're not the type. You're a drinker. You're a blackout drinker, that's a boy. And constant pussy's another way. Fuck yourself silly. Just don't own a gun, okay?*

LONG BEACH IS a hole. It's been a sailor's hangout for nearly a century. All the businesses around Long Beach cater to sailors with a barely veiled contempt. They call them names behind their backs, roll them when they're drunk.

This very drunk gunner's mate starts talking about *hippie chicks*.

We're listening.

"Got to watch them," he says. "They'll drop acid in your drink and then you're fucked."

I think, *Where can I find some hippie chicks?*

In the morning we are invited to a reenlistment lecture. A very young lieutenant, junior grade, tells us what kind of benefits we can expect when we ship over. He must feel strange when he looks out at this singularly uninterested group of combat vets. One is falling asleep. I'm hungover with my head in my hands.

Afterwards I call my friend Ron Hackberry in Tucson.

"Hey, can I stay with you for a week?"

13

I'M ABOUT AS far as you can get from the jungle. Through
the window I see the north side of the Catalina range, then the
Tucson Mountains coming up in the west. In 1968, there is still
some water—a trickle in the Rillito—and on the river's banks,
a fine grass. The desert gives off the funk of mesquite and creosote. There is a kind of bone-healing heat in Tucson. It feels good
when I get off the plane. It's March, and the hills are covered with
wildflowers.

When I enter the waiting area, there is a man with a cowboy
hat and thick, tooled belt who has never been nor will ever be a
cowboy. There is a little man with thick glasses, vigilantly waiting
for someone, his bolo tie sporting a scorpion encased in plastic. I
hear Spanish being spoken. Along with the desert tans there are a
few plain old pasty gringos, probably out from the east to see the
flowers.

I see Ron, his dark red straight hair and toothy grin. He looks
just the same, expectant, wanting to please. He bombards me with
questions about the war, and I keep changing the subject.

"Tell me about you," I say.

He tells me about girlfriend troubles.

"I'm telling you," he says.

"Same one? Helen?"

"Yeah her."

I say, "You can find another one."

"Skank."

"Well, she's not *that* bad."

We drive slowly through Tucson, past the sprawling University of Arizona campus and its red-brick buildings. We cut over to Route 10 and head up past Picacho Peak toward Marana, where he lives. I let the desert heat bathe me, and we become silent for the drive.

That night at dinner Ron and his father keep pushing me. They want to hear about the war from someone who knows, someone who's seen it. So I tell them.

"You're going to hear a lot of things from a lot of grunts, but here's my take."

I get it over with. I talk about what's actually happening and not what the press says. I tell them that they should give the protesters the time of day because they may be right. I tell them about the lies, the stupidity, the failed tactics, and the American politicians scrambling for damage control. I tell them about demoralized troops and dead civilians, about how we are fighting the war for the Saigon government and not the people of Vietnam, that we can hardly say anymore that we are protecting the Vietnamese from the Communists because we are killing more civilians than the Communists ever did. The more civilians we kill, the more the Cong look like liberators and the war swings their way. I tell them the Saigon regime's days are numbered. I tell them the war has made me sick in the soul.

Snake winks.

Ron is speechless. We'd hung out before the war with a guy named Terry who'd become a Green Beret and was stationed somewhere near Long Binh. We'd been patriots. We'd wallowed in the glow of our untried masculinity.

Ron's father asks the first intelligent question of the evening.

"Well, hell, what are we doing there?" But he is clearly upset. This does not fit anywhere in his idea of his country. It does not go with his time in the army in World War II. It doesn't fit in his head at all. He finishes his beer and goes to bed, earlier, I think, than he intended. I think, *He'll lie there in the dark.*

I say, "I'm going to hit the rack. See you tomorrow."

Ron turns the television on and shakes his head.

I FIND AN apartment on North Tyndall Avenue just southwest of the University of Arizona, where I plan to enroll in the fall. It's a little stucco one bedroom for eighty dollars a month. It isn't much, but it isn't a barracks and I can shut the door and nobody will bother me. I have a phone put in and fill the refrigerator with beer.

I walk north to the little Mexican buffet just outside the university's main gate and meet my old friend Angela Birk, ordering food. Angela and I had been close before I went over.

"Why, look at you. You're so skinny. Where have you been? You need somebody to feed you." Her Texas accent was unchanged.

I avoid saying Vietnam. I say, ambiguously, "Southeast Asia."

"Oh, that place." She lets the subject slide away. It seems as if I'd only been away a week and that nothing had changed. After lunch we walk to her place holding hands. I know from her hot, moist palm what is going to happen.

I see my sun-darkened arm against her pale skin, and again I feel like my arm belongs to someone else. After we've made love she tells me she wants me to get some decent clothes. She says that she has an instinct about people, and that I am going to become famous and make a lot of money. I have no idea what she could be talking about.

She says, "I'm going to start grooming you for my friend Shelley." Then she tells me about her boyfriend, Peter, whom she plans to marry when he comes back from Europe. We begin drinking wine and that's all I remember.

Next morning she says, "I didn't mind it when you passed out on top of me. I thought you were kind of sweet. But then you started making those *mooing* noises."

"Mooing?"

She tells me about the long, grievous moans I was making all night. She tells me her boyfriend is coming home Saturday, but that I can stay until Friday. I say, "That's cutting it pretty close." She kisses me and we make love again. It takes the edge off my hangover.

I pick up the phone and call my friend Alan Sorokin, who spent the war in the Haight Ashbury district in San Francisco. He'd written me during the war, hoping that I would accept his political opinions. In these letters he told me about hallucinogenic drugs, the Mothers of Invention, and the Straight Theater. He told me about Janis Joplin and Big Brother and the Holding Company. He told me about the VD he was trying to get rid of and the wild sex he was going to have when he did.

When I get to his place later in the afternoon, Alan is wearing a tie-dye T-shirt and a very baroque string of beads, sucking on a tiny roach affixed to a silver clip on a chain around his neck. Jefferson Airplane is playing and Alan's girlfriend, Seglinde, who is a whole head taller than him, is brushing her long blonde hair, her breasts swaying beneath a peasant blouse. Alan's friend, Charlie, is visiting, and we are packing his bright blue former milk delivery truck for a trip down to the Patagonia area, between Tucson and the Mexican border. We load up the Coleman stove, the candles, the chicken, the beans, the beer, and the marijuana and head south.

Arizona is not yet overdeveloped and the sheer physical beauty of the place fills me with something like happiness. I don't understand happiness. It's lighter than the rut of sex, and it dizzies me. *Snake says, I'll fix that. You can't have pleasure without the pain—that's the whole point of it. I'll give you a little heaven, and then fuck it up. Hey, do you feel like you are all brain and spine and fire, sort of like a luminous seahorse? Wait till you take that acid. Patience: This happiness will pass.*

Alan hands me a little square of paper with a half-inch dot on it. "Blotter acid," he says. "It will take about an hour to come on."

"You realize who you're giving drugs to?"

"You'll be fine," he says. "You're in good company."

Seglinde takes off her shirt and frees her Valkyrie breasts. Alan lights a joint and hands it to me. We search for a place without people, finally stop in a little ghost town with disintegrating nineteenth-century buildings of stucco and mud brick.

We lug the food and camp stove into one of the old buildings and find a place where the floor hasn't caved in. There is tall grass here, and old fences with rusting barbed wire. An old windmill squeaks and flaps its loose tin when the wind blows. Charlie, a gymnast, is doing a handstand on a fence post.

I feel suddenly strange.

Alan says, "Your jaw will feel a little stiff at first. How are you doing?"

"I feel like I'm welded together in one piece."

"That's good. Haven't heard that one."

"Like a seahorse: all brain and spine."

Seglinde is laughing at me. "What does a seahorse feel like?"

"Like a coil of sex."

Charlie is doing a one-armed handstand now.

Seglinde is doubled over, laughing.

Alan is trying, unsuccessfully, to assemble the Coleman stove, and howling with laughter. The wind blows the grass the wrong way, and it is silver.

THE SUMMER DAYS run together. Tucson is hot, but it's not jungle hot. It's like a big kiln and if you go out in the desert and die, it will mummify you. There is no humidity to remind you of how hot it is. It is wonderfully opposite of jungle. *Snake says, Did you know the sidewinder has no eyelids? Can you imagine? Yes you can, you don't sleep well, do you? That's why you drink yourself to sleep.* The pot is plentiful and the police, at least for now, have given up enforcing the laws against it. There are not enough jails, and somehow pot doesn't warrant a prison camp. I roll a joint, then go to the fridge for beer.

Angela knocks at the screen door and starts undressing when I open it. "My, my," she says. "Boys." She nods at the dishes in the sink as we head toward the bedroom. Later, after she's used the bathroom, she says, "Are you sick?"

"Why?"

"Your toilet doesn't smell good."

I tell her I'm fine, and go dump some Lysol in the toilet.

NOW IT IS the Fourth of July, 1968. I am napping when they start the fireworks in the university football stadium. I am awake listening to artillery. *Snake says, They're close.* The late sun coming through my window turns the whole room red. I smell the blood. *There, what did I tell you?* I look down and I am ankle deep in blood. I pull my feet up onto the bed and smear blood on the sheets. I start screaming. I get up and slosh through the blood and call Angela. Nobody's home. I call Alan. No answer. Then I remember I'm supposed to go to a barbeque, and I look down for my shoes. The blood is gone.

The days are made fluid by the seemingly endless supply of drugs. A bumper sticker reads, DOPE WILL GET YOU THROUGH TIMES OF NO MONEY BETTER THAN MONEY WILL GET YOU THROUGH TIMES OF NO DOPE.

Alan and Seglinde come by, and we drive to the foothills west of the Catalinas and eat mushrooms. The Indian petroglyphs on the rocks dance. We jump from rock to rock. We take our clothes off. The creosote trees smell sweet from the rain. Thick, heavy clouds hang against the mountains. We are laughing hard, our whole bodies laughing. *Did you know the devil was the funniest character in the medieval drama, he and the cuckold, Joseph?* Seglinde is talking and her mouth is moving. Her jaw is hinged like a puppet. I touch her and it goes away. I seem to be receiving thoughts before they become words. In my peripheral vision I see skulls. When I look, they are rocks. *Ha! See us in the retablo inside the little glass box.* La familia de muerte. *Snake side-swaggers and drinks the tequila worm straight from the bottle.* Then it is raining and we are running back to the car before the arroyos start to boil with water.

IT IS SEPTEMBER and I register for school. I enroll in theater classes. I'd been a decent actor in high school, with good comic timing, and the memory of all the laughter made me happy. Tuition is seventy dollars for state residents. I have GI Bill checks coming in monthly. Life is good. Arizona is hot in September and people don't wear a lot of clothes. The campus of thirty-six thousand students is swarming with beautiful women with burnt honey skin and sun-brightened hair. I'm feeling a little crazy, and I walk down Third Street through the smell of suntan lotion and patchouli, brushing bare flesh amid halter tops and body heat.

Among them is a slender woman with waist-length hair walking with a short man with a goatee who is much older. They touch now and again, as if to maintain the obvious erotic connection. I remembered the man from a party I had gone to before going to boot camp. He was introduced to me as Matt Hines. He was known in the area as someone who could take you down into Mexico for a nontourist kind of tour that involved butterflies and going to places gringos didn't get to see. At the party, he had objected to my service in an unjust war. I would now agree with him.

I see them at intervals throughout the day. I see them in Louie's Lower Level, a huge cafeteria and coffee shop that has become the center of student activism since the war started. Coffee is five cents per cup. The place is a hive of subversion and fuck-me energy. I keep looking at the redhead and she keeps looking away. I sit with a group of students and somehow wind up next to her. She is skeptical of a lot of the student politics, finds them immature and unstudied, and is resisting pressure to become an instant Maoist, Marxist, or anarchist. But we are all caught up in being young, and our energies form themselves around causes, some sincere, the others just swept up in the need to belong. I want her very badly, the woman with the red hair. I'm having trouble sitting still.

I am introduced to others I will spend a lot of time with. There is Gerhardt Linz, Sam Epstein, Jim Hood, John Banks, and his girl-friend, Bren, a pneumatic, sleepy looking, and utterly adorable little woman whose big heart I would come to appreciate. The two of them were charismatic together and apart. I like them instantly.

There are Jim and Harriet Marquette, older than the rest of us, and, I would find, the people I would turn to when things got too insane, their father/mother presence comforting. We uncon-sciously defer to them.

I feel her against my arm. *Yes.*

The conversation has turned to the origin of the word *hippie.*

Jim is proclaiming, "I'm not a hippie; I'm a beatnik," with a slight smirk at the historically new. Jim has a goatee like Matt Hines's, a trimmed sophistication amid anarchical formless bush beards and scraggle.

"We're old farts," says Harriet. We laugh. "Once you have a history of your own, history gets ironic." We don't get that. They have an "open marriage," something I will come to know as the beginning of the end of a relationship, however, theirs will survive the sixties. They've left room for some madness so that the seams don't rip.

Gerhardt, the anarchist, is talking about Bakunin, of whom I know nothing, and somebody else is responding with something about "substructure and superstructure." John says that anarchists ultimately cannot accomplish anything after the initial necessary dissolution of the power structure. Gerhardt is responding that anarchism is an element that seeks to rebel as soon as the revolu-tionary forms begin to calcify. I'm trying desperately to hang on to what they're saying, knowing that my success in this group depends on being able to talk the talk. I am also deeply moved by the ideas. They make sense. To me, they have blood and bones. *Snake says, Shake out your spine or tow the line. Mr. Charles has trained you fine.*

I am becoming disoriented by the redhead's warm presence, and the next thing I know we've left together, are walking out the front gate of the university, down Third to Tyndall, across Sixth to my apartment. I forget what we're talking about, because words just fill the gap until we're in bed, and now we are in bed and our clothes are flung all over. The sun has gone down, and I turn on the light so I can see her. Her hair is dark, auburn, waist length. Her skin is apricot-colored from the sun. I want her again and say so and she grins and we make love. *Snake says, Hey, you've pushed your snake juice down your spine and out the other end. I'm jealous. But I'll be back.*

14

BEFORE I WENT to Vietnam, I'd been a music major at the University of Arizona. Then I'd tried acting, playing the small comic role of one of Dogberry's three watchmen in *Much Ado About Nothing*. When I returned to the university after the war, I picked up where I'd left off. I was cast as Pizarro in Peter Schaffer's *The Royal Hunt of the Sun*. I was passionate about this role. A former Spanish peasant, now a general, Francisco Pizarro subdued an Inca kingdom and its king, Atahualpa, for the glory of Spain, but at the same time he became so fascinated with Atahualpa that it changed him. The relationship between the Spaniards and the Incas was, for me, reprised by the invading Americans and the Vietcong. I had not yet heard of Hegel's master and slave dialectic, but I instinctively understood how an invader can begin to respect his enemy, how Pizarro came to understand that Atahualpa's cause was more just than Spain's gold-driven colonialism.

The local critics did not appreciate the connection between the Spanish conquest of Peru and the American war in Vietnam—the press had not yet turned against the war—but the audience did, and packed the theater every night of the run.

IT WAS A different time in America. University faculties were getting out into the streets. For once, separate departments got to know each other in ways that had nothing to do with turf or budget. Chemistry professors became heroes. The age of psychopharmacology had arrived, and otherwise conservative people stepped out of the straight and narrow with a kind of innocent glee, grew their hair long and joined the party. Blake's imaginative landscape became extremely popular in English departments. Universities became centers of political and cultural activity in a way that has never happened again, at least in this country. Students read and attended plays and poetry readings in huge numbers and congregated in the streets afterward. Fraternities and sororities dwindled to skeleton crews of Ivy League wannabes. They represented a bourgeois mind that was part of the problem; besides, in order to get laid you had to get involved in some aspect of the movement.

Poets like Galway Kinnell could pack a large auditorium, and students and faculty alike walked around campus carrying copies of *Body Rags*. W.S. Merwin was another star, and *The Lice* was everywhere, as was Sylvia Plath's *Ariel*.

I took a course with Richard Shelton, warmed to his desert surrealism, and became passionate about poetry. I studied fiction writing and wrote a story called "The Journal of Nguyen Mai," about a corpsman who found the journals of a Vietcong cadre, and found empathy for him. The story was published in the university literary magazine, at that time called *The Tongue*.

I seemed to have unlimited energy in those days. I could go to a demonstration, get stoned, drunk, blasted, stay out all night, show up the next day for rehearsals, quickly memorize lines and blocking, have more than one sexual relationship, and still function. In the beginning, before the drugs and the booze became debilitating, I had a purpose and kept it in sharp focus. I was a witness looking for a form.

I had a new girlfriend during this time, Amanda Blunt. I was attracted to her freckled voluptuousness and her native happiness. I basked in her ability to find good in things, even though I frequently became cynical about her positive attitude. I don't remember where I met Amanda, but I think it was because of *The Royal Hunt of the Sun* and the aura surrounding the production's success. Amanda would not, finally, accept me as I was. She lectured me on my mood swings, which were considerable, and was concerned about my getting up in the night with the horrors, and my sudden bursts of neediness. She referred to me on one occasion as "dark Doug." I had not yet considered that I had post-traumatic stress disorder, indeed, the condition was years away from its medical adoption, and most people didn't know what to do with me when I got crazy.

One day she said, with schoolgirl sincerity, "You know, I really think you can be happy, if you want." I tried on and briefly rejected the idea that you could be happy by an act of will, and went on being me. I had little choice but to be me. I had no understanding of my unconscious, no capacity to question my often violent emotions. I was impulsive, sexually and otherwise, and would explode if anyone tried to get underneath my defenses. I had a horrible fear of abandonment, which I projected onto my lovers as their inherent dishonesty, and yet I would leave my lovers without notice, and did so several times in those years. But Amanda was not easy to manipulate, and our relationship was on and off for about two years. We were good together sexually, and when you are young, that is often enough to keep an otherwise doomed relationship going.

In my theater studies I became fascinated with Brecht and Beckett and Shakespeare. Shakespeare was a philosopher's machine. High seriousness always had a fool in its shadow.

The moment one man ascended, his power was already beginning to erode. Brecht and Beckett had some of the same qualities, although more philosophically framed in the case of Beckett, and ideologically in the case of Brecht. But even Brecht, wary of Stalin and McCarthy, finally distrusted ideology, and there was always irony in his plays and poems to offset politics. Beckett became my specialty. I played Vladimir in a student production of *Waiting for Godot*. What moved me was the character's constant reaching for meaning that was never fulfilled. One night, performing to a packed house of stoned and very responsive students, I delivered the line, "We give birth astride of a grave, the light gleams an instant, then it's night once more," and a student with hair like a black tumbleweed ran screaming out of the theater. It took a few beats for the audience to stop laughing, then we resumed.

In the sixties the boundaries between life and performance became blurred. The political theater in the streets became more interesting than on stage. Elsewhere, the San Francisco Mime Troupe was appearing at demonstrations, doing performances within performances. César Chávez was doing the same thing farther south, as was the Bread and Puppet Theater in New York. I wrote a piece of agitprop for a group of actors, directed by Francesa Jarvis, that was performed in Armory Park during a demonstration. It concerned two samurai types whose penises were equated to the length of their swords, the longest sword winning the day. The play is now, fortunately, lost.

The "stars" of the Tucson student movement were larger than life. John Banks, a thirty-six-year-old philosophy grad student with a white man's afro, became our de facto student leader on the basis of his charisma and sense of performance. John had been a Dominican monk, and then, lapsed, had become the road manager for a rock band. The band had been born from an East Village vortex that included Allen Ginsberg and the group who used to hang around the Peace Eye bookstore. The group would help power antiwar and other movements for years to come.

When John picked up the bullhorn at a demonstration, people listened. There had been no election, or selection process, for John. He was our year king, spawned by a huge energy looking for a persona. I liked John, his grin, his love of Wild Turkey, and his unbuttoned humor.

One afternoon I go with John to a party over on Pima Avenue to drink beer. The host used to be in the band John used to manage. It is sweltering. The host, who affects a Hell's Angels—like look—big, hairy and unbathed—enters the room with beer foam in his beard and announces, "I'M GONNA GO GET ME A BIG FAT INDIAN WOMAN AND GO FUCK ALL DAY IN

THE ATTIC SO I CAN LOSE THIS GODDAMN BEER GUT. SWEAT IT THE FUCK OUT!" He then pulls a huge hunting knife from somewhere and sticks it in the table in front of me. He knows I am new to the assembled group and wants to give me a scare. I know it's bullshit so I just look at him. *Snake says, He don't mean shit. He's an actor.* He mumbles something and walks away. We drink, sweat, piss, drink some more. The heat is vengeful and the swamp cooler on the roof is useless.

The social theater we are involved in is too big, too out of control, to fit on a stage. It is a great unmasking that becomes a mask of nudity. Taking off one's clothes is putting on the skin of the age. One day in front of Old Main on the university campus there are about thirty men and women, butt naked, splashing in the fountain. The campus police are looking on helplessly. A spontaneous piece of political theater.

Nude parties began to be the rage. Go to the party, take off your clothes, enter the living room where there are a large number of people, attractive or not, drinking beer or fibrillating under the rush of oncoming acid.

At one such party, a young woman with waist-length blonde hair goes out in the backyard to have a cigarette. She is completely naked and is dragged off into the bushes and raped by someone in the alley behind the house, a nonstudent who had stopped to watch the party through the rear windows. Imagine reporting this to the police, who don't like us much anyhow, explaining that yes, she was naked, but that was no reason to rape her.

At one party, held at a huge mansion off Sunrise Drive in the Catalina foothills and reputedly owned by a member of an organized crime family, I arrived to see an Olympic-sized swimming pool packed with naked people, possibly a hundred of them, chattering, drinking, and toking up. Cecile B. DeMille could not have done it better.

At a party at Alan Sorokin's house I met a woman who had just come unglued from her husband. We took a walk out back. Alan had stolen a gazebo from a musical stage set and moved it into his backyard next to his circular prefab swimming pool. We walked toward the pool, and then we were naked and entangled on the ground. We had been at it a while when I saw Alan in my peripheral vision, walking toward us. He had come out to smoke and had stumbled upon us. He tried to walk by as if he didn't see, but then he just stopped and watched. We had come from the fifties with no pill and lots of fear into whatever was next. We are both ashamed and unabashed, both lusty and sentimental for erotic order. This split condition is a consequence of what the Chinese, in the curse, refer to as "interesting times."

There was continuous theater. While visiting a friend, two bare-breasted women with austere expressions emerged from the bedroom carrying rifles, a .223 and a .22. Somebody told me they were Diggers from San Francisco, and somebody else told me they were in the Weather Underground, but I never saw them again.

I HAVE ACQUIRED a motorcycle, an old Ducati 125 that will barely make it up Mount Lemmon. Then I get a Suzuki 250 that is very fast and pollutes a lot. One day I am extremely drunk, run a stop sign, and hit a car broadside. Neither of us was going very fast. I don't remember any of this, but I apparently got up and left the scene and the motorcycle, coming back to get it later when somebody said they'd seen it. I left the damaged bike at home and forgot about it.

About three months later I am walking up Park Avenue to a bar called the Green Dolphin and a cop stops me, asks to see some identification. I give him my license, and in a few minutes, the cop is telling me to put my hands on the car. He tells me there is an outstanding warrant on me for leaving the scene of an accident and not paying the fine for running a stop sign. On the way down to be booked, the cop tells me that he felt bad about picking me up, that I seemed like a nice guy and should call somebody to bail me out.

It would only be about forty dollars, but it was late and I was too embarrassed to call somebody such for a trivial offense. If I'd been picked up for something political, maybe, but leaving the scene of an accident? How stupid.

Inside, while I was being printed and booked, a long line of freshly arrested Latinos come in. The deputy at the booking desk says something about "wetbacks" and "spics." He looks at me and tells me that I'll be at home with them. He thinks I'm in for drugs, and I don't disabuse him of this. I can't very well say I'm in for running a stop sign.

One very tough looking Latino shares a set of handcuffs with a heavily made-up drag queen. The deputies think this is funny, and the young Latino is obviously humiliated, ready to kill. The drag queen is careful not to make eye contact with him, hums "La Donna é Mobile" from *Rigoletto,* and stares at the ceiling. I am put in a holding cell with several passed-out drunks and a man who has just tried to kill his wife. She had locked herself in the bathroom and cowered in the tub as he fired one .357-magnum round after the other through the door. He, too, was passed out, and two guys are stealing his shoes. I wonder if they'll wear one shoe each, but they give them to another guy, who slips them what I think is money.

There were seven Mexicans who, according to the deputies, had just "swum the river." What river? There's no river on the Arizona–Mexico border. I ask one guy for a cigarette and he just stares at me, like *I don't know shit.* It's a class thing. He's been out panhandling and now this gringo wants a cigarette. He gives me one, reluctantly. I had quit smoking, but the situation calls for me to start again. I measure myself against the men in the room and conclude I can take most of them singly, but not in groups, so I am very courteous. *Snake says, You know where you are, son. Keep me down until you need me, then go for the throat the balls the eyes and don't quit until they back off. After all, you are cute enough to fuck.*

The cell is overcrowded, with stone benches against the walls. I understand that I'm going to sleep on concrete. *Snake says, You've slept on rocks. Quit bitching.* There is a stainless steel combination urinal-sink near the door that is plugged up and filled with vomit. The guy who gave me the cigarette tells me I'm going to be there all weekend because judges don't work on Saturday. *Long time for you to go without a beer.*

Two and a half days of hard benches and an ever-shifting cell population and I'm up before a judge. The Immigration and Naturalization Service is there for the Mexicans, and the rest of us have to say our piece. Nobody has a lawyer except the guy who tried to murder his wife, and he's bailed out. I'm sitting there mulling how I'm going to tell this judge I'm a nice guy. When my turn comes I say, "Your Honor, I'm a student at the University of Arizona and. . . ."

"Congratulations. Forty-five dollars or thirty days. Next."

This time I made the call. I asked Channing Smith, one of the theater department faculty, to come down and bail me out.

I HAVE GROWN wary of hallucinogenic drugs because they take me places I can't control. I don't mind it when I close my eyes and see the words that someone is speaking appear in gold neon. But when I feel a sinking into darkness I get crazy. *Snake says, I can't help you there. You've changed the rules.*

When I am coming down from hallucinogens, I become obsessed with order. I clean my room. It is the only time I clean anything. I also start drinking if I want to get back to plain old visceral reality. It does not help, however, and I become a hallucinating drunk, which is a little hard on my friends. I manage somehow not to use hard drugs. I often think heroin would have taken away the pain, for a while at least.

There is darkness coming our way, even in Tucson. Robert Kennedy and Martin Luther King are assassinated my first year back from Vietnam. Students are beaten by police in Chicago and Paris.

Locally, agent provocateurs are sent from the Phoenix police department to create pretexts for police action, but nothing much happens. Pastor Don Eckerstrom discovers a Molotov cocktail in the Campus Christian Center, but no one knows anything about it, and most of us think it's a police plant.

Even the usually cheerful John Banks has a grim look about him. He is now a Maoist and has become a severe ideologue. He believes the police are watching and listening to him. They were watching and listening to all of us, but John seemed to think he was the center of the surveillance.

One day in a bar I was talking to John about Samuel Beckett, whom we had often discussed with enthusiasm, when I saw another John emerge. He said, very seriously, "I sure hope we can let Beckett live after the revolution." Something is happening to John.

Snake says, Here I am in the strawberries. Here I am in the Boone's Farm strawberry wine. Here I am in the heated spoon. Here I am with the heavy metal cudgel. Flower power grows in the same shit as any other dream. Ask that guy in the elevator shoes with the withered arm. You know, Stalin.

15

THROUGH THE REDHEAD I meet Darrell and Nancy. Darrell lives in an alley apartment, writes poetry, and practices Buddhism. He has a large Mexican jug in the corner from which he drinks water, telling me the natural bacteria that flourish in such a jug are good for your innards. He says that bacteria are part of us. He says that all reality is interdependent. He says that antibiotics are ruining our relationship with bacteria, and for that reason Americans can't drink the water when they travel. He says, by way of demonstrating the interdependence of all life, that science and Hindu religious concepts are frequently compatible, and that physics and monism have a lot in common. He says the Hindu concepts of *prakriti* and *purusha* (matter and spirit) are an analogue of what's being seen under an electron microscope, with finer and finer matter being discovered with each advance in optics. He says everything is alive and part of everything else and the dust particles we breathe today may be the dust of the bones of Genghis Khan, and that if we understood this, we would all love one another.

Hereafter follows an interlude of group sex.

When I get up to go to the bathroom, I meet Clyde. Clyde is Darrell's alligator. Clyde is female, named before Darrell learned how to determine sex in alligators. Clyde is becoming too large for the bathtub—nearly five feet. Lying on her stomach, she is becoming concave, and Batwoman is complaining that he should move her to a larger containment. Clyde's serrated jaws are inches from my penis as I piss. She stares at me with her slitty eyes. I zip quickly and leave.

NOVEMBER IS PERFECT in Tucson, and there is a strange dissonance between the crisp but sun-hot day and the antiwar demonstration of nearly ten thousand students faced off with police at a downtown intersection. There were still downtowns in those days, and the shopkeepers and restaurateurs laze in their doorways and watch.

The Tucson police are not yet in riot gear, and it seems unlikely that anything ugly will happen today. Nevertheless, we have been ordered to clear the intersection and we do not. They do not rush us. A bare-breasted woman strokes the neck of a policeman's horse, and I wonder if behind the silver aviators his eyes are not in fact riveted on her, but he appears unaffected.

These articulate students intimidate me with their knowledge of issues, their deft phrases, their witty rejoinders. I become silent in their presence and, privately, read everything I can get my hands on. I am completely stumped by Marx's *Kapital* and put it aside, but I zoom through Joyce's *Ulysses.*

These students seem so sincere. I've got work to do. The reasons I have become adamant against the war hold the smell of blood and the vision of mangled flesh. *Snake says, Lookie there. Rub their noses in it.* But there is no way for me to communicate this yet. Do they experience three-dimensional images? *Snake says, Get down.*

By now the cops have formed a line and we are being backed out of the intersection. The speakers have had their say, and no one is resisting. The crowd moves to Armory Park for a rally. There will be no blood spilled today. *Aw, shucks, says Snake.*

DARRELL IS LOOKING a bit mournful. He has been forced to part with Clyde. He tells me the story. Darrell had been picking Clyde up and carrying her outside to lie in the sun in the backyard. There is no water in Tucson, and therefore no means of escape for Clyde, who is seemingly content to lie in the deep heat of the Arizona sun, as if she were digesting leisurely on the banks of the Nile. Since she seemed so peaceful, Darrell became confident enough to leave her in the yard and go back inside. *Heh, says Snake.* One day he was in the kitchen rolling a joint when he heard a fierce yipping in the backyard and looked out the window to see the neighbor's little rug dog running in circles around Clyde, moving in to nip at her tail. Darrell ran outside to behold the following: Clyde, who had hitherto shown little motivation to do anything, rose five feet off the ground, spun around with a whip of her tail, and chomped the little rug dog. She then shook her head a few times and spat out the bloody pelt. This all took less than five seconds. The dog's owner, who had been watering some suffering flowers in the next yard, began screaming uncontrollably.

The police were called, and Darrell had to get rid of Clyde. Clyde wound up in a cattle rancher's watering tank, scaring off coyotes. *She's happy, yeah, eyes above the water, waiting.*

REDHEAD AND I move into a little house in an alley on the north side of Speedway near Cherry and attempt to have something like a home. I have no idea what that is. All my life I've shuttled back and forth between relatives, done the custody agreement dance, but have acquired very little sense of home.

I become instantly uncomfortable. We do not want to have a baby; this would put us into domesticity and debt, away from friends we value. Redhead gets a monkey and the monkey learns to hate us. The monkey bites. The monkey retreats to the ceiling fixtures when he does not wish to be caught. The monkey masturbates openly in the presence of guests. The monkey leaves his shit all over. The monkey does not bring out our nurturing and parenting energies. The monkey has to go.

But the force of sex supplanted any notions I might have briefly entertained about fidelity and a sane, comfortable relationship. I couldn't stop. I'd go to do my laundry and end up going home with somebody I'd met there. I never did this because I wanted to hurt anybody, leastwise myself. I did it because I was out of control. Needless to say, the relationship did not last.

Every time I'd relax, stop the constant input of my senses, the war would rise into the present. The war that was still going on, that would go on, until April 1975. The dream came back: me naked and wandering the road in the rain.

SNAKE'S LECTURE ON *the Central Nervous System*

It's like a big tree with long roots and branches, but at the end of each root and branch there's an extension, at least the length of the real branch or root that snakes out like ectoplasm way beyond your body. That's your central nervous system, boy. It's been stretched beyond normal. It's huge, and every time some little thing comes along, some little click or bang, some little fragment of anger from somebody else, you light up the whole tree. Some medieval cat said the soul surrounds the body, contains the body, so your soul is touching things before your body arrives on site. That is why you are so crazy, bro. That's why you followed those people home the other day when they cut you off in traffic. You just stepped off your bike and stood in their front yard and menaced them big time. You need to find a bridle for your idle. But you don't know that and I can't tell you. You're going to have to run into something that doesn't give. You're going to have to hit your head, hard.

WHEN I WAS without a lover, I started to go to people's houses and stay with them because I couldn't be alone. When they wouldn't let me in, I slept on their porches. Tucson is warm most of the year. You can sleep outside. It was about then I began having the dreams about Richard Nixon.

I'd be walking along the street and this big, black-glass limo would slow down and stop, like a mafioso would step out who asks you to go for a ride between two thugs. But when the door swings open, it's Richard Nixon sitting alone at the other end of the seat, kind of hunched, like he expected somebody to swat him with a newspaper because he peed in the wrong place. He always had that look about him. But he said, "Get in, Doug," in that Nixon voice we all came to know, that humorless semi-quaver that was accompanied by his eyebrows coming together. I'd get in. Then he'd look at me, almost piteously, and say, "You just don't know how it is, Doug." And I felt guilty because I'd been trashing him at every opportunity. But when I woke, I knew I hated him with a passion that I would only feel again years later at the president who lied us into another war.

I STUDIED PHILOSOPHY because I thought I could figure things out and feel better. I thought there was a reasonable answer to the insanity of the war. But it was hard and my mind was unfocused and disassociated half the time and I had to work like hell just to pass. I took a course called Existentialism and Phenomenology from a guy named Charles Berringer who'd written extensively about Karl Jaspers. Not only was I expected to understand the reading, I was expected to understand all the other philosophers whose work had informed those philosophers—Hegel and Kant. I had never read either, and it killed me when I tried.

Berringer himself fascinated me. I also distrusted him. He'd been an American student at the University of Heidelberg during World War II and had decided to stay in spite of the war. His German friends hid him when the SS came to visit, and he managed to complete his studies. Heidelberg was not bombed, and Berringer's experience of the war was secondhand: it never touched him; he never saw death and maiming. Presumably he never minded that the Jews were rounded up from the university, as they must have been. He, like many existentialists, referred to the war, and the political circumstances of the war, as *absurd*. I wondered if it was possible to think that anything was absurd while people were trying to kill you, if that notion required a certain amount of detachment. After all, Sartre had taken a stand and joined the French Resistance. Not Berringer.

I squeaked by with a D.

My fascination with Brecht and Beckett continued. I could make sense out of poetry, even if I could not quite articulate just what that was. Maybe metaphor is the proper vehicle for chaos and despair. I was fascinated with the idea that life was absurd, although this wasn't quite what Beckett meant. I was more drawn to Brecht's poetic Marxism. In his plays, it was always the little guys who had something to say, and the self-important powerful were vulnerable to the craftiness of the disenfranchised. That made sense to me. I'd take it up with Nixon next time I dreamed my way into his limo (the dream repeated three times, with variants of the same conversation).

My mind was not working in an orderly fashion. It never has. I would struggle with anything that had to be figured out, but I could understand things in terms of imaginative counterpoint. I could put images next to one another and get them to add up to something.

I was also a romantic. I believed that it was possible to arrive somewhere, somewhere that made sense, somewhere that knowledge alleviated suffering. I liked the idea that by participating in the world of hallucinogenic drugs I was working toward a higher consciousness that would transcend everything. I had bought into the great hippie peripatetic romance. I believed, along with most of my friends, that we were ushering in a new consciousness by a *revolution of the spirit* that would supercede all previous revolutions because of an all-encompassing love. I had not read William James yet, who would have advised me that human progress is a meliorative myth, that human beings do not improve simply because time has passed, and that in spite of more knowledge, things remain pretty much the same.

I was listening constantly to conversations that went by just a little too fast and presupposed ideas I'd never heard of, like I was learning a language and everybody was talking too fast. I read difficult texts. Unfazed by my near failure in Berringer's philosophy class, I read Kant, Spinoza, and Leibniz. I was unable to bring their abstractions to earth. If I'd been able to understand, for example, that we cannot see *the thing itself* because our mind is too busy making up things about the thing, I would have understood a great deal about myself and others. But that would come later. If I had been able to understand that the violent yawing of my emotions had a dialectical reality, I'd have healed myself of much of the mental mess I'd brought home with me. My problem was deeply *moral*— not in the sense of moralizing, but in terms of trying to make sense of genuine evil and the human capacity for endless destruction.

I had stopped talking about the war entirely, and nobody asked me about it. I pushed the war outside of me, as if I'd never been there. I was guilty for having gone. Every day I'd hear the soldiers in Vietnam referred to as war criminals. A year after I came back, the My Lai massacre happened, and I withdrew further and further from my identity as a veteran.

One afternoon I was riding a bus to a doctor's appointment. I thought I recognized a guy seated near the side doors as I got on, but I couldn't place him. I kept turning around and looking at him, and he finally said, "Hello, Doc."

He had a glass eye and some scarring on his cheek. He said, "You put me on a chopper after I got shrapnel in my eye." Then I remembered him.

He'd been with a squad from another platoon, one that had lost its corpsman, and I was called over to look at him. I'd treated him and sent him off to the hospital, the war over for him then.

We rode in silence, forcing out a few words of conversation, but we were watching the students marching down the street on the right carrying signs with photos of the massacred villagers of My Lai, with the caption, AND BABIES TOO? YES, AND BABIES TOO.

He leaned over to me and said, "You ever kill any babies?"

I said, "Not a one."

"Me neither."

And we were quiet until I got off on Speedway at Country Club. We shook hands, hard. I never saw him again.

———

GERHARDT LINZ, THE anarchist and publisher of *The Match*, was a tall, tow blond with shoulder-length hair, big-lensed glasses, and a stark, antiestablishment scowl. He skulked. I liked Gerhardt because he had a sense of humor, and because he took me seriously.

I was talking with Gerhardt about Arizona's extremely conservative governor, Jack Williams, who had one eye and wore a patch. Gerhardt leaned forward and asked, with intensity, "What is written on the inside of Governor Wilson's eye patch?"

I leaned forward and said, equally seriously, "You Are Standing on the Inside of a Leibnizian Monad." I had located Gerhardt's sense of humor.

So went my education. I became a pretentious babbler and sat in the student union with the others, saving the world from itself.

16

BATWOMAN IS TWO years older than me, angry at her last lover, and fond of motorcycles. She puts on her leathers and rides sixty miles south to Mexico with her bat nets tied to the rear luggage rack. She goes during the full moon, crosses the border on dirt roads without detection, deep down into Sonora where the bats that live off the cactus fruits swarm and squeak.

She spreads the bat nets over the mouth of the cave and waits. Some Yaquis out on the road see this tall woman backlit by the moon and shout *Bruja, Bruja,* and she touches the .357 magnum she's stuffed down the front of her Levis, but they walk on, and soon she's got specimens to bring back, this during a time before *La Migra* began to stalk the border looking for illegals and it became harder to cross. Bats are her dissertation, and she's unconsciously developing a study of bat sonar she'll sell to the navy long after we've split.

She's got mood swings that leave me speechless. She's my older woman, although she's not that much older. She's got some scars like my scars but I'm too busy trying to bury mine to see hers.

And she's hard on the heart. I'm working hard to keep the horrors caged, and she's fucking with my emotional flak jacket. She's got a hold of something other than my cock and it's making me nuts. She's a jungle.

Batwoman drinks tequila and has an owl named Hoot perched on top of her refrigerator. When I come over, Hoot does this side-to-side thing with his neck that means *Try to pet me and I'll take your finger off.* She's also got snakes. *Snake says, Unhunh. Snake says, You sure know how to make me happy.*

We fuck and I'm happy and then we get into an argument because I say that writing is a miserable process, like an oyster making a pearl. She says, "Oysters don't feel a damn thing. Don't throw metaphors around like that." Then we fuck again and I'm okay. Then I'm not okay.

DRUGS DON'T FEEL good anymore. Pot loosens the flak jacket and I float where I don't want to. I'm starting to have the dream, the one that will stay with me for years. It's night, and I know the Cong are close. I'm naked and I have no weapon. I shake myself awake and go to the fridge for beer. I chug a quart of Coors. But the shakes don't subside and memory starts to bleed through into real time.

There's a new guy in the platoon named Paulhus who's got a tattoo of a little red devil on his left shoulder blade. I've gone with him to check out a small ville just east of the desert position. No one's there but an old man. The other villagers are gone—they always see us coming. But the old man has refused to leave. He's plainly senile. Paulhus is enraged. I don't know why—he hasn't been here long enough for that—but he grabs the old man by his shirt and shoves him down into the family bunker dug under his hooch. He yanks a grenade off his belt and pulls the pin, waits two, then rolls the grenade into the hole. The white flash, the blast of dirt and blood. I shake myself awake and go get another beer. It's a beautiful night in Tucson, but there's a red spiderweb stretched across the sky. No no no no no. That thing doesn't belong there.

I'M IN THE Student Health Center. The psychiatrist is asking me if I've had any homosexual feelings. He tells me I have to be realistic about my fantasies. I tell him I've been in a war.

He cocks his head and raises both eyebrows. "Really," he says.

I tell him I've had LSD on a number of occasions. He says, "You mean that didn't help you?" I have no idea what he means. Maybe he's tight with Timothy Leary. I say, "I feel like a reactionary," by which I mean that I don't want to take any more drugs, even at the price of seeming unhip, but he laughs like I said something funny.

Then he asks me about my mother. This is another one of those questions they have to ask. My mother is a long way away, physically and psychically.

He writes me a scrip for something called Stelazine. He picks up the phone. I try to make out what he's written on his notepad. I can only decipher the last line. It says, "Acute anxiety reaction." He puts down the phone and tells me to come Tuesdays at seven.

That night she comes by. We are naked and she hugs me from behind and takes my cock in both of her hands. I don't think anything can be better. It's the orgone fix, the rush. The pain is gone and we are fucking.

She says, "You can't think worth a damn, but you're a serious piece of ass." Then her face darkens. She tells me she wants to kill her lover's wife. "Simpering little bitch," she says. "Dresses like Joni Mitchell. Can't sing." She can sing.

"What are you doing with him?"

"I love him. I love his mind."

I'm getting depressed, and then she reaches between my legs and cups my balls.

Next day there's a huge rally at the university main gate at Park and Third. The police have just got new riot gear and they're showing it off. John Banks, our de facto Maoist movement leader, is there with a bullhorn, dressed in a Mexican wedding shirt. *One Two Three Four We Don't Want Your Fucking War.* The police start to move to clear the intersection and John calls for us to get out of the way. They've never seen the cops with riot helmets and batons. They've never seen tear gas canisters. This is 1969.

Someone breaks a drugstore window, and the cops charge the crowd. We've never seen plastic handcuffs.

I see Bob Epstein on his face with a cop kneeling on his back. A number of people are staggering and spluttering after a good dose of tear gas. We run to the Campus Christian Center. Don Eckerstrom is there—these are the days before he's traded in his priest's collar for a tie-dye T-shirt—and he's directing the tear gas victims into the kitchen, where they're spraying their faces with a dish-washing nozzle. I shout, "Don't rub your eyes." Something in the way my voice feels when I shout makes me smell rice paddies.

Outside the police have dispersed the demonstrators. There's a T-shirt lying in the street, a couple of placards with slogans. There's a pickup truck driven by a guy with curly red hair stopped in the intersection. He's screaming at the straggling demonstrators. There's a sticker on the rear window, below the rifle racks, that reads "University of South Vietnam School of Jungle Warfare." I walk over to him.

I say, "Hey, brother."

"Fucking goddamn faggots. Wish I had me a goddamn M79."

I say, "What you don't know is you've been fucked."

"What?"

"You've been fucked, brother."

"How'd you like your teeth in a doggy bag, asshole?"

"Third Battalion, First Marines, I-Corps," I say.

He looks at me incredulously, "What?"

"Just like you. We were fucked, brother."

"Shit," he says, and glares at me. His mouth drops open. He pops the clutch, leaves a long burn around the corner onto Third. "Fuck you," he shouts. "Fuck you, fuck you, you fuck . . ."

MY FRIEND JOHN BANKS was getting stranger, and people were saying things about him I didn't like. I'd always liked John, he was larger than life to me, and I enjoyed his company, but when somebody said he was getting paranoid and carrying a gun, I became concerned.

John lived in a little apartment over behind some stores and the Loft Movie Theater on Sixth Street. Friends of his who ran a head shop just around the corner asked him to look after their store while they were in Mexico. One night John was sitting out on his porch when he noticed somebody breaking into the head shop. He picked up his pistol, walked over to the shop, and shot the burglar dead. Immediately he became a cause célèbre for the local police, who were very much in favor of this way of dealing with criminals, but John was charged with murder. While waiting for his trial to begin, Bren drove him to Miami, where he got on a plane for South America and disappeared. Things were starting to go bad everywhere.

I LOVE THE way Lizzi hangs on to me on the back of the motorcycle I've just bought with my GI Bill check. We've been up to Mount Lemon and are a little drunk. She's hanging on to me tight, writhing against me, trembling. I mistake this for love. I think about what we'll do when we get to her place. I park the bike and we go inside. She puts on tea. I put my arms around her and hold her breasts.

She says, "I came about five times from the vibration of the bike. Try me later."

I AM DEPRESSED and out of beer when Batwoman shows up in her VW and shouts for me to get in. We're going down near the border.

The desert smells sweet from the rain. Tarantulas swarm across the old two-lane highway that heads south into Sonora. She stops the car and gets out. Low rumble of thunder over the Chiracahuas. *Snake says, Arc light.* She stoops and lets a tarantula crawl onto her hand, a big hairy one with a six-inch leg span. She walks over to me and tells me to open my hand. It's spring, two years since I came home.

I WOULD DRINK, take speed and quaaludes, find the temporary warmth of a woman's bed, and move on. When I visited Tucson years later I would occasionally see a woman I knew from that period and realize that I didn't know her name or she mine. We'd stare at each other across a sea of hallucinations and fragmented memory. My friend Steve Romaniello says that he thinks he slept with a hundred women during that time. I tried to count once and stopped at fifty. I was not proud; I was embarrassed, especially when I now admit that I can remember nothing else about these women. The adolescent dream of endless sex had become hollow. I was running, running as fast as I could, and when I could no longer run, I medicated to get through the night.

I kept dropping out of college and going back over a period of about seven years. The GI Bill and the theater scholarships I kept getting were enabling me to avoid the real world and the necessity of excelling at something in order to at least live. I had grandiose dreams that were safer than the brutal self-knowledge that came with testing myself in the world.

I had become something of a ghost. Most of my friends had graduated and moved on, and I found myself much older than the new students, who were changing in their worldview. They seemed less interested in politics and more interested in actually focusing on their studies. I had become history and so had the war. As I write this, I realize I am writing history of a sort, even if it is a history of fragments.

On campus, the radical image had exhausted its sexiness and the hard, long work of real politics had discouraged all but a few. Most of the activists my age had either turned in their tie-dye for ties, or settled into what Gerhardt called a "comfortable liberalism."

The romance was over. Woodstock had come and gone and the grim Altamont festival featuring the Rolling Stones had disintegrated into riot and murder. In a fit of hippie idealism, the Stones had paid the Hells Angels five hundred dollars and all the beer they could drink to work security for the concert, and they had taken their jobs a bit too seriously.

Herpes and venereal warts had taken the glow off sexual spontaneity, and free love had become as quaint as a Peter Max poster. The quality of street drugs was declining, and hard drugs were making profitable inroads into the pyschedelic culture, bringing some ugly predatory types along with them.

But most of the darkness I was feeling was of my own making.

I was spending a lot of time in bars. Gerhardt Linz was bartending at Mrs. O'Leary's Cow, a bar on Fourth Street that had remained popular with students through several name changes. Gerhardt still had the gritty energy, the drive of the professional activist, and as I write this, still does.

I was a regular at the bars, and was turning into a chronic, maudlin drunk. I'd begin by glad-handing everyone I had the faintest acquaintance with then spiral down into a depression and start sobbing at the bar. Or I'd make really clumsy attempts to pick up women, telling them how unhappy I was and hoping to awaken their mother mojos. Friends who had not left Tucson had pulled away from me. I was an embarrassment to have around, and I didn't care whose wife or girlfriend I passed out with. I still had not yet met my other who walked behind me carrying the war, and when in a lucid moment I glimpsed him, I quickened my pace. *Snake says, We comin'.*

Bad things were happening to people generally. One of the regulars at the bar, Bart Everett, whom I'd known as a great pool player from the student union, blew his brains out in his Volkswagen. A woman friend who frequented the bar, woozy on booze and quaaludes, was gang-raped on the way to her car. And John Banks got into even deeper trouble.

After he fled the country, John put on his monk's robes again and traveled from monastery to monastery all the way down to Chile. He arrived in time to get involved with the Allende regime, and when the coups came found himself arrested, tortured, and interned in the infamous soccer stadium in Santiago.

With the help of his family, John managed to be brought back to the United States to face the music. It was better than being a political prisoner of Augusto Pinochet.

THREE

17

SNAKE IS NOW like that little patch of fire dormant in the ashes, waiting for a breeze to flash full. I tried to put him out with alcohol, but that's like pouring gasoline on a fire. He hung smug in my every move, my stumbling love and my mumbling non-sleep with a faucet dripping enough to make me homicidal.

The people who tried to love me got burned. Some were stronger than others, like that good woman in Memphis who used to let me be who I was. She had this big piece of butcher paper on her wall. It read ACCEPTANCE in big block letters. She had a lot of that, maybe too much. She should have kicked me out.

I still looked good in those days and could leave one relationship and cross the street into another without too much bother, unless I was the one who got left and then all the old wounds opened and I was down for the count. It's amazing what you can do to yourself when you're young and still function.

It was the rage Snake fed on. There was plenty of it. I'd trained myself as a child to be depressed rather than act out my anger, because it was dangerous to assert myself. I'd get knocked into a funk at the first snarly word.

But I could scarcely keep the rage down now. One way to keep level was to channel it out through my groin. The times were right for that. We were the biggest bunch of fuckers that ever lived since that prehistoric crew you find on Hindu temple walls all twisted together in a frozen orgy. But we were on fire, and I was burning, running scared.

I showed up on my Uncle Fred's doorstep in Memphis with

black circles under my eyes and shoulder-length hair. I chose Memphis for no other reason than I knew I had a place to stay. I stayed in their house, ate their food, drank their booze, and hung out with their children, Jerry and Norma Lou, who were a lot younger than me and just coming of age at the tail end of hippiedom, anxious to get in their licks. Jerry was a stoner, and his father would shine a flashlight in his eyes when he came home. They had lost one child, Freddy, during a tonsillectomy, and weren't interested in losing any more children in any way. Like many, they saw the sixties as the end of everything wholesome and American.

I worked at a marble mill for a while, pulling up old piss-soaked tile in company bathrooms and laying new. I lifted big slabs of marble onto washing racks. I worked in cemeteries, sanding and polishing the places inside mausoleums where the coffins had leaked and stained the marble. I worked there with an old black man named Thomas who hated going in the tombs and looked at me sideways like he could see Snake sitting there, opening and closing his elliptical eye. Thomas, according to the boss, had been "born down at the end of a row of cotton," and did not know how old he was. I guessed eighty, but he could outwork anybody on the crew if he didn't slink off someplace. Thomas had something I wanted but I didn't know what. Peace? An intact soul? His presence was calming. He let me and Snake be.

I wore out my welcome at my uncle's and showed up at my father's house a little later, his third wife again angry at my presence. I stayed with them, got a job bartending out near the airport, and stayed drunk most of the time. Snake's rhythms rattled their sense of order and I moved on.

I did theater for a while at the Circuit Playhouse. I acted, directed plays, and fell into one relationship after another. I followed one woman to San Antonio, where she had enrolled at Trinity. I got a bartending job at the Crystal Pistol, a place that had a big sign on the front door saying how many years in prison you could get for bringing a gun into the bar. I served drinks to bikers and college kids and dodged pool cues swung during fights. Snake helped me sniff out when a fight was going to flash. People would leave drinks on the bar untouched and go home and I'd drink them. I could pour a mean tequila sunrise and goosed them a little just in case I ended up drinking them.

I REMEMBER ONE night after work I was drifting in and out, unable to sleep, with the horrors coming up through the dream and waking me. My girlfriend's friends were talking in the living room, not loud, a private conversation, but to me it sounded like shouting. I kicked the door open and came out naked, screaming, "Shut the fuck up." They froze.

I couldn't stand any kind of extra noise, noise that didn't belong there, tapping noises, clicking noises, and backfires, they'd send me cold. I flew into a rage when jets came over too low. People knew not to wake me up. I was a mess, but it was the sixties, even though it was really the seventies. You ask me, the sixties lasted until 1975 when the last chopper lifted off the roof of the embassy in Saigon.

I became a "maintenance" drinker and learned the rules of control, somebody who knows how to put one foot in front of the other and get through life, keeps a job, but needs control. A maintenance drinker thinks he's got it together and doesn't know people see right through him. He does damage merely by his absent presence, his quiet despair, and the spiritual pain that pervades the air around him. He survives by means of a series of phony selves that mask the one in Hell. He controls feelings through alcohol, alcohol with drugs, and drugs through alcohol, and alcohol through sex.

I'D GET UP in the morning feeling like shit and pop some speed to burn off the hangover. That would give me the shakes, and I'd smoke a joint to take the edge off. That would make my mouth dry, and I'd drink a half quart of ice-cold Coors. This would mellow me out till I had to go to the bar, then I'd take a hit of speed to pick me up and repeat the whole cycle. I'd come back to the apartment drunk but flying and take a quaalude to come down and sleep. I'd sleep fitfully. Snake would work his way up my spine and into my medulla and set off a starlight scope of clarity and I'd pop awake, dry-mouthed and heart pounding.

In another bar where I drank there was this postmaster who came for happy hour, sat down with his back to the door so the bright sun from the street wouldn't hit him in the face every time somebody came in. He'd order black Russians and the bartender would set him up four at a time. This was before responsible bartending etiquette. They knew why he was there, this postmaster, this man with organizational skills and a sharp eye. He'd drink for a while and begin to fantasize, to talk to someone who was standing right where the bartender stood. But it wasn't the bartender. Maybe the bartender's apron was a screen upon which he projected whomever he was talking to with such eloquence. The bartender, deadpan, would refill his drinks.

When happy hour was over the postmaster would pay up and go back out into the blinding sunlight and somehow manage to get home. These were before the days when if you got caught driving drunk you'd go right to jail. I laughed at him and could not see that I could wind up there, sitting on that same stool, disconnected and pathetic.

I had developed a fierce longing for something that I couldn't explain. I found a bookstore that sold spiritual and occult books. I read a book on Sufism by Idries Shah and was fascinated. There was a natural foods restaurant across the street run by Sufis of the Chistia order. I became friendly with Sarmad, the sheik who ran the restaurant, and began to attend their meetings. I seemed to be responding to something I would find much later in life, an exchange of *spirits* for *spirit,* a kind of longing known by alcoholics who are at the end of their capacity to function, who have wrecked their lives and finally seek outside themselves for help. I didn't know that any spirituality I might genuinely pursue would involve hav-

ing real relationships with other human beings. I thought somehow God would just beam me up above it all.

I was attracted to mystery, always have been. It was merely the
notion that there is always something just beyond our grasp, something protean that will always change when named, something
larger than the figuring-out part of the brain could apprehend. But
there was no quiet in me, no "Be still and know that I am God."
One of the things Sarmad tried to teach me in his gentle way was
that I was just fine the way I was if only I knew *what* that was. *Snake
says, You fracture the prism, you don't know simple, you don't know quiet,
but what you do know is if you cut a grape in half you'll see veins of light-
ning. You know that. But you can't see for all the hoopla.*

The war continued but nobody talked about it. I'd see it on
television once in a while at other people's houses. In those days
they allowed camera teams to go on combat operations. I'd watch
the squad of marines suddenly drop to a crouch under sniper fire.
I'd watch the lines of bodies covered with ponchos. Was I there?
Did this happen? This war, reduced to twenty-five inches at most,
and the folks I'm visiting chewing through their dinner, rolling a
joint after, ignoring the television. Walter Cronkite telling us how
it was. I'd even stopped paying attention to politics at this point.
My objectives were determined by booze and addictive relationships. It was even getting harder to read.

The hot event in San Antonio then was the arrival of *The Exor-
cist.* The first week I saw a ticket line all around the building at one
theater. People were fainting in line, they were so terrified of pos-
session. Latinas in early adolescence were especially vulnerable, the
alchemy of hormones and Catholicism stirred the pot. We'd stand
and watch them faint and laugh.

I was as miserable in San Antonio as I was any other place, and
so I thought a return to Tucson might mean happiness. *Snake said,
Here we go.* Tucson was even bleaker than before. Gerhardt Linz,
the anarchist, was still bartending at Mrs. O'Leary's Cow. There was
someone to talk to at least. The artists at Rancho Linda Vista had

become more serious about their work and less interested in the soft revolution of the sixties. More of my friends had moved away.

MY MOTHER HAD been assigned to USAID in Pakistan, and when she wrote me from Islamabad in 1972 and invited me to come for a visit, I was relieved to be getting out of Tucson. It was typical of her to alternate her disdain for me with acts of generosity. Part of this was because she wanted to be seen as a mother who had a son she could be proud of. This desire did not extend to actually loving and accepting me, but more often was a matter of her becoming frustrated and angry that her efforts to turn me into something she could understand did not work. Nevertheless, I went. I was running from myself and thought a foreign country would be a good place to hide.

The passport picture I had taken looked like the mug shot of a small-time drug dealer. What immigration official in whatever country would *not* look at me with attention? I got on a plane for Hong Kong and ended up with a flight attendant ("stewardess" then) during a twenty-four-hour "layover." I had come through Hong Kong on the way to Vietnam and it seemed pretty much the same.

I went to a bar that was full of British businessmen. There was a very loud Brit a few tables over who started shouting, "We go all over the world, we fuck everything that moves, then we go home and want to marry *virgins.*" There followed a burst of laughter. This phrase was repeated, word for word, every few minutes, with more slurring and less mirth. It was his one good line for the evening and he was going to work it for everything he could.

Hong Kong was still British, and the streets were maintained by British police in khaki shirts and shorts, with Chinese police in a slightly different shade of the same. They all had a diagonal belt across their chests, and a kind of ritual bandolier without bullets that seemed to say, "We're British, we don't need much ammunition, we have class."

I ate Mongolian barbecue and took the ferry to Kowloon, where I ate at the floating restaurants. Traveling loosens the soul. My body was detached from the familiar, anchored in new smells, new colors. The experience was unlike Vietnam, because no one was shooting at me and my imagination could supersede my fear. *Snake says, You ain't been here very long, that's all.* I thought, for a short period of time, that I might be happy.

I met my mother at the airport in Islamabad. Security was tight; a religious "fanatic" climbed into a baggage cart and ran over a Polish diplomat. The anti-Western feelings in Pakistan were not as focused as they are now, but foreigners were generally resented by much of the population. A Moroccan embassy employee had been attacked with rocks for wearing a miniskirt in downtown Islamabad. Violence was always just below the surface, even in 1972.

My mother first took me to visit her office and introduced me to her fellow USAID workers. When she got to her office and closed the door, her first words to me were, "You're losing your hair." Before I could respond, she drew her hand back as if to hit me, then withdrew it. She said, "If you'd just wash it," and glared at me. I had the same pattern baldness as my paternal grandfather, but to her, I was the cause of my own hair loss, the implication being that I never washed my hair. It had taken only the drive from the airport for the old dynamics to emerge.

My mother lived in a diplomatic community of elegant, two-story houses complete with gate guards, groundskeepers, and house servants. The house had a marble staircase and a veranda on the second floor. She had decorated it with beautiful rugs and furniture that could be had for a song in Pakistan in those days.

Every morning Aziz, the house servant, would bring my tea, which appalled me, but it was his job. I might as well have been part of the British Raj, the way he deferred to me. He had tuberculosis but refused to go to the doctor, because he would then be quarantined and couldn't work.

My mother introduced me to Julian Samuels, a Pakistani about my age who went by "Coxy." He was from a Christian family and worked at the interagency motor pool, where all the embassy cars were serviced and repaired. One night he suggested that we take a walk. He reached in his pocket and produced some British Gold Leaf cigarettes and offered me one. After the first inhalation I knew that the cigarettes were loaded with hash, and soon we were laughing. Later, Coxy showed me how he loaded the cigarettes. He'd roll them between his fingers and then shake out the tobacco. Then he'd take a centimeter-sized chunk of hash and heat it over a match. He'd crush the hash between his fingers and sprinkle it in the loose tobacco. Finally, he reloaded the cigarette. He smoked these all day long, during work, especially. I imagined him singing to himself softly as he worked on the Mercedes of the Russians, the Koreans, the Americans.

One morning Coxy and I drove to Peshawar, located just east of Kabul, Afghanistan, which in those days was a bandit town. Pashtun bandits from Afghanistan and Pakistan came there to sell their booty. Banditry was an honorable profession, tolerated by both governments. You could buy anything there. I saw a tribes-man with an old Martini rifle left over from the British days. There were horses tethered here and there, and loudly deco-rated trucks. The bandits wore long knives and carried their rifles openly.

We ate a wok-fried dinner in a restaurant in a cave in the side of a hill, one of the best meals of my life. While we were eating I looked up to see the whole room staring at me. No women, just bandits. We ordered a tray of treats served to their table and they saluted us. One said, "An Englishman," and toasted me with his tea. *Snake says, Don't you dare get ironic. Don't you dare.* Being referred to as an Englishman did not make me feel safe at all. Then the same bandit said, "I think you are very high class," which made me more nervous. *Snake says, Smile back, idiot. This is where you need me.* I smiled and returned his toast.

On the way back we got out the hash.

At home, we sat on the veranda and smoked, my mother long gone to bed. It was a star-infested night and someone was singing on the road to the north.

Coxy said, "He is singing because he is afraid." *Snake said, It's cultural. You ought to try it.*

My mother wanted to take a trip to India. We flew to New Delhi and checked into a hotel. New Delhi in those days was, and perhaps still is, a city of stark contrasts. There were businessmen in silk suits stepping over the homeless. I had never seen homeless people; my own country, at the time, had a small homeless population, and the mentally ill were safely ensconced in state hospitals which had not yet gone belly-up. Hobos were perceived as men who had *chosen* to live that way. When on the way out of New Delhi toward Agra we rounded one of the many rotaries in the city, and I saw a completely naked man with waist-length hair and beard standing in the grassy center. He had a white stripe down his face and was shouting at the top of his lungs. The driver, a Sikh, gestured that he was mad. It would not be long before this was a common sight in my own country, but that day it was something out of the biblical imagination.

We headed toward Agra to see the Taj Mahal, but the best was not the Taj: the best was the trip itself. Halfway there, near sunset, a cow wandered suddenly onto the road and the driver could not avoid hitting it. The impact knocked the cow down, but it got up and wandered off. The problem, however, had just begun. The cowherd came from the trees in a rage, shaking his staff at the Sikh. The Sikh was trying to calm him down. This was all weighted by the fact that Sikhs eat meat and Hindus are not only vegetarian, but consider the cow sacred. The argument lasted for a half an hour, until the cowherd became exhausted. The Sikh driver was powerfully built, but his presence was calming. The two men stood and talked for the better part of an hour.

I almost didn't see the troop of monkeys until they were on top of us, running over the car, bouncing off the hood, chattering,

reaching into the car, then disappearing as quickly as they came
into the trees.

Just before the sun went out of sight, driver and cowherd
embraced each other and we were on our way again. We had been
there nearly two hours but it had been out of time. It took two
hours to set things right, and the men acted as if it was all worth it.

Back in New Delhi, I wandered in the bazaar and had my fortune told. An old man stuck out his tongue at me against the evil
eye. In the Hilton, I ran into a guy who looked like a smaller, kinder
Norman Mailer, who said he worked for Amnesty International but
would not speak of why he was in India. I went to see *Tora! Tora!
Tora!* with a young CIA agent my mother had introduced me to.
And when we left on Pakistan International Airlines to return to
Pakistan, the CIA agent was going through customs just in front of
me, and the Amnesty International guy was behind me. *Snake says,
Keep your mouth shut and watch. Try to stay sober.* I felt as if I were in
some kind of secret conduit. We flew to Amritsar and stayed at Mrs.
Bandhari's Guest House where, blessedly, I could drink beer. *Snake
says, The fog, The fog.*

Back in Islamabad, I prepared to leave for Russia. Coxy drove me
to Karachi, where I was to board an Aeroflot flight to Tashkent and
then Moscow. When I went through customs, I was ushered into a
private room by two agents with identical mustaches and identical
dark rings under their eyes and asked the following questions.

"How much money did you make from the car you brought
here and sold?"

Coxy translated.

I said, "What?"

Coxy could see me getting angry, and made palms-down *calm
down* gestures at me.

I explained that my mother had given me money to go to
Russia.

They didn't believe me.

"How come you are leaving Pakistan with more money than when you entered?"

Snake says, Relax, they just want a little baksheesh. Fork it over.

I was innocently indignant. I thought I could smack their heads together. They weren't wearing guns. Coxy had his hands on my shoulders now.

I managed to get out of there because they really didn't have any kind of evidence, and Coxy told them my mother was in the State Department, and I didn't have any idea what baksheesh was, and I was young and had things to learn, and when I returned to Pakistan I would pay them a visit (I wasn't coming back). On the way to the plane Coxy explained about baksheesh.

Before I got on the plane, Coxy said, "I told your mother that she would never understand you."

Finally, in the air, the flight attendants brought us eggs and heaping mounds of caviar. They were showing off. When the seat belt sign went off and I got up to wander a bit, I saw the Amnesty International guy seated next to two Vietnamese in combat fatigues, no rank insignias, looking straight ahead. *Snake says, Ho!* The war was still raging at this time, and when the Amnesty International guy got up to come shake my hand, I asked him what the Vietnamese were doing on the flight. He gave me a look that said, gently, Please don't ask about the Vietnamese.

DO I THINK YET? Or do I simply manage my confusion better? What I am able to do at this point is to place one thing next to another; some call it montage. Some call it poetry, whereby apparently unlike things make sense together by virtue of a leap, where images that are not logically combined stir the fire. *Snake says, You can fit the green eye in the cat, the diamond in the dung heap, the fang in the saint, the light in the gun barrel, the mind in the rock split sidewise oh geode of wisdom in thy babble-tongued song. This is the brain you came with.*

Fuck me, it's the brain I've got and I'm trying to understand these old potato-shaped women I am dancing with along Leningrad Prospect, sharing a bottle, laughing. I'm trying to understand why the kid with the Elvis haircut whispering through my hotel room door wants to buy my shoes, rain damage and all, or why the woman in the dining room wants me to cut her steak for her— maybe because it is tough, maybe she's trying to tell me something about meat in Russia. I don't know why I can't get booze after dark in this town, or why the subways with the wood paneling remind me of the czar.

The Intourist guide, Marina, tells me as we pass a huge bookstore that you can get any book you want there (the subtitle says, "contrary to your capitalist propaganda"). She's defensive before the fact, wants to burn her bridges before she comes to them. I tell her I had a hard time getting a cab the previous night, and she snaps back, "You should try to get one in New York!" What is this woman, KGB? Propaganda wing? Ministry of knee-jerk defense?

We visit Lenin's tomb, and she wonders why I don't have a camera. I tell her I don't believe in cameras because I want pure experience of a place without having to take a picture. *Snake says, Poser.* Marina looks at me as if I were some Victorian Brit who's never seen a giraffe.

And then I'm in the Warsaw airport hotel with pneumonia. And then I'm in Frankfurt sleeping at the Jugendherberge and checking out the women. I am reading *The Gulag Archipelago.* The French girl walks over, looks at my book, sniffs once, and walks away. The pretty blonde German girl a fellow hostel member has picked up decides she wants me instead, and he and I nearly have an Apfelwine-inspired fight. The hamburgers in Frankfurt are terrible. Are there frankfurters here?

The Goethe House is dull, but the zoo isn't. I'm wandering through the zoo before it opens, hungover and cranky, but I'm cheered by the lions. A male lion gets up and walks over to a female and mounts her. The female merely moves her tail aside for him, her paws tucked under like a purring house cat. It takes a few seconds, and when he's done, he opens his mouth wide, raises his head, and roars. Then he walks over to the other side of the enclosure and repeats the act with another lioness. And roars.

I am in the business of remembering the things between the things that are supposed to be important. Not the Bolshoi, but the potato-shaped ladies in the street. Not the Kremlin, but the bus driver asleep in the rear seat.

I go to Munich and get kicked off the train for having no ticket by a short inspector with what looks like a gray Nazi hat with a little red dot in the front center. I sleep in a Jugendherberge where they make you get up and make your bed at six AM to marching music, and then you're out of the place till evening, where, prior to dinner, I am ordered to peel potatoes in the kitchen in the preparation of Eintopf mit Wurst.

I get drunk with a German guy at the Hofbrau House who asks me if we are still having problems with "the neegers" in my country. I go to Mannheim, which is as dull as Springfield, Massachusetts, and I get back on the train and go to Heidelberg, where you can smoke hash at the Melanie bar and buy carpets sold by Turks, and then go out and watch the barges churn up soap suds in the Necker. All the students seem to speak English and French, and I am embarrassed that I cannot speak French or German.

Back in Frankfurt I meet a sylph of a American woman who wants to talk to me about Melville (I'm reading *Moby-Dick*), and things are getting friendly but it's time for me to go to London— I'm running out of money—but the snow is so bad the planes are grounded and I go back to the Jugendherberge and find the American woman still there and we get a room in a pensionne and take our clothes off immediately. I watch the snow fall on the gargoyles on the building across the way, and I feel so good I am willing the gargoyles to spread their stone wings and lift off into the swirling snow.

And then, finally London. Not Big Ben, but the pensionne in

Earls Court, where I put shillings in the heater. Not the Tower of London, but the IRA types in the Prince's Bar who look mean enough to break one finger at a time but who, because I'm a Yank, buy me a Guinness or four. Not the Globe Theater, but the As You Like It dress shop in the basement of Judith Shakespeare's house.

I looked up my mother's anthropologist friends in Oxford, a married couple who taught at the college, who put me up in the Queen Elizabeth House for scholars. I lied at tea and told them I was working on a paper about Brecht. I knew enough about him to talk the talk. The guy in the room next to me is writing a book and scarcely leaves his room. I ask him at tea if he works all the time in there and he says, "Well, I get up and scratch my balls, you know." I go to the Bodleian, to Blackwell's bookstore, but best is the barmaid who's just got her master's in American literature. We go to midnight mass together at the central church. Outside, demonstrators chant, "Two, four, six, eight, don't forget to smash the state, Merry Christmas!" Afterward we go to her place for some cross-cultural synthesis.

Stoned in Wheatly trying to play bridge. Back to London where I see a young Judi Dench as Viola and John Dench as Aguecheek in a brilliantly funny *Twelfth Night*.

Out of money and back to Tucson.

18

I SEE A thin trickle of piss coming down the old marble steps leading up to the lobby of the Kingston Hotel in Times Square. I mount the steps and stop in front of the night clerk who sits behind a thick sheet of bullet-proof glass. He is Latino, in his twenties, wearing blue eye shadow. He looks at me with something like tenderness. "You ever stay in a place like this?" he says.

"Sure," I lie.

He shakes his head. He knows I don't know that this hotel is for hookers and their johns. All I saw in the paper was a room for seventeen dollars and ninety-five cents a night.

I pass him a twenty for which he returns a key attached to a rectangular piece of wood and two dollars and five cents change. I have twenty dollars left, enough for a six-pack, breakfast, and subway fare to my temp job the next morning. I don't know where lunch is going to come from, but there may be donuts in the office.

It is September, 1977, in New York.

I pick up my key and walk toward the single, ancient elevator, the kind that is operated by a handle attached to a steel wheel. Sitting in front of the elevator is a huge black man. The revolver tucked in his belt seems tiny, his eyes small in his blue-black, frown-muscled face. He gets up slowly and follows me into the elevator. I show him the number on my key, and he takes me to the third floor.

In my room, an elongated closet, the bed takes up nearly the whole space. There are holes in the door like the holes punched in a pet's travel carrier. The one window looks out on an airshaft at the bottom of which is a concrete atrium, its floor covered with shattered bottles. Voices come up the airshaft. A woman's laugh. A man's shout.

I pick up the bleached rag of a towel folded on my bed and walk to the big communal bathroom at the center of the corridor. Might as well shower before the rush. The bathroom has two opposing banks of urinals and open showers at the back. I stop when I see the huge mound of human shit in the center of the hexagonal tiled floor. I stand for a moment, then walk back to my room. I lock my door, push the elevator button, and go down. The elevator operator/bouncer is not pleased to see me. I have caused him to get up twice in one hour.

I go around the corner and get a six-pack of Budweiser and a bag of chips. It's going to be a long night.

My next hotel is an SRO near Washington Square Park. It is run by an ancient, troll-like couple with Eastern European accents who charge by the day. Its rooms are full of the indigent and the slightly mad who live on Social Security. Some of the bathrooms work, and there is an old-fashioned party-line phone system linked to the main desk through which all calls must be placed, and for which the old trolls charge exorbitant rates. One night I tried to use the phone to call out. Someone else picked up the receiver at the same time. "Excuse me, I'm trying to get out."

A female voice responded, "He's trying to get it up," and disintegrated into squeals of laughter.

A male voice cut in, "You tryin' to get it up? Take it back to yo mama—maybe she can get it up for you."

I tell myself, this is temporary. All I need is some money. But I'm more alive than I've been since the war. New York is like a hit of speed. For once the noise outside my head is equal to the noise inside. *Snake says, Is that so?* I feel like my brain is being sharpened by the sheer compression of the place, by the propinquity of smart, articulate, and ballsy people. I will always be economically marginal here, but in a while, less marginal, indeed, almost steady. Almost.

Close Encounters of the Third Kind has just opened in New York. "You Light Up My Life" is echoing up every airshaft in the city. My theater friends are sanding their apartment floors, spackling walls, working as waiters, hoping for the big break. Most of them will gradually fade from that brutal profession into just living and working and feeling like they're going somewhere just because they live in the great hive of heart heat called New York.

Roller disco is the rage and anyone with skates is gliding through the streets. Young black men are break-dancing on the corners, their hats filling with money. A woman sits on the sidewalk in front of Crazy Eddie and sings opera arias so badly, in a half-tone-flat vibrato, that people give her money to shut up. Crazy Eddie himself, enjoying his unindicted heyday, is being touted in the *Village Voice* as a performance artist, his grotesque mug on nightly on television shilling electronics: "Crazy Eddie is *insane.*"

Moondog, ghosting his way in from another age, can still be seen on Eighth Street, standing on store stoops, with his staff and biblical-looking headdress. An advertising executive who calls himself Roller Arena floats through the Village on skates, dressed as Tinker Bell, wand and all. One day I am walking along Hudson near Fourteenth Street and this black kid in a white tux, white shoes, white vest, and white top hat is standing there like a royal guard with a white telephone in his hand, the long white cord coiled down into his fly. When I pass, he thrusts the receiver at me and says, "It's for you. It's the White House." And all of this is *all right*. What might have got you arrested in Podunk is *normal* here.

If you hang out in the Village long enough you will see everybody. One day I see John Ehrlichman of Watergate fame crossing the street from Crazy Eddie. He has grown a beard but is still very recognizable, scowling out over the heads of the crowd. One day I see Orson Welles waddling slowly down the steps of an East Village film memorabilia shop. He is so fat he can scarcely walk.

In those early, lonely days I hung out in the Bagel Buffet near Eighth Street. Or I went to the Peacock, the great Italian coffee shop across on Greenwich where the owners would play opera all day. There I sat, read, and drank cappuccino. I met women there, and in the great bookstores that used to be in the Village—the one just off the Avenue of the Americas, and the one on Christopher Street. Sometimes I'd wake up in a strange woman's apartment and think, I could like this. *Snake says, You have no idea.*

I GOT A job at Spring Street Books in Soho. Especially in the evening, the store was full of extraordinary looking people and celebrities. I would routinely see Kate Millet and others—one day Norman Mailer. We hoped they would come in at the same time, but they never did. The filmmaker Nicholas Ray, now ailing, lived upstairs with his young girlfriend. The job alternately exhilarated me and made me feel like a rube.

I found an apartment on Twelfth Street right across from John's Italian Restaurant, and freelanced as a story analyst for United Artists, supplementing with temp work. I worked in telephone sales, where I met other out-of-work theater people hustling up the rent. I acted in a few plays off-Broadway, but was becoming less interested in acting. I was, without knowing it, looking for something other than mimetic creativity. I began writing.

When I first moved to the East Village, it was still the old East Village. You could see Sam Shepard or Willem Dafoe on the street. I ate at Veselka or Kiev two days a week. I hung out at the coffee shops, especially the Fregata on Eighth between Second and First.

I went with writer Al Santoli, who would later edit *Everything We Had,* to visit Allen Ginsberg and Peter Orlovsky in their Twelfth Street apartment. I only knew Allen by reputation. I expected to find a couple of laid-back vegetarian meditators, but they were seated at the kitchen table eating very bloody steaks and nothing else. The house was almost bare, except for unsheeted mattresses on the wood floors. Allen and Peter were very warm and unpretentious and I liked them immediately.

I liked staying up all night. I liked to pick up the Sunday *Times* at the Gem Spa at Eighth and Second and spend the whole morning reading it. I loved wandering down St. Mark's Place on a Saturday night in the swarm of performing selves, the punks who drifted over from CBGB, the girl with the pink hair and the white rat on her shoulder. The deadpan Korean and Arab merchants selling hats and sunglasses and the bikers who drifted over from the Hells Angels headquarters. St. Mark's bookstore was still on St. Mark's Place in those days, and I would spend hours in there, wanting to devour everything I saw.

I was optimistic, excited by the new world, and spent less time in bars. I went to the theater as much as I could. A friend had convinced me (and I was easily convinced then) that the only real creativity happening in New York theater was the off-Broadway avant garde. Lee Breuer and Mabou Mines were doing things I'd never seen before. I was amazed by *Shaggy Dog Animation,* with its principal characters played by bunraku puppets and its world created by electronic layers and synthesizers. Spalding Gray and Willem Dafoe were doing a lot of "auto performance" with the Performance Group on Wooster Street. They were dramatizing autobiography in a way I'd never seen. One summer I bought Sade's *Juliette, The Spiritual Exercises of St. Ignatius of Loyola,* and Fourier's utopian writings. I bought them because Roland Barthes had written a book called *Sade/Fourier/Loyola,* which I devoured, along with his selected texts. Something, some stricture, loosened in my head. It changed my thinking, my writing.

I ran into Matthew Causey, a writer and director I'd done theater with in Chicago. He'd become fascinated with the theater of Richard Foreman and created his own hybrid form. While Foreman did not use actors in the traditional sense of creating characters, Matthew kept the idea of characterization and adapted classical texts to avant-garde ends. At the Performing Garage, I played the Prophet Ezekiel in his staging of the biblical text, and Satan in his mounting of Milton's *Paradise Regained*. I was a good madman and, according to one critic, "a great loser." Once, during the Ezekiel play, I accidentally stabbed myself in the hand with a long knife and was cabbed to the emergency room at St. Vincent. There I sat, dressed as the prophet Ezekiel with a vicious knife on my lap. A weary young doctor came out to get me, looked at the knife, and said, "Is that what you used on yourself?"

"SERIAL MONOGAMY" WAS very fashionable, and that suited my inability to have sustained relationships; in fact, it gave me permission to move from bed to bed and be hip. This was either hard on the women in my life or hard on me, depending on who left first. Just when you thought you'd become worldly enough, something would surprise you.

I did temp work for extra money and in the late seventies, while working with the Veterans Ensemble Theater Company—begun by Vietnam vets—I wrote a play called *Short Timers*. It was about a maimed Vietnam vet in a locked ward. He was missing arms, legs, genitals, and eyes. Influenced by *Johnny Got His Gun*, Joe related the events of the play in a hallucinatory flashback. As writing, it was both sloppy and talented. I had not yet developed any discipline. I considered revision to be anti-romantic and had to force myself to do it. Emotionally the play brought up stuff I hadn't dealt with since the war, and I was not ready for what I felt. *Snake says, Rain on the thick leaves, mosquitoes, smell of blood and cordite, three AM up and awake and the room moon-cold, the shadows forming themselves into knives. the . . .* Any excitement I felt about getting a play produced in New York was nullified by paranoia that came with the play's subject.

I was also creatively confused. I had trouble squaring the emotional volatility of the play with the detached ironies of the avant-garde strategies in which I had been immersed. I was trying for something like Brecht's *verfremdungs-effeckt* without really knowing how. The result was a fugue of styles within a single text that only occasionally worked. I was also too dependent on the opinions of others, too unsure of myself to make the kind of strong choices needed to make the play cohere.

Nevertheless, with generous help, I was able to put together a cast and director and find a venue. I had an excellent director, John Pynchon Holmes, who had worked at the Manhattan Project with Andre Gregory, and some well-known actors—Gale Garnet, David Brisbin, and Aki Aleong. In April 1981, *Short Timers* was produced by Crystal Field and George Bartenieff at The Theater for the New City, which at that time was on Second Avenue across from St. Mark's church. It broke even and got mixed or bad reviews. Its emotional power was admired, but its structural inconsistencies and occasional bathetic language were noted. The pressure of the play's production, my paranoia, and erratic behavior, destroyed friendships and love relationships and finally wore me out. *Snake says, What did you expect, serenity?*

By that time I had given up drinking and had developed a valium habit. I became skillful at going to different doctors in order to get the drug prescribed as if for the first time. I thought I was recovering from alcoholism, but I was merely numb and crazy, alternately, and what passed for a self was a rigid mask cobbled together from clichés. I had yet to be naked with what I was hiding from. *Snake says, Get honest, even if it's late.* It had been a long time since I'd connected with anyone at a human level. Sex, as always, was the substitute for love. At least it made me feel whole for an hour or so after.

After my last lover kicked me out, I moved to Prospect Park with a friend. It seems ironic now that, even with a play produced, I was coming unglued. I was incapable of building on anything, of feeling a sense of accomplishment. It is no small matter to write a play and have it produced in New York City. I should have been able to feel proud of this, however imperfect an accomplishment.

But I was in trouble. I could no longer really take care of myself in the city.

I'M WORKING WITH George Bartenieff and Crystal Field's summer street theater, heading out to the projects and the boroughs to do political satire from a stage on the back of a flatbed truck. We arrive unannounced, set up big speakers, and pipe bass-heavy funk out into the echoing canyons of housing projects. The crowd begins to show. They look at us deadpan. We do broad satires of the Reagan administration. The plays are built from improvisations and held together by musical routines. I have created for myself an old cracker cockroach who has survived the nuclear holocaust, who carps about the state of the world, and who smokes a pipe.

The local residents continue to look at us deadpan. It doesn't matter who's president, they get fucked just the same. What are all these sweet-smelling white people doing up there preaching to us? Vote for what? The smell of marijuana begins to drift over the concrete basketball courts.

I'm coming home one night from rehearsal and stop to withdraw rent money for my landlady, who likes cash. I get off at Prospect Park and walk from the IND station down Flatbush to Lefferts and head home. In the middle of the next block there is a rustling sound and someone grabs me around the chest from behind. Somebody else places a knife at my throat: "Freeze mutherfucker. I'll cut your jugular vein." *Snake says, Believe it. Don't move. It's only money.*

I freeze. *Snake says, Don't say it. Don't tell him he means carotid artery, the sorry fuck.*

They push me down a driveway behind a house and go through my pockets and my backpack.

"How much money you got?"

"Two hundred dollars."

"Whoa, we doin' good tonight."

I see him out of the corner of my eye. I recognize him as somebody who panhandled me last week and to whom I gave some change. No good deed goes unpunished.

"Don't look at me," he says, the tip of the knife on the back of my neck. I turn away from him.

He hisses, "Climb that fence."

I'm standing in front of a six-foot fence with pickets on top. *Snake says, Don't think: do it.*

"Climb it, mutherfucker."

He gives me a quick jab with the knife tip, and suddenly I'm over the fence and standing by myself in the alley.

When the cops arrive at my apartment I tell them what happened.

One of them asks me if either of them were Panamanian.

"How do I tell?"

The cop shrugs.

I show the cops the palms of my hands, bruised from the pickets. I say, "White man's stigmata."

No response from cops.

Next day I am invited to the local precinct to look at a line of mugshots. I think I recognize the guy who panhandled me, but the detective shakes his head.

The detective says, "*You* don't have a record. I checked."

I ask him how hard it is to get a permit for a gun.

"Very tough," he says. Under the *very tough* is perhaps the subtitle *it takes money.*

I am walking down Lefferts Avenue on the way to the D train, and this black guy comes out of the house where I was mugged. He has my backpack. He hands it to me, says, "You get mugged?"

I say, yeah.

He says, "I'm sorry."

I thank him and move on. He doesn't say anything about it happening behind his house.

I am getting pissed. I am tapping into a great vat of pissed off energy that goes back some. I know the Jamaicans in the area are fond of machetes for protecting their houses. I consider it. *Snake says, Ain't no sentimental education here.*

THE CAST OF the street theater takes up a collection to replace my rent money, and we are back out in the projects trying to tell the locals how evil oil money is. We set up the speakers and turn on the funk, the bass rattling windows. Nobody dances.

I think about leaving New York.

Snake says, You got to get me out where I can roam. Discontent gonna overflow your ability to be civilized.

I GET MYSELF some jumbo blue Valiums and climb on a Greyhound for Tucson. The bus winds its way through places I'd never otherwise see. I sleep most of the way, drugged. About three o'clock one morning we stop somewhere in the Midwest and I get off the bus to eat. The bus stop restaurant is full of heavyset old ladies with aprons and big grins. They call me honey. They have a glass display case full of homemade pies, the kind where the fruit slices are huge and fresh off the tree, covered with sugar and cinnamon. I order some apple pie and a glass of milk. It seems the thing to do in such a place.

"Here y'are, honey."

I wash down a Valium with the rest of the milk.

Back on the bus there is a young blonde sylph with big blue eyes in the seat next to me. I go back to sleep. When a bump wakes me up, I realize my head has slid onto her shoulder. She is reading something. I lift my head and say, "Sorry."

She says, "That's okay," and smiles one of those smiles that is so sweet I want to kiss her on the mouth. She goes back to her reading.

Why don't I get off the bus with her? Why don't I marry and settle down, somewhere around here and live simply? Why does everything have to be a war? It occurred to me that there are people who are content to be who they are, to live in their own skins, and who never make demands on life. Maybe I've got it backward. What is the desire to accomplish something, to leave a mark, but the fear of emptiness?

Why not stop here, wherever we were, and have every man's dream? This woman with the gentle smile. Have children with her. Watch the days lengthen into mystery and silence in the stubble fields across the endless flatness of the land? *Snake says, I'll just hang out here in this blue baby blanket moment. Heh.*

I was disappointed when I looked down at her hand and saw either an engagement or wedding ring. What kind of married person would let my head rest on her shoulder and fear no complication? But she was not afraid of me. I felt that she knew me, or some part of me I kept hidden under the whirl of selves I picked from to dress for life. Maybe she had brothers, maybe she knew men. Maybe I was a better person than I thought.

I went back to sleep and my head slid back to her shoulder. When I woke up the bus was in Texas and she was gone. I wondered if I had imagined her out of my longing.

IT WAS ALWAYS good to return to Tucson, at least for the first few weeks, until I got into another jackpot. I was still alcohol abstinent but taking barbiturates. I enrolled in the master's program in the theater department at the University of Arizona, with a focus on playwriting. I did a lot of acting as well, and got involved in relationships with younger women that almost immediately blew up.

Snake says, Don't forget the karate.

I began studying karate at a Kenpo studio out on Speedway Boulevard. The sensei of the studio had been in the marine raiders in China during World War II. He described Kenpo as a collection of the world's nastiest dirty fighting woven into a science. The form was descended from Chinese kung fu, Okinawan karate, Mongolian wrestling, and other lethal forms. For someone with untreated post-traumatic stress disorder who had recently been mugged, this was heaven. I got into the best shape of my life, sparred, ran, broke fingers and toes and, after a year and a half, tore a hamstring so badly I had to quit.

After another bad relationship, I started drinking again. My work at the university began to suffer. I became scary or pathetic by turns and, by the time I'd written my thesis play—about two muggers in New York City—they were happy to see me go. I may have been the only student they ever had who used the word "mutherfucker" during my master's orals.

I RETURNED TO New York in 1983, hoping to continue writing for the theater, but I was not up to it. It took all my energy to stay housed and tolerably drunk. I got a job driving a yellow cab. If there is any job that will push you over the edge, it is cab driving in New York. *Snake says, Believe it. I sit just behind you where the guy who's got it in his mind to rob you will sit, the guy with the cold steel pressed behind your ear. Maybe he'll kill you, maybe he won't. Just like old times, hunh?* I stayed stoned during the daytime and drunk at night, after my shift.

I remember the day I quit. I picked up a woman on Lexington and Fiftieth who was in a hurry to get to the Port Authority. Her bus was in five minutes, she said. I told her I'd try, but I wasn't optimistic. I could tell she was in a snarly mood the minute she got in the cab. When we got caught in traffic in front of Grand Central, she began beating on the Plexiglas behind my head and shouting. I pulled to the curb, walked around, and opened the door. I said, "No charge. Get out."

I left her standing white-faced on the curb, drove the cab to the garage, and never went back.

I learned to use a word processor and began to temp for better money. I worked as a computer operator at Pfizer and was fired because I was making too many mistakes, was hungover at work, and was generally hard to deal with. Once I destroyed a disc pack with huge amounts of important data on it.

I moved in with a woman whom I'd known in Tucson. She had a condo on the West Side, and for a while we were snug, happy, and co-alcoholic.

I tried to quit drinking over and over again. I'd last a month. An alcoholic who tries to get sober without help is almost as bad as one who won't stop drinking. I would reach the condition of "stark raving sober" and become impossible to live with. After a week sober, I'd have so much energy I couldn't sleep, and so much anger that I'd attack inanimate objects like kitchen cabinet doors. I'd last almost a month, then I'd start going to the Korean grocery across the street to buy huge bunches of grapes. By the time I'd got to the Häagen-Dazs rum-raisin ice cream, I knew a drunk was coming. I tried quitting about three times this way, and my lover couldn't take it anymore. She said, "I don't know which is worse, you out of control, or in."

After two years, she had had enough of me. She was better at handling her booze, more emotionally equable, and I had become just plain mean and nasty.

ONCE, IN NEW YORK, at Seventy-second and Broadway, I kicked in a car window. I was trying to cross the street and a car turning right forced me back onto the curb. I shattered that window into little cubes. The driver gaped at me and kept going, probably to look for a cop. I ran into the subway to get away, got on the downtown local. Might as well go down to the Village for a while.

I sat down next to a Chinese man. The train had been held in the station.

A few minutes later a gristly plainclothes cop came steaming down the stairs and into the idle subway car. I thought, *This is it*. But it wasn't. He stopped in front of the Chinese man and said something to him. The Chinese man looked puzzled. The cop took out his badge and shoved it in his face. "You understand *this*, you chinee fuck?" Two black men on my left looked at each other and laughed. The cop pushed the Chinese man off the train, hand on his belt.

In August 1986, I said goodbye to my lover, packed a U-Haul and moved to Northampton, Massachusetts.

Four

19

THERE ARE A lot of stories being told here and I'm struggling to hear them. I hear, "cops." I hear, "pancreas," "locked ward,"
"vehicular manslaughter," but I only hear fragments. I don't know
why people are laughing, but I recognize the tone. It's the deep *haw*
laugh of those who've pushed things to the edge and looked over
it. I have boils on my forearms, my thighs, my cheeks, my eyelids.
They bleed. They are red lumps on otherwise very white skin. My
body's not used to being without alcohol and is punishing me,
squeezing the toxins out through my skin.

A guy in a pinstripe suit puts his hand on my shoulder, says to
me, "You might be better off in detox, take care of those runny
sores." He's looking at the one on my eyelid, which has nearly
closed the eye with swelling.

A voice of compassion, trying to suggest without judging.

"Detox is for winos," I say to the guy whose name I don't know.
"I'm not a wino."

He chuckles to himself, shakes his head, pats me on the back.
"Keep coming," he says.

I hear, "pray." I hear, "let go." But I can't hear very well because
my mind keeps slipping away, back to my searing obsessions. I hear,
"self-pity," I hear, "bullshit."

Then it's time to hold hands and pray, time to leave the church
basement. It was cool and dark in the basement. When I come outside, the sun blinds me. It's like coming out of any number of bars
on any number of bright afternoons. Only I'm walking straight.

I've been sitting in a room with ex-cons, lawyers, cops, college students from Smith, professors, radical feminists, reformed pimps. They are just like me, holding on by a frayed rope, walking a razor from the three AM waking terror to the time when, previously, I'd drink myself to sleep. Here are the tattooed and the tweedy. I don't know how I will spend the time between now and the next meeting.

At a meeting again I try to listen to people but my mind flies away, back to the string of broken relationships, or back to a child's corpse in Quang Nam Province in 1967. One day it is so bad that I'm sitting in a meeting, and I am so far outside myself I think *I've got to get to a meeting.* I'm sitting in a meeting longing for a meeting. That's crazy. I've got a college degree. I've survived a war. I'm disassociated?

Snake says, You sat on that stuff for all those years. You can't self-medicate anymore, so there it is, just like you left it: a cage full of fanged crazies. Ha! Now you can dance. I'll be watching, catch you when you fall.

I'm sitting with my friend David Bourbeau in Bart's. I've ordered a tuna-salad sandwich. I'm hungry. No booze, you get hungry. *If you want a drink, eat something with sugar,* somebody said. *It will take the edge off.* I can scarcely sit still. Twenty minutes after I order, the fey teenage waiter with a scraggly goatee, who does not make eye contact, returns to tell me that they don't have any tuna salad. I stare at him. *Snake says, Yo, somebody lit the fuse in your tailbone, and it fizzed straight up your spine.*

I say, "You tell me twenty minutes after you take my order you don't have what I ordered?"

The waiter stiffens at my tone.

"What kind of moron are you?" I say.

The waiter backs up a step.

David puts his hand on my arm. "Doug," he says. "Doug . . ."

I get up and stomp out. Hungry. Full of rage.

After a few minutes David follows me out of the restaurant. I haven't been in Northampton very long. I was in New York just over a year ago, and now I'm in a place that if you yell on the street, the police will notice you. In New York they wouldn't give a shit.

I think, *You used to be a nice person.*

My mind won't keep still; it keeps going places I don't want it to go.

David brings me back to the present. He says, "Hey man, you're not in New York anymore." He says, "Look, it's a great day."

I don't think it's a great day; there's a dark film over everything I see. But I need the film, its reflective surface: life is too bright, like an ice-cream headache; but now my mind is veering sideways, to years wasted, to death and mutilation, to a crushing shame. Back down there in the shit where I understand things.

Guy at a meeting says, "If you love God, you can become holy in ten years; if you hate him, you can do it in *two*." Honesty is a stinging black fly.

That night I try to read. I keep reading the same line over and over. I've always been able to go into a book to escape, but I can't now. I used to be able to flip a switch and go cold, but the switch is broken. I lie down and try to sleep. I couldn't sleep at all the previous night and, theoretically, I should be really tired. I should just fall out.

I worry about the court date I have. Drunk, tore the side off a car in a parking lot, don't remember doing it. I was arrested the following week.

I sob for a while and go to asleep. *Snake says, Puke it up, sweat it out. You've got a long walk in the desert ahead of you.*

But when I sleep all the controls break down. My mind goes where it wants to. Grief opens up the whole can of worms and you can't just pick which worm you want to deal with. No place to hide. I'm drifting and I dream of my last lover in that soft gold light I always imagine her in, that alcoholic special effect for romance; but it's realer than that. I wanted it to work with her. I wanted it to work so bad I had to have two or three shots of cognac before going over to her house.

And then the dream takes a sharp turn, as if she has opened the door on the locked room. There's the child again with the exposed intestines. Then I'm walking down a muddy village road in the rain. I am naked and I don't have a weapon. I am so afraid my body feels like a claw.

I'm sitting up with my heart pounding. There is blood on my pillow where a boil has drained. The clock reads two AM. This is the time to go to the fridge and get a beer. But there's no beer and it's too late to go to the 7-Eleven to buy it. Wait, aren't I trying to stay sober? Here is where I'm supposed to call my sponsor. Here is where I am supposed to pray instead of going to the fridge. I pray. What a strange, awkward thing it is to pray. "God," I say. How strange it is to say this. "Help me." That's simple. "God help me." That will do. That will have to do; I can't pay attention long enough for more than that. *Snake says, Did you forget me? Light me a candle, fool.* I try to sleep again, but I lie awake until it's time to go to the seven o'clock meeting where I'll sit and try to listen, my mind cutting me to pieces from the inside.

AFTER THE MEETING, I go to a bookstore in Amherst to buy something to read. I won't read it. It will be one of those books I've always wanted to read but can't concentrate long enough to get through. I can scarcely read the spines on the shelves. I walk back to my truck and reach for my keys. I've locked them inside. This small event is suddenly gigantic. I cock my arm to punch a hole in the driver's side window and catch myself at the last minute.

I'm parked on Pleasant Street across from the Amherst Police Department, so I walk into the station and up to the desk sergeant. I say, "Can you help me break into my truck?"

He puts on a cop face. He says, "Just what do you mean, 'Break into your truck'?"

I almost say it. I almost say *What the fuck other reason would I want help breaking into my truck than because I left my keys, you fucking sub-*

moron. But I don't. I'm practicing restraint. Besides, he's got a gun, and the police know who I am anyhow. *Snake says, Good boy.*

I try to keep a condescending tone out of my voice. "I locked my keys in my truck. I'm wondering if you have a slim jim so I can pop the lock up."

He looks at me a moment, deciding just how nuts I am. "We don't do that anymore. If we break something, we get sued."

I go back to the truck. The driver's side window is open a crack, but I can't reach in. I hear someone say, "You want some help?" I turn around and see a guy in brown polyester pants, a tropical print shirt, and badly scuffed wing tips. He's got yellow nicotine stains on his fingers.

I say, "You got a slim jim?"

"No, but I got a coat hanger." He walks back to his car and returns with a coat hanger, bending it out straight as he walks. He makes a loop on the end of the unfolded hanger wire and in seconds he's slipped it through the window and pulled the lock up.

"You're pretty good at this," I say.

"I oughta be. Used to steal cars."

"Coat hanger, too. You do abortions?"

He flinches. Then he laughs, like he suddenly doesn't know what to make of me. "That's sick," he says, grinning.

I thank him and shake hands. He walks away.

I'll see him that evening at a meeting. We nod at each other across the long table.

For a few minutes at least I've escaped the tyranny of my emotions. On the way back to Northampton on Route 9, I reenter Hell. I don't have any idea what happiness is. No, I don't have any idea what the absence of pain is. *Snake says, It may be shit, but it's your neighborhood. You can navigate without street signs.*

I'M AT A meeting on Ward Eight at the VA hospital. Most of the guys at the meeting are in-patient Vietnam vets with substance abuse and psychiatric issues. I'm talking about how bad it feels to remember the guys I couldn't do anything for, the guys who bled out on me.

A guy with very white hair and a southern accent says, "You were there so he wouldn't have to die alone." I'd never thought of it. Never thought that my presence would ever mean a damn thing to anyone, much less a dying marine. I started to cry.

I went home and sobbed for an hour and fell asleep. I woke at three AM wanting a beer, a shot and a beer, a quart of beer, a quart and a fifth. No place to get it at this hour. Besides, aren't I supposed to be sober?

Toward dawn, I go back to sleep. There's the child again, his parents unrolling him from the bamboo mat, the extruded intestines, the smell of the paddies. I jerk myself awake. It's past seven. I'm late for the meeting.

AFTERWARD I'M DRIVING, going somewhere, to the store—somewhere—but I can't remember now. I drive out Route 9 past Smith College. Then I turn around and go back through town, under the railroad tracks, toward Hadley. I'm driving to be driving because it won't feel any better if I stop. It's the four-wheeled version of pacing.

I turn off on a side road in Hadley and drive past the farms. The fan belt breaks and flops around under the hood. I stop the truck, leave the engine running, and raise the hood. I can drive a little while without a fan belt. I reach in to pull a frayed piece of belt loose from where it's wedged in near the crankshaft seal and the fan. I misjudge the distance and a blade whacks my hand. I pull my hand back and one of my fingers is broken, stuck out sideways at a ninety-degree angle. "Fuck!" I shout. "Fuck!" I get in the truck, turn around and head back to Cooley Dickenson Hospital.

I don't have insurance. I sit for four hours. People try to not look at my L-shaped finger. I don't know which is worse, the shit in my head or my finger. When finally I'm seen I walk back through the

ER and get my finger set, get a scrip for Percocet. I tell the doctor I can't have the Percocet because I'm a recovering drunk and addict. *What a good boy you are, says Snake.* The doctor tears it up and writes me one for naproxen.

I pick up my scrip and take several naproxen, hoping they'll make me drowsy. They don't. I'm up all night. Ah, the luminous glow of Snakebrain. Any little thing can set it off. It makes everything bright; I miss nothing.

At the meeting the next night I can scarcely stay awake. Somebody says, "Missing a night's sleep never killed anybody." I'm nodding. I put my head down on the formica table. I sleep through the meeting and am awakened by chairs scraping the floor.

The day outside is bright as a toothache.

THE DREAM RECURS.

I am naked. The wind whips the rain and it stings my skin. My legs are calf-deep in mud. I am walking through the village alone. There is no one, but I know that in the brush at the side of the road, and in the tree lines set back from the road, there are eyes among the thick, rain-whipped leaves. They follow my every move. The rain is so thick it cannot be distinguished from the rest of the gunmetal day and there is no horizon, only hanging curtains of water.

20

I BEGIN WRITING again. I join one of Pat Schneider's writing workshops in Amherst, which turns out to be exactly the right thing. We write from prompts and share the results immediately. No negative critique follows and the focus is on "what stays with you." A lot of what I hear stays with me. The group encourages me to be honest, to write without stopping to edit myself.

I find out about a poetry workshop at the home of Jim and Susan Finnegan. When I join the group, I meet Jack Gilbert, Linda Gregg, Robert Hill Long, Margaret Lloyd, and Jim Anderson. They are formidable, committed poets. Jack Gilbert is the de facto group leader and the others instinctively defer to him. The poems he is bringing into the group will become *The Great Fires*. He describes them as meditations. He alludes to the particular process of these poems as "carving with an axe." He is at the top of his form and writing the best poems of his life. I learn from observing his craft. I absorb the physicality of the poems, the incandescent images. The way I describe to myself Jack's revision process is *dropping the poems into an acid bath, and when they are plucked out they are free of everything but the poetry.*

The first thing I bring in is a fourteen-page poem, a kind of mini-*Iliad* about Vietnam. Jack encourages me to break the poem down into the incidents that form the narrative. These poems will become my first chapbook, *Bamboo Bridge*, and, finally, my first full-length book, *The Moon Reflected Fire*. The workshop is known as Group Eighteen, because it meets at 18 Perkins Street. The feedback is fierce, and not everybody is able to stand it. Some leave. I hang in there. I start publishing. I read my poems in the group and my hands shake.

INFANTRY ASSAULT
The way he made that corpse dance
by emptying one magazine after another into it
and the way the corpse's face began to peel off
like a mask because the skull had been shattered, brains
spilled out, but he couldn't stop killing that corpse . . .

These poems are written quickly and scoop up with them two or three incidents, melding them together in a synesthetic pectin, the way poems do. I'm not even thinking; the poem seemed to be written by my body without my permission. All I had to do was provide the lens that would find the memory. In addition to the original fourteen, other poems come from this same high-pressure zone.

I have a memory of how swollen my lips would get from mosquito bites. I write from this body image and get a poem.

We are still, lips swollen with mosquito bites.
A tree line opens out onto paddies
quartered by dikes, a moon in each . . .

An academic in California will one day ask me if the swollen lips were a symbol of "the wounded healer." I told him, "No, the swollen lips were from mosquito bites." He was well-intentioned, certainly, and he may have been right about the unconscious level of the poem, but the poem was written from a specific body image. I received a lot of encouragement from the group for following my instincts, especially from Jack, who believed that the clear apprehension of real things was the point in poetry. I would read somewhere in Ezra Pound's letters that the best metaphors were also real things.

Later, I will add a poem about Goya's *Los Desastres de la Guerre*. I will people *The Iliad* with my own grunts:

A BAR IN ARGOS
They'll tell you it was a wooden horse;
I'll tell you it was not.
We gutted twenty oxen,
and slid inside their empty bellies,
but for our short swords, naked . . .

The poem is a conflation of an actual special forces operation and the story of the Trojan horse. In Vietnam, a group of special operators had hid inside the gutted bellies of water buffalo and waited in ambush.

I had taught *The Iliad* that year and discovered that apart from the hunchback Thersites, no one doubted or faltered in their warrior ethic. I thought that the average Greek foot soldier, unlike his princely commanders, might not be as in love with the war, which began over a stolen wife and lasted more than ten years, and was likely to have a few unprincely comments to make about war in general. And then there were many passages in *The Iliad* that closed with "the circling dogs" knowing, beneath the bravado, that death waited. I gave these grunts a voice. This, of course, was the view of a Vietnam veteran. In the following excerpt, I contrast the hero's homecoming with that of the common grunt.

on the gull-spattered cliffs above the sea
he waits at the door of his stone hut
for his wife to recognize him,
Not as Penelope knew Odysseus disguised
but as a woman who sees a husband, only older,
something unnamable gone out of him.

The veterans returning from the Vietnam War came home sometimes to hostility, but mostly to indifference or a vague curiosity that stopped just short of a real question. Those who most fervently supported the war were the chief offenders. They simply did not want to be reminded of the consequences of their actions. The vets' lives were frequently wrecked by the war; they had difficulties with their marriages, their girlfriends. The pyscho vet became so mythologized that every time a television drama needed a crazy they'd make him a Vietnam vet. He was a loser, probably a junkie, a remnant of a lost war. He lived in the woods and talked to himself and grew hairy and smelly. These were the stereotypes. No World War II victory parades, no welcoming our boys home, except by the immediate family, and sometimes not even them.

The Odyssey becomes the archetype here. It took Odysseus ten years to get home from the war. On the way back he encountered every kind of horror. With Vietnam vets, the Cyclops and Circe were inside their heads. Circe is like heroin and the Cyclops the huge eye of scorn. In a slightly different way, the psychiatrist Jonathan Shay, in his books *Achilles* and *Odysseus in America*, has worked Homer for a convincing thaumaturgy. He argues in *Achilles* that the most deeply traumatized vets were the ones who had acted against their own gut morality in Vietnam, either because they were following orders or because they were in a situation in which conventional morality collides with survival.

I wanted to speak for vets and also for the Vietnamese in these poems, although at the time I wrote them I most likely would not have been able to articulate it. Time is a great editor.

An image that still haunts me found its way into "Xin Loi":

The man and woman, Vietnamese,
come up the hill,
carry something slung between them on a bamboo mat,
unroll it at my feet:
The child, iron gray, long dead,
flies have made him home . . .

My sanity seems to be growing in relation to my writing. *Snake says, Unhunh, you're makin' me happy bro, makin' me want to dance.*

And some of the music came back in the poems. Playing jazz had been good training for a form that depends on the ability to make the same kind of surprising artistic choices that good jazz musicians make when they improvise.

The prerequisite to healing is to tell the truth. No way around it. Place realities into words and put them outside the body a little more each time. The poems I wrote then seemed to come from just-opened veins.

21

IN JANUARY 2000, I sat in the Cathay Pacific departure lounge at Los Angeles International Airport, waiting with about thirty Vietnamese for a flight to Vietnam, smelling the pungent *nuoc mam* from their bon voyage dinners. *Snake opens one eye.* I felt the undertow of something pulling me out past the familiar markers. The waiting Vietnamese seemed happy, animated, some a little drunk. They were going home, but not for good. They were exiles, "boat people," or people who had left during the war for business, to go to college, and found themselves caught outside the country in April 1975, when the Communists took over. Since 1994, when President Clinton lifted the embargo, Vietnamese had begun to trickle back to find family, friends, lovers, to find out who was still alive, who had been interned in "re-education" camps, and to find out if Vietnam was still home. These Vietnamese were now referred to as *Viet Kieu,* the Vietnamese community in exile. Most were people who had been run over by history. The wealthy among them were able to escape easily in or before 1975, their destinations softened by foreign friends and offshore bank accounts.

The Vietnamese waiting with me were not wealthy. Some of them had carry-on luggage that was tied together with heavy twine. Like Vietnamese everywhere, they were warm and open and full of humor. Here were very old men and women, and here also were bright-eyed grandchildren who knew Vietnam only as a mythic homeland.

The Vietnamese I was on my way to spend two weeks with were my former enemies. The last time I'd been with them they were trying to kill me. Now I was reading their books, and they mine. We were reaching out to each other across vast historical improbabilities. If during the war someone had suggested that I would be making this trip someday, I would have laughed in his face.

The flight to Hong Kong was sixteen hours. I had come prepared with sleeping pills, books, and a journal to write in. I did not, however, read or write on the trip over and slept fitfully. Time zones blurred. The seats were too small. The Taiwanese businessman next to me had dressed for comfort in a pair of silk jogging shorts and tropical print shirt. He was sporting a Rolex watch and Dior sunglasses. He tried to talk to me about golf, but soon became discouraged at my indifference and began talking in Chinese to the woman on his other side.

I was continually distracted by the flight attendants, all women: Vietnamese, Chinese, Filipina, Thai, Indian, Malaysian, all handpicked, I imagined, by some white-haired mandarin pointing one long pinky nail into the multitude of peasant Cinderellas and saying, *Her, her, and yes, that one.* Their presence was about beauty and grace. Their uniforms were hybrids of the *xuan xam,* the *ao dai,* the kimono, the sari, unified by something from *Star Trek,* dress which required a certain carriage, a certain length of stride, an obligatory femininity. They were warm, courteous, multilingual, and a little cautious.

In my nodding in and out of time and sleep I remembered a girl in third grade I had a crush on. She was a good reader, and therefore had been enlisted by the teacher to help others. I would call her over to my desk and ask her to help me spell words I already knew, just to feel her hair brush up against me, to smell the soap she'd bathed with, until, one day she said, "You already know these words," lifted her chin, and stalked off. I restrained myself from pushing the flight attendant button to ask for more magazines, more tea, to ask about our arrival time in Hong Kong (which I already knew), to ask her where she was born, or what her deepest longings were. These women became part of a dream fugue that enveloped me in my intermittent naps, waking me into yet another dream, one who came with orange juice and a muffin, or my favorite—the one who covered me with the blanket that had fallen to my feet.

I met the rest of the delegation in the departure lounge at the Hong Kong airport. They had come from Boston and I from Los Angeles, so they'd had eight more hours in the air. Of the veterans in the group, all had made a return trip to Vietnam but me, some several times, and some even before the embargo had been lifted. When we boarded the plane for Hanoi, I sat next to the poet Bruce Weigl and his adopted Vietnamese daughter, Hanh, who was on her way back to meet her mother after fourteen years' separation.

On the last leg of the trip I had trouble staying in my seat. *Snake says, Unhunh, dig it.* The cabin was chilled with air-conditioning, but I was covered with sweat. The familiar unfamiliar was crawling up into my heart. I looked over at Weigl, who was grinning at me. "You'll be fine," he said.

The only Americans who had been in Hanoi during the war were POWs and Jane Fonda. During the war, Hanoi was "the north," a place we bombed, a place we hoped to invade and sub-due to release our POWs, but we never got there. And even now I expected to see a city reduced to rubble and hostile young men with AK47s coming for me. As the plane rolled to stop at Noi Bai Airport and I looked out through the window at the low, French-built stucco buildings, the red dirt surrounding the airstrip, I felt Snake fill my spine. *We're here, he says. Stay cool. I've got you covered.*

When the door swung open and I smelled the funk of the rice paddies mixed with city smells of oil and motorbike exhaust, I felt strangely like I'd come home, although it had never been my home; rather, I had come home to a part of myself that was full of a longing without a name. Inside we waited in line to be pro-cessed by customs officers who, in their green uniforms with red epaulets, reminded me of the stern young men in the newsreels I'd seen escorting American POWs through the streets. The officer who took my passport was as young as some of my students—and had certainly been born after the war. He held the passport up to my face, looked at the picture, then me, then the picture, and then just me for an interminable ten seconds. He disappeared below his window where I imagined him checking a special list, then rose and nodded for me to step through.

At the baggage claim, only one of my bags came through. Weigl assured me that someone always loses a bag between Hong Kong and Hanoi. It had happened to Yusef Komunyakaa the year before. One bag had my clothes, the other books and broadsides of my poems, gifts for my Vietnamese friends. The one with my clothes was missing. I had brought a pack with my two cameras and thirty-six rolls of film with me on the plane. I slipped the bag off my shoulders and got into an air-conditioned van. When I dropped my pack, the body memory hit me hard.

Snake says, Good thing you stopped drinking. But from the moment I climbed in the van I felt as good as I'd felt in years. *Snake says, Solid.*

22

DUAT WAS MOVIE-STAR handsome; my age, or older, dyed hair. The most famous poet of the war years, he had a profile and a nose that made me wonder if way back some gringo hadn't slipped into the gene pool. Tapes and CDs of his poems, sung in his fine tenor, were played in restaurants throughout Hanoi. Tonight he was dressed in a white jacket and tie. Hoa, poet and translator, was short, busty, and, as I would discover over the next two weeks, brilliant. She spoke English, German, and Russian and was in the process of translating Vietnamese poetry into English. Both poets were members of the Vietnam Writers Association.

We drove through the fields on the northern edge of Hanoi. An old French tank sat rusting in a rice paddy, its engines silent since 1954, when the French were defeated at Dien Bien Phu and nearly all of the French Foreign Legion in-country were killed or taken prisoner. We passed the remains of one of the turreted, triangular concrete forts the French had built all over Vietnam, remnants of a feudal Europe. Signs of the foreign regimes involved in Vietnam's wars were still present. Aging Russian trucks rumbled through the sea of motorbikes. Farther out in the countryside shells of American helicopters or amtracs, stripped of recyclables, lay rusting in the fields. The tunnel complexes dug by the Japanese during World War II, extended and renovated by the Vietnamese during the American War, had gradually filled with water and snakes.

The Vietnamese are *bricoleurs*. They do not reject on principle anything inherited from a colonialist regime, but weave it into their history in a way that is difficult for non-Vietnamese to understand.

The poet Vo Que told me, with neither shame nor pride, "The French taught us how to grow cotton." His tone was subtle, factual. It said to me, *What life has handed us is hard. We use what is at hand. There is no shame in this.* Chung pointed out to me during the trip south that an engine salvaged from the wreck of a Russian truck was now running an irrigation pump for a system of rice paddies.

We were taken to a pension in the center of Hanoi. Weigl had told me that Hanoi was a big village. It was true. The stores, the streets, are animated by people who seem to have none of what Americans would know as big city chilliness. They all seem to know each other. If someone's child gets lost at play and wanders three streets off, she will be passed from family to family until she is deposited in her mother's arms again, much in the same way it would be done in a mountain village. The Hanoians had to pull together to survive the continuous bombing. The bond still holds. They were relatively prosperous compared to the people in the central provinces. Lady Borton, the director of the American Friends Service Committee in Hanoi, said to me one summer in Boston, "They are bingeing." Vietnam has been a unified country only since April 1975, and they are still celebrating.

It is important to remember that they were under the heel of the Chinese for two thousand years, until they threw them out. Then there were the Japanese, until they surrendered, then the French, until they threw them out. Americans were merely the last.

Hanoians were not rich, or even comfortable by American standards, but they were joyously full of their new lives. There were more beautiful women in Hanoi than I have seen in one place in a long time. I said to Weigl in the van, "How could we bomb these people?" Charlie Desmond overheard me and said, "It was a war." And so it was. But still. And *cafe sua*; how could we bomb anyone who knew how to make Vietnamese coffee? I tried to make it in my own kitchen for months after I returned and failed every time.

We had the rest of the day to wander through the streets. The motorbikes moved like schools of fish that changed direction instantly and gracefully. Crossing the street in Hanoi required you to walk calmly through the shoals of motorbikes at a predictable pace so that the bikers would know how to accommodate you. If you stopped or sped up you caused a snarl. If you were calm and predictable, the bikes opened to admit you and closed behind you as you crossed. Horns blared constantly. It was not the horn language I was used to from city driving. Having once been a New York cabbie, I remember our horns as long blasts of rage and retribution. Here the horns were short taps and bleats, merely signal systems that said, "coming up the left now," or "don't turn in front of me."

The pollution was fierce and unregulated and many bikers, particularly the women and their children, wore kerchiefs or masks. The women wore long gloves to keep the sun off their arms so that they would not look like women who worked in the rice paddies.

There were no regulations to determine how many people could ride on a motorbike, and I have seen five: a beautiful mother (or older sister), one teenage boy, and three small children, hanging on, squinting against the wind. There was a box in the basket, which I imagined might contain a sixth child. One American friend who had lived and worked in Hanoi for a year claimed to have seen six on a motorbike. There were occasional accidents; I saw one. Two bikes collided and a woman was hurt. There were no ambulances or police. A young man stepped into the street and helped the woman up. The traffic around her stopped, and people gazed at her with quiet respect. The man who helped her righted her motorbike and she sat down on it. She was in pain with her eyes closed, but she did not cry out. She was aware of the public place she was in. She was graceful in her pain and sat for quite some time, the crowd watching quietly. Finally, she nodded and thanked the young man and started her bike. I don't know how badly she was hurt, but I suspect that she had broken something. I imagined her taking herself to the hospital, where she would wait a long time to be seen. I imagined her sitting quietly with her pain.

I walked alone around the lake in the center of Hanoi. Vietnamese were not camera-shy. They had not yet been conditioned to pose when they saw a camera, or to fear it as a personal invasion. Occasionally people from outlying villages did not wish to be photographed, for religious or superstitious reasons. They waved their hands or shook their heads, and I let them be. But most Vietnamese would look directly into the lens with fearless curiosity. This candor made me like them immensely. The camera was frequently a pretext for conversation. *Where are you from? How do you like Hanoi?* Some wanted to have their picture taken with me, and I would hand my camera to one of their friends and put my arm around their shoulders. It warms me to look at my collection of photographs with cab drivers, students, and children selling postcards. A young girl gave me the peace sign when I photographed her. It might have meant victory, but her smile was kind and the war remote.

Toward evening three young men approached me and asked me to have tea with them. We went to a three-story coffee shop on a back street that I would have missed without their help. They spoke slow and proper English and were intent on practicing. Typically, and I would find this especially so with the young Vietnamese, they were not terribly interested in the war and were very much rooted in the present. One of them, a skinny kid from Hanoi University was very shy and took a while to compose his first question in English.

He said, "What do you think of Madeleine Albright?" I had to think for a minute, and then realized I'd never had a single thought about her. This compelled me to explain my personal politics. I went on to say that I was sorry there had been a war. The young men looked at each other the way young people look at each other when their parents are getting ready to bore them.

Pham, the most talkative and the de facto group spokesman, sighed and asked me, "Were you a pilot?" I thought of the Hanoi Hilton, where captured American pilots were held during the war. I told them no, I had been a medic, a *bacsi,* with an infantry unit down south. This led to a conversation in which I felt compelled to say that I thought the war had been wrong. They were getting impatient with me. The war was over before they were born. They were not interested in the war. They wanted to talk about MTV.

Pham asked, "Do you know personally any rock stars?" I answered that I had gone to high school with Linda Ronstadt. They had never heard of Linda Ronstadt. I felt old. They knew the Beatles, but I had never met one.

Pham pointed to my top pocket. "May I have please your pen?"

I thought at first that he wanted to write something with it, but when I handed it to him he put it in his top pocket and smiled at me.

I bought them another round of tea. We exchanged addresses, and I walked back into the streets of Hanoi. It was getting dark, and the motorbike traffic had increased. Was it the weekend? I'd forgotten what day it was. The young people on their bikes were now immaculately dressed—the women in their *ao dai*s and the men in jackets, some in ties. They were, in a word, beautiful. I felt good. I felt the war go away. I felt alive.

That night we had dinner with Duat. He arrived on a motorbike in his white jacket. As we entered the restaurant, the maître d' ejected the tape that was playing and inserted one of Duat singing his poems. The opening poem was accompanied by martial music, appropriate to his military career, but somewhat reductive of his fine poetry. He is an extraordinary poet, and his poems will last longer than their political context. He speaks of the jungle he spent ten years in.

Here the tomato is a small lantern
to warm the long winter night,

the pepper, the flame of an oil lamp,
so hot it will burn your tongue.
Our land, so filled with life,
one branch might light a field.
But men travel across oceans,
their planes swarm through the night fog,
loom out of the darkness
like fireflies over fresh dug graves.

Duat poured the wine, and when I refused a glass, he stared at me and uttered in a long, descending glissando, *"hmmmmm."* This was the first of many occasions in which I experienced the awkwardness of refusing a drink, as I have done for many years.

The poet Nguyen Ba Chung translated bits and pieces as we listened. Kevin Bowen leaned over and told me about Duat's long years in an NVA unit on the Ho Chi Minh Trail. The Vietnamese losses greatly exceeded ours during the war, and body count had been the means of keeping score, we most certainly would have been the winners, but that was never the point. I remembered reading once that an American general visiting Vietnam years after the war said to his Communist counterpart, "You know, militarily, we beat you." The Vietnamese general responded, "That may be true, and it is also irrelevant." In those two lines are the Vietnamese secret of victory: their willingness to expend large numbers of lives was equal to their commitment to reunite their country. Our willingness to withdraw with fewer losses was a measure of the political fogginess of our goals, from beginning to end.

But the price paid was staggering. Three million Vietnamese, military *and* civilian, died during the war. I don't know the statistics on Vietnamese wounded, but the number of wounded is often triple the number of dead. Four hundred thousand are still missing in the North alone. When I think now of the black POW flags I've seen flying from police and fire stations mourning the two thousand missing Americans, a number that is much smaller compared to other wars, especially in a jungle war where the retrieval of bodies was more difficult, I wonder what the POW issue is really about. I don't believe that Communist Vietnam held back some POWs for political reasons, or for perverse "Oriental" reasons. I think simply that they are dead, and that keeping hope alive for their families is perverse.

What I was to learn on this trip about the suffering of the Vietnamese during the war would make me silent for a long time. The Vietnamese are modest when asked about the war. Several, when I asked them what the war was like, answered, "It wasn't so bad." The understatement was stunning.

We parted with Duat when it was still light, watched him, reeling a little from the whiskey, start his motorbike and ride away, gaining balance as he went.

As we walked slowly through the streets I was once more struck by the demeanor of the women. During the war, while the men were away, the women became the doctors, teachers, shopkeepers, and administrators of the country. The confidence gained from those years still shows in their faces. Women in peasant pants and shirts, carrying baskets of produce to sell on the street, crossed paths with professional women in suits and sunglasses riding on motorbikes. When they met in the streets they seemed always to cross at an angle, as if gliding through some obliqueness of time in which the historical distance between them suddenly increased. I saw in them the gap of a thousand years.

Hanoi was a big village and the streets were neighborhoods. There were still remnants of this kind of life in the East Village of New York, or in the barrios of the southwest, but the sight of people congregating in the cool of the evening to gossip and drink tea while their children played on the sidewalk, or in the streets near the curb, has all but vanished from American culture, where even suburban families seldom talk to one another. I can't help but feel that we have lost something valuable, and that the Vietnamese, perhaps because of what they have endured, have it in great supply.

Lady Borton describes the Vietnamese as a *we* culture. The actions of one person affect the whole in ways that Americans, with their cherished tradition of individuality, cannot understand.

The next day was sweltering. We were scheduled to give lectures at the Vietnam Writers Association. I had heard that Vietnamese academics and writers were more formal than Americans. I had written a lecture on the populist poetry movement in America, the poetry slams and the culture that had grown up with them, its purported causes, and its relation to mainstream poetry. Within two pages, everyone in the room was fanning themselves, clearly bored, the translators droning on as I spoke. I put away the paper and summarized the lecture. The rest of the delegation gave their presentations, and finally the Vietnamese poet Nguyen Duc Mau, as if in response to our long-windedness, spoke one line that distilled the subject into a phrase. He said, "Life is the rice, poetry is the liquor." Afterward we filed out to be interviewed by Hanoi radio and television reporters.

There was more blessed, unstructured time wandering the streets of Hanoi, buying bright green oranges that were gold inside, or Vietnamese grapefruit, huge and sweet, called *bui*. I could not get enough *cafe sua*.

I had gone as far as to ask someone how much it would cost to rent an apartment in downtown Hanoi. I was told it would be expensive, maybe a thousand dollars a month, US. But one could build a house out in the rural areas for four hundred dollars. There was no land to buy, because under socialism there was no private real estate. I thought it might be where I would like to end up as an old man, in a culture that respected age, just outside of Hanoi, perhaps within cycling distance.

All the bomb damage from the war had been repaired long ago, and the city seemed downright sexy in its hopefulness. Just beyond the water-puppet theater near the lake I saw a wedding party with young men in suits carrying huge, covered silver trays, and then the bride and groom emerged from a door, delectable and grinning.

It was the end of January, the beginning of Tet, the Vietnamese new year, a propitious time for new undertakings. There would be many marriages. The photographers arrived and I shot the scene from the outer circle, beyond them, so that I got the photographers photographing. The camera has become for me a way of slowing down time in order to see what is present. So much of my life is a blur. The war years are veiled in fear and confusion. Just as poetry stops time and allows images of a moment to unfold, so does the camera. I am not describing the tourist's method, by which one imposes upon the subject the idea one had of it in advance merely to confirm one's worldview. I use the camera to help me see what I do not see. Subjects on which I often turn a critical eye are benevolently transformed through the lens. Details I missed in the original composition surprise me in the print. The lens is a metaphor for a spaciousness of mind that lets the world in, unmediated. Of course a lens is not completely neutral—the photographer chooses the subject and the composition—but it is more neutral than the mind, which always imposes something. A lens is an opening, the film a tabula rasa.

I look at the photographs I brought back from the trip now and wish I had images from the war years. Not the standard shots of guys leaning up against sandbags, smoking or posturing, but images of the events themselves, to check against my memory, which is always revising itself, often skewing things in the direction of comfort or too-succinct formulations. But not even the most courageous of the great combat photographers can see what the unmediated mind sees. In *Snakebrain*, all is luminous and indelible. If I could attach a lens to that part of my mind . . .

That night we ate dinner in a Chinese restaurant with Hu'u Thinh, former tank commander, now poet, novelist, and president of the Vietnam Writers Association. The Vietnamese are great toasters, and Hu'u Thinh had many for us. "We soldiers understand each other," he said to me when he shook my hand. He was not talking about male bonding, or the insular world created by soldiers after the war. He was talking about facts that are so dark or poignant as to make fashionable concepts silly.

The next morning we visited the outlying village of Dong Ho. I saw a Vietnamese market that brought the war back to me. The new items in the market were plastic washtubs. Everything else was the same: the handmade brooms, the baskets, the fish traps. Among the crowd were several young men wearing the green pith helmets the NVA used to wear. *Snake says, Army surplus. Don't freak.*

On the other side of the Yellow River, at the entrance to another village, was a ramada of bamboo and grass beneath which was an old pool table on a dirt floor. Young men were playing pool and swaggering a little. They were wearing long-sleeved white or striped Western shirts, untucked at the waist, and Levis or chinos. One had a long silver chain hanging between his wallet and his front pocket. They were the age of the young men we'd killed and had been killed by in the war, tough farm kids with incredible endurance who could run their bodies on a handful of rice a day, or a piece of sugar cane, or a small fish scooped from a stream. There is nothing extra on Vietnamese bodies, at least in the rural areas. The heat and the lack of Western excesses have kept them trim.

After a week we reluctantly said goodbye to Hanoi and flew to Phu Bai. The airport, a one-story stucco building, looked like a set that Humphrey Bogart would frequent. But for the others the associations were not cinematic. They had all been in the First Air Cav there, and seen heavy fighting against large NVA units. We drove through Phu Bai and the outer villages to Hue, and on the way tried unsuccessfully to find their old army base camp. No Vietnamese seemed to remember, or care, where it had been. The war was over for them, even if it is not for us.

23

DURING THE FAMOUS Tet Offensive of 1968, Communist forces penetrated every major city in Vietnam. They overran small military posts at the outskirts and fought small guerilla actions inside the cities, taking over radio stations and public offices, and penetrating even into the American embassy compound in Saigon. They knew they did not have to hold those positions to achieve their goals, and quickly faded back into the countryside. They suffered staggering losses, but they'd proven to the world that they were still powerful in spite of the propaganda spun by the US government to maintain the illusion of imminent American victory.

The Communists had learned how to fight the political war, and knew the power of symbolic actions and their effects upon an international media that was after many years turning against the war. In early 1968, the North Vietnamese overran the ancient imperial city of Hue and held it for two weeks against a powerful combined American and South Vietnamese counterattack. The two sides fought street by street and, finally, American marines drove the retreating NVA back into the citadel at the center of Hue, a monument of two thousand years of brutal Chinese rule, and the later colonialist regime of Bao Dai, the last emperor.

For the Communists, the citadel was a symbol of everything that was wrong with Vietnam, a reminder that the Chinese, Dutch, Japanese, French, and, finally, the Americans had kept the Vietnamese in a subservient posture, divided against themselves by class and ethnicity. The French war resulted in the partitioning of north and south at the thirty-eighth parallel during the Geneva accords. But this wasn't the same thing as the division along the seventeenth parallel at the end of the Korean War. Partitioning was nothing new to the Vietnamese. The Chinese and French had divided Vietnam into three regions according to the predominance of three ethnic groups. The northernmost region was called Tonkin, after the Tonkinese; the central Annam, after the Annamese; and the southern third, which included Saigon, Cochin China, after the remaining Chinese populations. There are also large numbers of Khmer in the south.

Tet of 1968 was a major shock to the Americans. Whoever was alive then cannot forget the famous newsreel footage of General Westmoreland being interviewed in downtown Saigon, telling the listeners that the city was under control, while simultaneously flinching at the sniper fire that was coming just a little too close. This footage made it into the film *Hearts and Minds*.

Meanwhile, in Hue, the citadel had begun to shimmer with ironies. The Communists knew that if the Americans called in air strikes the citadel would be destroyed, bringing the world's condemnation. All that dynastic architecture, sculpture, art—how could they? Of course, the Communists would have been delighted to see the cultural symbol in ruins, thus achieving the twofold victory of weakening the American position internationally, and destroying a classical symbol of foreign oppression. But the citadel survived and has come back to haunt the Vietnamese. It is now a major attraction. Only a few bullet holes remain unspackled, and tourists from all over the world come to Hue to spend money.

A sign in the center of Hue reads DMZ TOURS. A Vietnamese travel agency offers van trips to the former US bases at Khe Sanh—The Rockpile, Hill 881, Con Thien—and the old special forces camp at Lang Vei, site of a famous Alamo-style holdout of Americans against superior NVA forces. If these bases offer nostalgia to American veterans, they offer further ironies for the Vietnamese. Khe Sanh, in particular, is symbolic of American disaster and delusion in Vietnam. Through the early seventies, the Americans maintained the base at Khe Sanh to try to lure the North Vietnamese into a Dien Bien Phu–style seige, with the difference that the Americans would win this time by vaporizing the assaulting forces with two-thousand-pound bombs. The Vietnamese generals knew the Americans were thinking this and only appeared to take the bait, moving several divisions of crack troops into the surrounding area. The assault on Khe Sanh was a magnificent diversion from the troop build-up around the major southern cities in preparation for the big push that would end the war in 1975. Diversion or not, the fighting around Khe Sanh was bloody and costly for both sides, particularly the Vietnamese, who were willing to sacrifice large numbers of troops to preserve the grand illusion.

The novelist Bao Ninh, author of *The Sorrow of War,* was one of ten survivors of an entire division chopped to bits by the American B52s. The poet Nguyen Duc Mau's job at Khe Sanh was to assemble enough pieces of his comrades' bodies to approximate a burial. Neither has recovered from the experience. They are men of enormous talent, sharp wit, and deep sadness.

When American vets meet with their former enemies, the sadness pools between them and collects in the shadows around them. Politics go away. There is only one body of grief. Americans lost about fifty-nine thousand killed, more than three hundred thousand wounded, and it is estimated that another sixty thousand died of their wounds, or of the psychological damage they medicated with alcohol and street drugs. The Vietnamese lost three million killed, two-thirds of whom were civilians. Four hundred thousand are still missing in the north alone. They have no veterans administration and the families are supposed to take care of the maimed and maddened.

Today we find each other in our writing. Our host in Hue is Vo Que. He is a handsome, almost Latin-looking Vietnamese with a beautiful singing voice. Wounded by an American rocket during the siege of Hue, he was nearly disemboweled and spent a horrible week in a tunnel complex beneath the city while NVA medics

struggled to keep him alive. One night he took us out on the Per-
fume River on a small boat, cut the engines, and let the boat drift
as he sang to us, accompanied by traditional Vietnamese musicians.
Kevin Bowen's poem, "River Music," recounts the many trips on
the river with Vo Que.

> *One by one the lanterns*
> *swim off down river.*
> *A green one first, then red*
> *and yellow. Each one calls*
> *back a friend. Like dancers,*
> *they turn in circles.*

Among the vets, there are as many different opinions about
the war as there are vets, but a significant number of them have
been drawn back to Vietnam. Their actions are historically unprec-
edented. Why would veterans of a horrible lost war befriend their
former enemies? During the postwar US embargo of Vietnam—
another mindless and vindictive act against a devastated country—
some vets began to return to Vietnam with pockets full of medical
supplies that were otherwise unobtainable, since the Russian infra-
structure had begun to fail and slide toward glasnost. Anguished by
reports of Vietnamese still stepping on American mines, an army
engineering battalion returned with their charts and removed
them.

Some Americans were outraged at these vets, but for many the
war was already becoming historically remote. Who were these
vets? Certainly they were as strange to the conventional mind as
the scraggly and often homeless vets who had disappeared to live
in the woods after they had returned to "the world" and found
contempt and rejection. On this trip I was in the company of
Kevin Bowen, a poet and director of the William Joiner Center for
the Study of War and Its Social Consequences at the University of
Massachusetts, Boston. Bob Glassman is the president of a bank,

Charlie Desmond the vice chancellor of UMass Boston, and Bruce Weigl is a prolific and widely recognized poet.

The millions of American vets who came home from the war found a country turned upside down. The hawks who had been the war's architects turned their backs on them. Many in the antiwar movement, in an incredible act of naiveté, publically denounced vets as baby killers. At one small, elite college where I taught, both colleagues and students condemned men in general as the cause of the war while enjoying the privileges of the rich families they'd been born into. It remained for the vets themselves to carry the moral legacy of the war, and one by one by ten by a hundred they began going back.

Not all vets were up to the challenge. Some of them, after all these years, are still cursing Jane Fonda and, as I contact survivors of my unit to interview them, I find them suspicious of somebody who is writing what I am writing now. There is one thing any Vietnam vet, regardless of his political views, is sure of: The custodians of the official versions lie. Governments lie. Histories lie, and few people care that soldiers and others die for the lies.

Nor are the Vietnamese in exile pleased with us. Not all Viet Kieu are escaped torturers with Swiss bank accounts. Many of them were just people who, because there was no other way to make a living, had to live and work among the people the Communists were trying to drive from the land. They had to flee on or after April 1975 when the inevitable unjust reaction to the original injustice caught many innocents in a net while the real culprits slipped out of the country with American help. Some say that if Ho Chi Minh had been alive at the end of the war, this would not have happened. Those of us who love the Vietnamese do not love some of the things their government did after the war. But who are we to speak after what we wrought there?

There we were in Hue, a city trying to hide its wounds and be gracious to us. We walked with Vo Que and his friends to the Anh Mau restaurant on "Hell Street," so named by the Americans for the vicious fighting and heavy casualties, and equally respected by our Vietnamese hosts. Hell here contained all of us, as Heaven might have; but Hell was more recognizably human, as Dante knew. Like most people, we knew more people in Hell than we did in Heaven. We were perhaps purgatorial then, walking down Hell Street among the many beggars and war mangled who dogged us with their hands out. Central Vietnam was poor still, and the collapse of the Asian economy in the nineties did not help.

In front of the restaurant, a very old woman sat on the back of a bicycle being pushed by, presumably, her daughter. She was all hide and gristle stretched over bone. She looked at my camera lens as if to curse me, but maybe it was beyond a curse. Maybe there is no name for what she felt. Maybe age had taken her mind and she thought I was French. She was old enough to remember the French, the Japanese, and the American wars. Perhaps it had made her mad.

Pho, noodle soup, is the great Vietnamese food, eaten by everyone, sometimes twice a day. With chicken or beef broth, according to one's taste, with slivers of chicken or beef, it is garnished with basil and bean sprouts and seasoned with *nuoc mam* or chili sauce. It is a symbol of plenty in the wake of lack.

After lunch we were guests of the world literature faculty at the University of Hue. The campus was a staging area for the first marines during the siege, but, like the rest of the city, has mostly spackled its bullet holes and filled in its craters. The Vietnamese refer to those people who cannot get over the war as "the broken clock people." They have rebuilt as best they could. They are curious about all things American. Some of the faculty were born after the war, or were children during it.

I am lecturing, extemporaneously and with brevity this time, about populist "slam" poetry in the United States and how, although it represents a departure from the modernism long enshrined in the academy, it is mostly, alas, terrible. It is bad prose, I say. It has no poetry in it no matter how I much I wish the idea of it to succeed.

A young professor asked me, "By what criteria do you speak of this poetry?" I answered that the poetry of which I spoke had no art in it, no music, no compression, no visible energy and, most of all, no negative capability—all those things by which poetry is instinctively experienced. It was mostly a lot of shallow ranting about "issues," whether or not the poet actually had any grasp of those issues. I said I was not arguing for elitism, but the kind of literacy that could appreciate nuanced language. I felt strangely conservative saying that, a little stuffy. I just wished it weren't true. How could I explain to these young people who were fascinated with the images from America that came to them electronically that I thought that my country was in intellectual decline?

The last day in Hue, we visited the citadel. While walking through the ruins of the royal concubinage of a Chinese emperor, Hoa said to me of emperors, "They didn't live very long. Too many women." From time to time I received little glimmers of feminism from Hoa, as I would later that day from Lam Thi My Da at the Hue Writers Association. My Da was a combat engineer along the Ho Chi Minh Trail during the war. She built bridges or blew them up as required. Later in the war she was inserted into the south as an intelligence operative.

When you talk to Vietnamese men, they don't often mention the women who served with them. Women were couriers, doctors, engineers, nurses, cooks, snipers, and spies. They were famously good shots, and many of them died fighting side by side with the men. When Pham Tiem Duat visited a Buddhist monastery where there were women veterans of the war, he spoke of them with sadness. Many of them were disfigured or maimed and would never find husbands. His sadness was based on their non-marriagability, but he did not ask them to tell their own stories. Perhaps on another trip I will visit them.

My Da is a lovely, round-faced woman with a few gray streaks in her hair who seems to be beyond seeking battles of any kind, military or intellectual. She was a skilled navigator of grief, and one got the impression from being around her that she paced herself, understood there would be no end of grief, that it must be felt in portions meted out through all her days and poems. She wrote about women in the war. Vietnamese were all veterans of the war, because the war touched everybody and the front was everywhere. She wrote a poem about the young girls in the mountain villages who were ordered to run out into the fields at night with flashlights to attract the bombers, so that infantry and supplies could move down the mountain paths. These young women died like flies.

As I look in the bomb crater where you died
The rain water became a patch of sky
Our country is kind
Water from the sky washes pain away.

I have seen her sing this poem. She stands and makes her body small, like a girl's, and sings in a small voice.

That night I asked Chung about the mass graves in Hue. Everyone knew about them, and each side used these graves against the other politically. The Viet Kieu blame the Communists. The Communists blame the ARVN and Americans. Chung, in his gentle way, told me that during the siege there were so many bodies that something had to be done with them, so they dumped them all, Communist and non-Communist, into mass graves and spread lye over them. I appreciate the irony of this, and the historical typicality. They were all dead. And the reasons for their dying fade into the great absurdity of all wars.

Next morning we left Hue. We drove overland through the poorest part of central Vietnam, and by noon, in fog and rain, had arrived at the mountain pass that led down into Da Nang. We were nearing the area I had been in during the war. We drove through the traffic jams and coughed through the exhaust. There were trucks carrying decorations for Tet moving among the motorbikes like large insects among ants. We met the poet Ngan Vinh in front of a floating restaurant on the Da Nang River. A huge banner in English and Vietnamese hung in front of the restaurant: VIETNAM: A DESTINATION FOR THE NEW MILLENNIUM.

Ngan Vinh was in his sixties but, like many Vietnamese, looked half his age. He is proud of his service in the war. He was the first Vietnamese I talked to who retained a little swagger about his youth. I have a picture of me with my arm around Vinh, standing in front of the restaurant. I am a foot taller than him. When I asked him what he thought of the huge Americans swarming into his country in the midsixties, he replied, "Easier to hit."

We were waiting for lunch and talking about weapons.

"We had 81s," I said. "You had 82s as I recalled."

"We had some 81s too. I remember we had a problem when the ammunition got mixed up."

I said, "Well, from what I remember, you guys would always overrun an ARVN outpost when you needed resupply. Good place to get 81s."

Vinh grinned.

We were looking out over the Da Nang River at the Marble Mountains, on the other side of which my battalion had been stationed.

Vinh said, "When I was a young soldier at Nha Trang, before I came north, the first American marine units came ashore. The marines were very naive. When fired on, they'd drop to one knee to return fire. It was quite easy to pick them off."

I felt a little twist in my gut. *Snake says, Ho! What's this?*

I said, "By the time I got to Vietnam in 1967, they were down on their bellies."

Vinh laughed. He asked, "Did you carry an M16?"

"No. I had a pistol. Then a sawed-off shotgun."

I told him I had been a medic, a *bacsi,* which was confusing, because it also means doctor, which I most certainly was not.

"I couldn't hit anything with the pistol, so I got a shotgun," I said.

We got back in the van and drove down to Nui Kim Son. They had planned the trip especially for me, after I had refused to go down alone. I was feeling a little strange.

Nui Kim Son is the village at the base of Kim Son Mountain, one of the five Marble Mountains. To the east had been a leper colony. When I asked about it, Vinh told me there was no more leprosy in Vietnam. No more cholera, typhus, or typhoid, either. And no more plague. You could still get malaria and dengue fever if you spent some time in the bush.

Snake says, See those clouds building up? See that hazy, dusky kind of murky watercolor smear over the mountains? Don't you want to just shit? You remember that dream you have about once every six months where you're running through the village naked? No weapon, scared shit-less there's nothing between you and mutilation? Remember that? Well, cowboy, here's the village.

My breathing quickened. The village was larger and the main road had been paved, but it looked the same. There were electric lines running through it, but there were still the small red stars of betel nut spat in the road, the same smells.

Pop pop pop pop pop, pop-pop, says Snake. Get down and boogie, boy.

We were being shadowed by three boys, ranging from about seven to ten, who managed to get in every photo I shot. I would quickly turn away from them to get a picture of, say, a pagoda, and they would hustle to get in, sounding like the rustling of leaves. They struck kung fu poses and mugged for the camera. There are no shots of Nui Kim Son that they're not in. In one, they are lean-ing up against two palms at the edge of a fallow rice paddy, the other side of which had once stood the sand berm of the battalion command post. They were grinning, mischievously, as if they knew the terror I was just barely keeping down.

Snake says, Whoo haaa!

We were walking toward a pagoda that was built into the mountain, and a local monk joined us. He too seemed full of mischief. The Vietcong had hidden in the caves of the Marble Mountains. The caves were now part of the monastery. The monk guided us into the mouth of one and pointed to the various tunnels going deep into the rock. These tunnels had been mined at the entrance during the war, in case we followed them in. The monk asked us if we wanted to see some M79 rounds. *Snake says, Whoo-haa!* I told him I'd seen all that I'd ever wanted to see, and he laughed. I wondered about the Mad Seventy-Niner, who we'd finally killed a kilometer south of where we stood. I wondered if he was part of the local folklore.

I looked out over the rice paddy for the last time at the sand where I had once slept and shook and shat and hoped. We stopped and talked to an old couple who told us that once an American soldier had come to visit the temple and had stepped on a mine. The old man, who had been young then, had climbed to the top of Kim Son, where there was an air force communications compound, and got help. But that was in the seventies, long after the army units had replaced us, and the marines had moved north. I would not have known him. I found the story incredible, remembering how we had treated them.

We got into the van and drove back to Da Nang, where we would board a plane to Saigon.

24

NGUYEN QUANG SANG was a short, round-faced man with white hair and full lips who reminded me a little of pictures I'd seen General Pham Van Dong. Sang had directed National Liberation Front operations in Saigon during the fifteen-year war without being detected by the Americans or the South Vietnamese. Now he was a grandfather with a grand piano in the front room of his ground-floor apartment on a quiet side street.

When we arrived, he sent his grandson to tell the neighbor children to be quiet so he could toast us properly. We sat in the little patio in front of his house and drank toasts, me with my mineral water, the rest with rice liquor. His sons brought out a roast pig, and we sat and told stories late into the night. Sang lived well, if modestly. Former NLF fighters had been treated well after the war and given amenities, but nothing resembling wealth.

Sang had the serenity of a man who had lived every day with certain death and somehow survived. But, unlike others I'd met, he didn't have that sense of being surprised to be alive. Nor did he appear traumatized.

Sang had not met me before and made a point of sitting next to me at dinner. In the manner of Vietnamese men, he held my hand. I remembered how horrified the marines in my unit had been at the sight of two ARVN soldiers who had walked by one day, BARs across their shoulders, holding hands. I can still hear a Mississippi accent saying, *Got-damn. Got-damn. You see that?*

We drove back to the hotel and I went up to my room. There were burns all over the carpet, as if hundreds of customers had simply stomped out their cigarettes on the floor. The shower was a cold trickle. There was no top sheet on the bed, but a thin spread against the fiercely effective air-conditioning. I thought about the pointlessness of top sheets. What is the purpose of a top sheet? Who invented top sheets? I lay down and fell into deep sleep.

SAIGON IS NOW called Ho Chi Minh City, but only for the sake of protocol. Most Vietnamese still call it Saigon, even loyal Communists. After all, Ho Chi Minh City has five syllables in English and four in Vietnamese, a number excessive for the poetic phrase or the street corner conversation, especially in a tonal language where a whole world can be invoked by the lift and drop of a monosyllable.

There is a saying in Spanish, *La vida es corta, pero amplia,* Life is short but wide. The war was like this for many vets. Time experienced at that intensity, with the whole being, created a sphere that surrounded the experiencer that is at first unavailable to memory. During our combat tours, while we moved through the months toward the day we would go home, parts of us moved out to the sides, above and beneath, and fastened tendrils there. Most of us were in-country for only thirteen months, but that time has taken most of a lifetime to understand. The war tore up everything we had believed about our country and ourselves.

Saigon has always been out of control. In April 1975, when the Communists overran the city, they attempted to put an end to the huge machinery of corruption and crime. Anyone who looked like a collaborator was shipped off to a re-education camp. Most of the cowboys—the young men who were famous for riding by on a bicycle and snatching the camera off your neck—were rounded up and shot. In the manner of all revolutions, there was an attempt to wipe the slate clean. But some parts of the city had returned to the old ways, and crime was alive and well.

We walked the streets of Saigon, past the old American embassy where the famous photos were taken of diplomats being helicoptered off the roof during the last hours of the war. We visited Tu Do Street, once famous for prostitution, now thriving with shops and street vendors. There were two American institutions: the Hard Rock Café and Thirty-One Flavors Ice Cream. "Thirty-one flavors" translated into Vietnamese as "thirty-one smells."

We visited the huge open market at Cholon, the Chinese section of the city. Hundreds of Chinese sat outside the honeycomb of three-story market buildings cooking food in woks to sell to the visitors. Lan Anh, the daughter of our host, Nguyen Duy, was walking with a girlfriend when two teenage boys ran at them aggressively, as if to do them harm, then stopped inches away. The two women did not flinch or turn their heads.

Inside the marketplace buildings was a labyrinth, a bazaar. Occasionally I would see a store full of clothes with American logos on them. On the way back to the van, a woman and a baby approached us. The woman held her hand out. Hoa said, "She has rented the baby to beg with. The baby is sedated with opium so it won't cry." I could see that this admission caused her pain. She said, softly, "We have our problems." I said, "So do we. We have a huge homeless population." And she said, "Yes, but it is not like this, not so extreme."

Hoa was a committed Communist and a daughter of a member of the politburo. My own thinking had been deeply shaped by Marx, although I did not see Marxism as a political ideology or utopian strategy, but an effective analytical tool. As Machiavelli is about how power works, Marx is about how capitalism dehumanizes. But I was also aware, as was anyone who'd lived during my time, that utopian visions are too easily hijacked by fascists. The history of Communist countries suggested that radical change was something like a stump of petrified wood: Minerals had replaced the rotten wood, but the exact form of the stump remained. Stalin became the czar.

Americans in the fifties and sixties, particularly conservatives, imagined communism as a single block, taking over one country after another, threatening to enslave the whole world. Equally naive were the American leftists who also imagined communism as a single block, liberating one country after another. But all communisms are different. Vietnamese communism is more the vehicle of Vietnamese nationalism than of theoretical communism. There is much conjecture that Ho Chi Minh, had he been taken seriously by the Americans after World War II, would have used democracy as a modus operandi of postcolonial Vietnam instead of communism. He needed the support of a major power to unify the country and, having been snubbed twice by the Americans, he wooed Russia.

In fact, in the final years of the French war, the CIA had been hard at work destabilizing the local regime and paying local bandits to commit acts of terrorism so they could blame it on the Communists. In *The Quiet American,* Graham Greene characterizes the American CIA agent, Pyle, with the line, "Innocence is like a blind leper who has lost his bell, roaming the earth, meaning no harm."

That night, Weigl and I rode through Saigon in a cylco—a bicycle cab. At one point we were surrounded by young men and women on motorbikes. The young men watched our faces intently. The women, perched sidesaddle on the back, were dressed in brightly colored *xuan xam*s slit all the way up the thigh to the hip. They were stunning. It took me a few seconds to understand that these were pimps and their girls. The cyclo driver was making negative gestures, saying, "Number ten, number ten!"—pidgin left over from the war which meant *very bad*. The driver continued, "Not girls, not girls," and shook his head vehemently. I guess he wanted to protect us from an unwanted surprise.

Transvestite prostitution is very popular in Saigon. Weigl informed me later that the problem with prostitution in Saigon was that you never knew what you were getting. If you didn't in fact get a transvestite, you were liable to get a considerably less appealing version of what you saw on the motorbike. The girls on the motorbikes (if they were girls) were strictly "demos." I could hear Hoa's voice saying, "We have our problems."

Next morning at the Saigon Writers Association we met Sang again, along with several other writers. There were two generations present at the reception, and some of the younger members—including a reporter from Saigon Television who had come to tape the event—seemed impatient with the writers of the war generation. When the poet Vien Phuong introduced himself as "the old man of the tunnels," the reporter rolled her eyes. He was a fading historical icon for her, but for me he was not.

There had been a tunnel complex underneath the American air base at Cu Chi that housed hundreds of NLF and NVA and was an important guerilla operations center between 1962 and 1975. The Americans never knew they were there. Phuong's poems chronicle that experience. He was a wiry little man, one who you might imagine was very good at living in tunnels. The tunnels at Cu Chi are now a principal tourist attraction; but their openings have been enlarged to accommodate obese Americans.

The rest of the afternoon I was on my own, photographing, napping, drinking *café sua* at the hotel. Every time I turned left out of the hotel there was a young girl selling postcards. She had a limp. She was, in fact, not a little girl but a stunted young woman. I thought, *Agent Orange, birth defects.* Every time I passed her she would ask me if I wanted postcards. I said, "No." Then she would say, "Why?" in an imploring voice. This is a disconcerting technique of Vietnamese street hawkers. You have to stop and give a reason, and that involves a conversation that makes it more difficult to refuse.

I pointed to the camera and said, "I'm working." She looked at me and said in American-accented English, *"Awwwwwwww God."* Each time I saw her she would stop me. She was no longer interested in selling me anything. I liked her. We never exchanged more than trivialities, but I still can't get her out of my mind. She seemed to embody some undying remnant of the American War, of damage that would not be healed in my lifetime.

That night we were invited to Nguyen Duy's house for dinner. Duy was a terrific poet, visual artist, photographer, and master cook. I have enjoyed his dinners both in Saigon and in Boston, where he came the following year as a member of the visiting international faculty at the Joiner Center.

It was a sweltering night. We had been walking all day and my shirt was foul and caked with salt. Earlier, at the hotel, Duy had looked at me mock-sternly and said, "You go take a bath." The shower in the hotel was again a cold trickle. I was reminded of how many things Americans take for granted. Five minutes outside the hotel and I was soaked with sweat again.

At Duy's we dined on the roof. On a side street, away from traffic, we could hear the children playing. Duy had prepared a generous spread. I missed being able to drink beer on such a night. I missed the fellowship of whiskey in a short glass. But I was serene without the booze and more than a little fascinated with Lan Anh, who was wearing a simple white dress and performing daughterly duties like pouring tea and passing appetizers. Her parents' presence brought out the traditional girl.

I slept heavily that night, and in the morning collected my laundry and began to pack. This was my last day in Vietnam. I did not want to leave. Because I had flown from the West Coast and the rest of the group from Boston, I was scheduled for a different flight, which gave me an extra day in Vietnam. I drove to the airport to see the rest of the delegation off. Hoa embarked for Hanoi, the others for the long flight home.

Duy arranged a dinner that night in the hotel. He had invited several younger Vietnamese writers. They drank heavily. When the waiter came to me with the bottle of rice liquor, Duy waved his hands. *Don't give alcohol to the big gringo he might misbehave.* My teetotaling had become a point of humor by then.

The poet Thu Bon arrived with his wife. I had met Thu Bon the previous year in Boston. He had a swirl of mad white hair and wore traditional silk shirts that buttoned just under the chin His two children were born with partial brains because of his ten-year exposure to Agent Orange during the war.

Later, Duy and Thu Bon said their goodbyes and left. Lan Anh stayed to keep me company and translate what the younger writers were saying. By now they were smashed. They were laughing so hard the tears ran down their cheeks. Lan Anh summarized the conversation as she translated.

"Now they are making fun of public figures," she said.

The waiter was pouring another round of drinks.

"Now they are making fun of literary contests."

A huge burst of laughter.

"Now they are making fun of socialism."

Afterwards, Lan Anh took me on a walking tour of Saigon. There were no Americans in the area, and we stood out. As a fifty-seven-year-old American and a twenty-year-old Vietnamese woman, we were a veritable projection screen for intercultural resentments. That I was behaving did not shield me from the gawks and censorious looks.

Lan Anh had pretty thick skin. She had seen more than most Americans her age.

"Have you ever eaten dog?" I asked.

"Oh, I love it," she said. "My father knows all the best dog restaurants. You go into the backyard where they have them in pens, and pick your dog. Then they kill it and cook it." She was not sentimental.

"That pushes the lobster envelope," I said. She asked me to explain the reference.

We began talking about the Clinton and Monica Lewinsky caper, which, in every country but the United States, had become a celebrated joke.

Lan Anh said, "We just think that very handsome people have

a lot of sex. Bill Clinton is very handsome, therefore he has a lot of sex."

As we passed a side street I saw an Afro-Vietnamese man, perhaps in his early thirties. He was looking right at me. Then he looked longer at Lan Anh. The Americans left roughly eighty thousand mixed-race children. These children did not fare well. They became symbols of everything the procession of foreign regimes had inflicted on Vietnam for the last three thousand years. Many of these children were finally relocated in the United States.

We stopped at a rotary and sat on a stone bench, surrounded by Vietnamese families and a swarm of delighted children. I was approached by panhandlers, both children and adults.

We talked about love, about Americans who came to Vietnam and took Vietnamese girls home with them, and of the people from the fashion magazines who came to Saigon and paid young Vietnamese girls unimaginable money to go to France, where their svelte bodies would animate French fashion with a combination of innocence and otherness. In a way, it seemed that the colonial powers had never left, but stayed on to extract the beautiful and precious for their own use. And nothing came back to the Vietnamese. All over Saigon, skyscrapers, built during the Asian boom of the nineties and abandoned after the collapse, stood empty. Vietnam still struggled, still sought to come into its own, and was forced to court the titans of multinational capital. After what they have suffered, this is a bitter pill indeed.

We talked about Lan Anh's desire to go to a university in the United States.

Lan Anh suddenly said, with some vehemence, "I would rather hang myself than become a traditional Vietnamese wife."

I asked her why, and she said, "When you marry, you become the property of your husband's family to whom you are the same as a servant."

She was studying for her English as a foreign language exams.

I looked at Lan Anh and wanted to rewind the tape, come to

Vietnam again as a young man and find someone like her. Not
to take her home, but to stay and understand. How much better
to come to Vietnam that way than the way we came, with all our
blindness and lethal force. We walked back to the hotel in silence.
Aware of the Vietnamese in the lobby, I kissed her lightly on the
cheek. Then she went outside and flagged a cab.

The next morning Duy, Lan Anh, and her brother took me to
the airport. I did not want to leave. Lan Anh presented me with a
little album of pictures her brother had taken of us during the time
we were there.

All during the short flight to Hong Kong I played back the two
weeks. The image of the woman with the rented baby, her sadness and grace, morphed with the lovely face of Lam Thi My Da.
The flight was full of Vietnamese returning to the United States.
Their language soothed me, and I knew that I would miss it when
I returned to California, where I would hear it only occasionally.
I tried to think ahead to the new semester at the college where I
taught, thought of the syllabi I had yet to write, the books I would
assign. These concerns seemed so insubstantial that I could scarcely
hold them in my mind, which kept slipping back to the trip. Hanh
standing at the huge caldron at Hue. Pham Tien Duat looking at
me incredulously when I refused a drink. The roast pig at Sang's
house, and the huge gold Buddha in the central temple. The kids
at Nui Kim Son grinning with gaps from missing baby teeth. Lan
Anh at her father's with a platter of spring rolls. I had been changed
by the trip. Often we think of ourselves as endlessly complicated
and hopeless, a mass of confusion and contradiction, and yet the
change in me seemed so simple. We cling to suffering because it is
familiar and because freedom is an unknown landscape. When we
visited the central Buddhist temple in Saigon there was an old man
and his daughter out front with a cage of birds. For one dollar, he
would release a bird. When we were leaving the temple, Lan Anh
touched my arm and pointed to the old man and his daughter: the
birds were returning to the cage.

I thought of Snake. He was hiding in the shadow of the tenderness I felt. From Hong Kong to Los Angeles, I slept.

During the first month of the new semester, I sat in my office, prepared classes, made adjustments in my syllabi, but did not feel as if I were actually there. I missed the smells of Vietnam, the voices. I promised myself to return. I wrote my first poem of the new year.

PETITIONARY PRAYER ON NGUYEN DUY'S ROOF
Saigon, January 2000

Black sky and moon of chipped ice.
We fall on the chicken, the shrimp,
the sliced melons. The whiskey
picks up the neon from the streets.
A sudden breeze cools our damp shirts.
Below, children play in the light
from open doorways.
The heat of the day has made us silent.
Lan Anh, in her simple white dress, pours tea.
God make me young again and not stupid.

FIVE

25

MY MOTHER'S FRIEND Kay called to talk about my mother. "She left a pot on the stove and it burned."

"Well *I've* done that."

"Yes, but she wouldn't, you see? That's not like her. And she's fallen a couple of times. They think she's having little strokes."

"She seemed all right at Christmas."

"Well, she's not. She takes off in the car and forgets where she's going."

I wanted to tell her I'd done that too.

I had been dreading this, denying it, pushing it away. I hoped she'd be lucky and go peacefully in her sleep, but for most it doesn't happen that way.

In recent years, every time I'd visit my mother, she'd make a point of showing me where all her papers were in case she died. I thought she was emotionally blackmailing me and ignored her. I was simply refusing to deal with it.

I said to Kay, "Maybe I'd better come."

"Maybe you'd better come."

I flew from Ontario, California, to Tucson.

I had lunch with Kay, my friend Berta, my mother, and our friends, Reverend Charles Ingram and his son Mark. My mother seemed very alert. She was suspicious. She didn't miss a word of the discussion about assisted living and nursing homes. Of course we meant to include her in the conversation, but she knew that a decision had already been made, and that her protestations wouldn't make any difference. I had already taken away her driver's license and made plans to sell her car.

She said, "You just want to put me away somewhere."

I tried to tell her that assisted living was not a nursing home, and that she'd have her freedom, but she'd also have people close by in case she needed them.

Later, I was trying to ease her mind about moving in and she noticed that I was wearing an earring in my left ear. She said, with a leer, "Does that *mean* anything?"

In principle, I am against putting old people out to pasture. I know cultures where it's never done. The Vietnamese take care of their old. But I knew that it would be a grievous mistake for me to live with my mother.

"You should have married that Mexican girl," she said. The subtitle would have read, *You should have had children. You should have had a family to continue on.* But there had never been any family. My father was gone by the time I was seven. My mother left the country when I was eighteen and was gone until she retired from the State Department when I was long out of college and living in New York. I had no siblings to share the load, and my aunt and uncle in Memphis were old and ailing themselves.

Kay and I visited several assisted-living homes. They were all about the same: private homes, licensed, refitted with wheelchair ramps. Such homes are a cottage industry in Tucson, where the old have always come in droves, fleeing the swollen joints of the East Coast winters and the bad air. Anyone with a house and the ability to negotiate the bureaucracy could open a home.

My mother had two pensions that would take care of her quite well, and we attempted to find a place at least one step upscale. I found one slightly more expensive, north of town, out in the Catalina foothills, where she had first lived when she'd moved to Tucson. The place was large and very pleasant, the staff smart and sophisticated. She would have her own apartment, bathroom, and kitchenette. It was a few blocks from church and a small shopping center where she could get a pedicure or get her hair done.

My mother scowled when we opened the door to show her the new apartment. It was cheerful and sun-drenched from the tall windows.

I said, and meant it, "I wouldn't mind living here myself." My apartment in California was shabby in comparison.

She scowled again.

During this time she wrote a poem which she then mailed to Charles Ingram, asking him to help with the title. The Ingrams have preserved it from oblivion.

> *I don't think I'm going*
> > *Incarceration is its real name.*
> *A dinky box of a room*
> > *Two hots and a cot*
> *Put your laundry out on Thursday—*
> > *If you want it done*
> *Maybe There'll be a friend.*
> > *How much did you say a month?*
> *Assisted what?*
> > *Just for that I won't take my pill.*

We moved her in.

I returned to teaching in California, relieved to have my mother housed in a good place. Then I got a call from Berta, who said that my mother had gotten drunk and fallen down the stairs at the home. She said that she had been miserable and lonely and was not in very good psychological shape.

I flew back to Tucson, and Berta and I went looking for nursing homes.

I asked her, "What's going to happen to us when we get old and sick?"

She said, "We'll go into a nursing home."

I thought, *I'd better apply for a gun permit now so I can shoot myself when the time comes.*

We found a nursing home in the east part of town. It was an old office building of some kind with a big sunlit atrium. In some ways it was a step down from the assisted-living home, but it was pleasant and staffed by large, cheerful women with tattoos, and a manager I liked right off. My mother was confined to a single room there, and we endeavored to make it hers with her shelf of favorite books and her favorite paintings. I had shot and framed a medium-format photo from Joshua Tree National Park, but she scoffed at it. As we were leaving she reminded me to put the bright Do Not Resuscitate form on her door.

The occupants of this home would not provide my mother with much conversation, although there was a common room with a television where they all gathered. There were two younger men in there who had been severely brain damaged. And there was one my age who claimed to have been in special operations in Vietnam and to have infiltrated the north. He was too young to have done such a thing, but I indulged him. Most of the occupants had long ago crossed the line.

My mother began to have conversations with the dead. In some cases they were people who had been gone over forty years. My mother told me she just had a conversation with one of them the previous day. It felt spooky. I wondered if the dead became finally available to the very old, waiting to help them over. I imagined two very old people listening to each other through a wall that had become thinner and thinner. In any case, my mother's ability to logically compartmentalize was deteriorating. She was still reading, however, her beloved Faulkner.

I returned once again to California, only to be called a few days later by the manager of the nursing home, who explained that my mother had died the previous night. Back to Tucson.

We had a service for my mother the next week.

Very few of her friends came, but a good many strangers did, or people she had known slightly. Bertha Martinez, an old friend with whom she had had a spat and stopped speaking to came and sat quietly. Then I realized that several of her friends weren't there because she'd outlived them.

I made a display in the back of St. Andrew's Church, which she had attended for many years before Charles Ingram retired. There were pictures of her as a child, as a strikingly beautiful young woman, and several passports fanned out together showing the places she had lived and worked in the Foreign Service: West Cameroon, Santo Domingo, Saigon, Santiago, Islamabad.

I eulogized her as a woman who had been born the last year of World War I and had never gone to college but could read Shakespeare and Faulkner in depth. Then I read her poem, to which there was choked laughter. She lived in the poem.

I placed her ashes in the church columbarium and kept a portion to take to Hickman, Kentucky, where she had been born. That night I stayed at Berta's house. We had gone out to get Ben and Jerry's ice cream and planned to sit in front of the television and eat the whole pint.

Berta had a parakeet, a cat, and a dog named Bongo. Suddenly the cat bounded from the chair where she had been sleeping, bounced off the couch, caromed off the birdcage and into the kitchen. The parakeet became hysterical, flew straight upward, and brained itself on the cage. It was stone dead. We began laughing and couldn't stop. We were convulsed and in tears with laughing, laughter that lets you know it is joined at the hip with grief, that anything that goes that deep, whether a laugh or a wail of sorrow, will touch the same place. It took us a long time to stop laughing.

I HAD BEEN unhappy in California for the five years I had been there. I resigned from my position at the college, packed a U-Haul, and hitched my pickup to the back on a towing trailer. I set out across the country determined to travel Route 66 as far as I could before I had to turn north up into Pennsylvania.

I met my Aunt Rose and Uncle Fred in Hickman. We went visiting kinfolk, and I heard stories about family members I scarcely knew or had never met, like my great-half-uncle Leonard. He'd been imprisoned four years for stealing hogs, and he came home to find his brother shacked up with his wife and a new kid. He killed them both and fled to Arkansas, where federal marshals killed him the following year.

I ate catfish and collards and photographed the old downtown, half of which had fallen into sinkholes caused by the Mississippi. This was worth a sermon or two about iniquity at local churches.

We met at the graveyard where many generations of Wisemans are buried, including my mother's little sister Mary, who had died of leukemia. We said a few words to my mother and sprinkled the handful of ashes I brought with me. Then they went back to Memphis and I headed northeast.

IT IS A *clear sunny summer day. My mother and father and I arrive at the Larose house. I am three. My grandmother picks me up and hugs me. I smell the lavender she wears. I like how warm and fleshy she is. Inside the house the conversation is roaring. There is laughing and the rattle of ice in glasses. Everyone is young or younger. Even my grandparents seem young, and my grandfather is up laughing and gesticulating with the rest.*

We move to the backyard where my grandfather and uncle start a roaring fire in the red-brick barbecue pit. Uncle George and Aunt Frances are there with my cousins, George and Freddy, who are boys too. Freddy is still a toddler.

The grass is very green under the bright sun and all the colors seem to be hotter than usual. There are plates of sliced tomatoes. My grandmother has begun to make ice cream, turning the crank over a wooden bucket.

The war is over. Everyone is happy. This is the only time I will see this.

The only image I have of being whole and being part of something. This image is incandescent and it is the only one.

September 11, 2001

On campus, several students who are in the National Guard are fully dressed in combat uniforms and black berets. They are clustered together, speaking softly. They do not yet know just how much the Guard will be involved in the coming war, or that their tours of duty will be extended, their lives turned upside down.

Snake says, Look at these boys. Look at how their eyes sparkle when they see those uniforms, those berets, that high-tech weaponry, those sexual constellations of lights on the control panels of tanks and fighter jets. Hell, these boys have been playing video games. This is a new generation. They're wired for it. They can put a smart bomb right up your nose, so nimble are those Nintendo nubs.

I am reminded of a poem by Nguyen Duy, who wrote "Meeting a Young Soldier" after he visited Moscow in 1985. "You look beautiful like a thorny cactus, . . . may you always look as beautiful as a show room plant. / Pray to God / You never have to go into battle."

In the English Department office, the secretaries, Rose and Doreen, look grim. Rose says, "And look who we've got for president."

I go downstairs to my office and call Martín Espada. He says, "Unbelievable. And there are still several planes out there." We don't know yet that there are only two more planes. One will hit the Pentagon, the other will go down in an open field.

Martín says, "And look who we've got for president."

We talk about how afraid we are for Arab students, for ourselves for that matter.

Before the week is done, about twelve foreigners, some of whom are not even Arab, are killed throughout the country. One of them is a Sikh, nowhere near an Arab, killed in Arizona, simply because he was wearing a turban. Network news channels are still playing the towers being hit by the planes, or falling down, or employees in lower Manhattan running, covered with ash. The whole thing has an apocalyptic feel to it.

I call a former student, a Saudi, and ask if he's all right. He tells me so far so good, but his father is calling him home.

It is clearly a new age. We have a new president that thinking people everywhere distrust. We don't yet know how bad it is going to get.

Before the semester is over, a student tells me that she can't come to class because she has relatives who died in the Towers, and that she'll try to complete the semester if I allow her some time off to deal with things. At the end of the semester, she turns in a plagiarized paper. I know I have been scammed. I do nothing. How can you possibly contest this paper? It was not the only scam that would ride the wave of the new patriotism.

Those of us who lived through the sixties and who believed that we had reached a plateau from which we would only rise upward—after all, two civil rights acts were ratified and the war in Vietnam was shut down by public pressure—now looked out into classes of students who seemed as far from that decade as one could possibly get, students who participated in no public forum, knew nothing of politics, and cared less. Would we have to learn it all over again? When I was young, I didn't understand history, because I didn't have a history of my own. When I was less young, I still loved being young too much to take history very seriously. History finally had me, sitting on my chest like a schoolyard bully. *Ho! says Snake.* Now in my sixth decade, I feel like an old fart standing by the road, waving his cane. Can it be that this is everyone's lot, eventually? That age dooms us to see repeated idiocies against which voices of experience have no weight? But there is something wrong with this formulation.

The students, even the graduate students, are clueless. I was having a discussion with one about President Bush. I was comparing him to Nixon, and he said, "I'm kind of fond of Richard Nixon." Since he wasn't alive during Nixon's presidency, I was astonished that he could make such a statement. Faced with this, with other students suddenly striking patriotic poses, one is tempted to go silent. Like a ship drifting without telemetry among the ghosts of other ships. This can't be happening, I think. We can't unlearn so quickly what we've paid for with our blood. *Ha! says Snake. Happens all the damn time.*

It was not long after that that President Bush was able to dupe the electorate into going to war in a country that had nothing to do with the attack on the World Trade Center, while letting the hunt for Osama bin Laden fade away into a spook war somewhere in the Pashtun tribal regions of Pakistan.

We are in it for the long run. "The arm of the moral universe is long, but it bends toward justice," wrote Martin Luther King. I type these words out in boldface, Xerox them, hand them out. I practice believing these words. Hope is exhausting when not held by faith. I want this man's faith. *Snake says, Down on your hands and knees lookin' for that mustard seed.*

26

IF ALL THE wars of our national history were invited to Christmas dinner in 2008 the Vietnam War would not be invited. Or
rather, it would be invited, grudgingly, and told to dress in such a
way as to resemble the other wars, with all their medals. It would
be told to cut its hair, control its mouth, change its attitude. The
others would tolerate no unpleasant conversation of the variety, say,
that might compare the war in Iraq to the Vietnam War. It would
not be allowed to mention any of the family secrets, such as the
lying and greed that kept the war going. But it would find a strange
ally. Suddenly Siegfried Sassoon, who had been lurking over near
the brandy next to World War I, for which he has so often been a
voice, would stand up and quote the following lines from his letter
to parliament:

> On behalf of those who are suffering now I make this protest
> against the deception that is being practiced on them; also I
> believe I may help to destroy the callous complacence with
> which the majority of those at home regard the continuance
> of agonies which they do not share, and which they have not
> sufficient imagination to realize.

Since he was a war hero and a favorite of his men, it would have
been impolitic to have him shot for treason, so the British high
command, aided by Sassoon's concerned friend Robert Graves,
had him interned in the Craiglockart War Hospital in Scotland.
Perhaps today he would be easily dismissed as homosexual—one

of the hate nodes in the neocon brain that George Bush so skill-fully manipulated to get elected.

But my imagined dinner guests would have given Sassoon a moment of silence, for they knew more than the politicians and the general public. The words that stand out for me, that are medicine against any lie, are "callous complacency" and "have not the imagination to realize."

The Vietnam War continues to resurface in ever more unexpected ways. There is a midwestern preacher named Phelps who has begun showing up at the funerals of Iraq soldiers killed in action with signs that read GOD HATES FAGS. He also preaches at these funerals. His latest tirade is that our boys are dying in Iraq because this country is soft on homosexuals. He has one sign that reads IED'S ARE A GIFT FROM GOD.

Into one instance of this malign inanity there came, suddenly, a Vietnam veterans motorcycle club, full of gray beards, arthritic knuckles, and scarred hearts, which effectively screened off this idiot and his followers from the rest of the funeral. They have done so at every funeral Phelps showed up at since. Whatever their politics, these veterans have had enough and do not wish the veterans of the Iraq War to suffer the inundating disrespect with which they were treated after they came home from an earlier, ill-conceived war.

SNAKE SAYS, HONOR ME. *Snake says, I have been your brother and your other and your own. I have glowed like a second spine when you have been spineless and I have spoken when you did not have words. Honor me. You have lit candles for the Buddha, for Mary, for Christ. Now honor me.*

I AM TALKING to the Batwoman on the phone. When I ask her if I can write about her she says, "I will neither hinder nor help you."

"Well. Would you consent to a few questions?"

"Shoot."

"I have depicted you as having a .357 magnum that you took on your trips to Mexico. Is that correct?"

"No. I had a .22 that I loaded with birdshot, for snakes."

"Well, the .357 stays in. You are a .357 magnum kind of woman."

(No response.)

"You know, I was crazy about you."

"I never knew that. I always thought you were too talented and too good looking to be interested in monogamy."

I have sent her "Don't Rub Your Eyes," reprinted here as Chapter 16, and which was published in *Ploughshares* in March 2005.

She says, "I never knew you were suffering so much."

"I probably didn't either. I was too drunk and drugged."

We get older. We accept. Our sharp edges are smoothed like a salt lick.

WHEN I CALLED my old platoon commander, whom I refer to as Shepard in this book, he remembered me well. We tried to square information on the action in June 1967, when my company killed thirty-nine Vietnamese. He said he didn't remember the bodies. He was calling in an air strike and was otherwise employed. He *knew* about the bodies though. They're in the morning report he wrote and signed.

He told me that he'd gotten the company radio operator's name on the Vietnam Veterans Memorial Wall in Washington. On another operation, the radio operator had been shot through the cervical spine and was instantly rendered quadriplegic. He had lived a long time in that condition.

Shepard said, at the end of our conversation, "You know, I've come to think that all the Vietnamese wanted was their independence." There was such gentleness in his voice. There was a thread that, from his voice on the phone, shot straight back to 1967, when I was in the field with him. He is a very good man.

Most of the men I served with were good men and the war

was a hard teacher. Their only misfortune was that they served in a dirty war. They were no better or worse than any other soldiers in any other war. All have coped in their own ways. I accept that many of them think differently than I do about the war. I carry them in my heart nonetheless.

THE CONSEQUENCES OF the war continue to manifest, nearly forty years later. Vietnamese women still comb the country-side for their missing husbands so they can bury them. They look for a fragment of clothing, a pair of glasses, a tooth, a bundle of letters, to go with the bones.

This is no small matter.

I GOT MARRIED in December 2006 for the first time, at the age of sixty-three, to Julie Janiszewski, a painter and activist, and got in the bargain a stepdaughter, Zofi, and two dogs. She was fifty and also marrying for the first time. What we have in common is the knowledge of which cages our demons are stored in, and a goodly dose of Snakebrain. She too has experienced extreme violence, and the things that years ago would have ensured the destruction of our relationship are now its bonding substance. She has managed a soup kitchen in a homeless shelter, been a mental-health worker, and is now director of an AIDS project in Hartford, Connecticut. She is an artist; her oil paintings remind me of my own poetry, the way they come from her body with unmediated force.

What do I want in the last years remaining to me? *Snake says, Hey, you've got a while.* I carry a sense of poetry like a small flame cupped in my hand. To write. To love in a real way: to accept the whole ripeness of another, to share silence, to move to a place beyond petty difference.

My poetry mentor Jack Gilbert, now struggling with the reali-ties of age, told me that he was happy to have lived when he did. He lived in Paris before McDonald's, and in Provence before SUVs. He lived in the Greek islands when it was still possible to live on fish brought up from the ocean, and to sleep on the roof of a stone hut. And he lived during the great years of modernism when art was going to change us all into enlightened beings.

Snake says, Hee hee.

What we have lost most tragically as a culture is interiority, the sense of depth the night sky can bring, the *Thou-ness* of things that poetry is best suited to discover. I was born before television and, in my solitude, became a reader early on. I can read *Moby-Dick* in a way that those who are trained to treat imaginative literature as artifact, cannot. My imagination is not pre-mapped with jargon and theory. I am not predisposed to multitask, but rather to stay with what is there, before me, human or object.

I have been a teaching affiliate of the William Joiner Center for the Study of War and Its Social Consequences for going on twelve years now. Each summer we come to be replenished and to help educate about the effects of war on the countries in which it is fought. We come to write together, pursue scholarship, and do service where we can. We have had many Vietnamese visitors, including some of Vietnam's most distinguished poets, writers, and scholars. In recent years, the center has moved beyond Vietnam to include writers, scholars, and filmmakers from Ireland, Bosnia, Rwanda, Israel, Palestine, and Latin America. The center is a well from which we all drink, a community which, each year, is recharged by the synergy we create together. We have grown old together and some, like Grace Paley and Pham Tiem Duat, are no longer with us. Three Iraq vets are now affiliated with the Joiner Center, and this year, we hosted a Palestinian and an Israeli filmmaker as Joiner Fellows. Most recently, Iraq vet and poet Brian Turner, author of *Here, Bullet* has joined the staff of teaching affiliates.

I HAVE SOMEHOW survived my life and lived on into another century, one in which the questions long outnumber the answers, and uncertainty grows daily. Much of what Orwell warned against in *1984* has long come to pass and the younger generations seem to accept it as a condition of life. Newspeak and double speak, against which poetry has always stood, are now the accepted tools of government. If we identify with certain thoughts we are labeled unpatriotic, although we are not yet being tortured for "thought crimes." At least not in this country. Yet.

Snake says, Somebody, somewhere, is fiddling with your future in the dark.

I wonder if the things I value will come full circle again and be at the center of our culture, rather than languishing at the margins: whether people will once again inhabit public forums together, and not online, will read poetry and care about the language they speak and write. Robert Stone, in *Prime Green,* writes, "Language is the process that lashes experience to the intellect." May we once again honor books. May our words be who we are. May we care when those in power lie. I realize I am writing a kind of prayer.

ACKNOWLEDGMENTS

Special thanks to my editor, Carol Houck Smith, for her brilliant insight, commitment to good writing, and her considerable patience. I am very lucky to have worked with her.

Thanks to editor Brendan Curry and editorial assistant Denise Scarfi for their close attention to the final stages of the book.

Thanks also to the following for their support, both professional and personal:

My agent, Victoria Sanders, Benee Knauer, and other members of her staff.

My writing group: Wally Lamb, Sari Rosenblatt, Leslie Johnson, Pam Lewis, Susanne Davis, and Susan Campbell.

My mentors at the University of Connecticut: Margaret Higonnet, Marilyn Nelson, Sam Pickering, Thomas Recchio, Thomas Jambeck, Bob Tilton, Penelope Pelizzon, and Ellen Litman.

My dear friends Dorianne Laux and Joe Millar, who read early drafts and shouted enouragement.

My friends Jim and Deb Bogan in whose living room the memoir began to grow.

Mi campanero, Martín Espada, for his long friendship and assistance.

Thanks to Mary Pellino for proofreading the manuscript.

My good friends Sandy Taylor and Judy Doyle.

Thanks and *thai binh* to Vietnamese friends, both in this country and in Vietnam, for their help with names and factual verification, their hospitality, writing and conversation: Nguyen Ba Chung, Minh Phuong, Pham Tien Duat, Van Kam Hai, Dao Kim Hoa, Nguyen Quang Sang, Vinh Dinh, Nguyen Ngoc, Nguyen Quang Thieu, Lam Thi My Da, Bao Ninh, Nguyen Duc Mau, Hu'u Thinh, Thu Bonn, Nguyen Lan Anh. Nguyen Duy and Nguyen Duc Mau for their poetry and great cooking.

Thanks to Iraq War veterans Steven Morrell, Chris Lacasse, and Brian Redmond for information you don't get from the mainstream media.

Thanks to Kevin Bowen, Director of the Joiner Center for the Study of

War and Social Consequences, University of Massachusetts, Boston, and to Lady Borton, Director of the American Friends Service Committee in Hanoi. Thanks to my Joiner Center colleagues Bruce Weigl, Larry Heineman, Preston Hood, and many others for their fellowship and support.

Thanks to Maureen O'Brien not only for her help with two drafts but also for her advice about agents and publishers.

And special thanks to my beloved wife, Julie Janiszewski, who has read and commented on several drafts of the memoir and put up with me while I was writing it.

Works by Doug Anderson

"Night Ambush," "A Bar in Argos," "Infantry Assault," "Homer Does Not Mention Him," and "Xin Loi" from *The Moon Reflected Fire*, Copyright © 1994 by Doug Anderson. Reprinted with the permission of Alice James Books.

"Petitionary Prayer on Nguyen Duy's Roof," from *Field*, Number 64, Spring 2001. Reprinted with the permission of Oberlin College Press.

"Don't Rub Your Eyes," chapter 16 of *Keep Your Head Down*, in another version, was published in *Ploughshares*, April 2005, edited by Martín Espada.

Parts of the following poems are reprinted with the permission of Curbstone Press

Lam Thi My Da, "Bomb-Crater Sky," from *Six Vietnamese Poets*, edited by Kevin Bowen and Nguyen Ba Chung, Curbstone Press, 2002.

Pham Tien Duat, "The Fire in the Lamps," from *Six Vietnamese Poets*, Curbstone Press, 2002.

Nguyen Duy, "Meeting a Young Soldier," from *Distant Road*, Curbstone Press, 1999.

Kevin Bowen, "River Music," from *Playing Basketball with the Vietcong*, Curbstone Press, 1994.